SUPPORTING SHRINKAGE

SUPPORTING SHRINKAGE

Planning and Decision Making for Legacy Cities

Michael P. Johnson, Justin B. Hollander,
Eliza W. Kinsey, and George R. Chichirau
with Charla Burnett

Published by State University of New York Press, Albany

© 2021 State University of New York

All rights reserved

Printed in the United States of America

No part of this book may be used or reproduced in any manner without written permission. No part of this book may be stored in a retrieval system or transmitted in any form or by any means including electronic, electrostatic, magnetic tape, mechanical, photocopying, recording, or otherwise without the prior permission in writing of the publisher.

For information, contact State University of New York Press, Albany, NY
www.sunypress.edu

Library of Congress Cataloging-in-Publication Data

Names: Johnson, Michael P., author | Hollander, Justin B., author | Kinsey, Eliza W., author | Chichirau, George R., author.
Title: Supporting shrinkage / Michael P. Johnson, Justin B. Hollander, Eliza W. Kinsey, and George R. Chichirau.
Description: Albany : State University of New York Press, [2021] | Includes bibliographical references and index.
Identifiers: ISBN 9781438483450 (hardcover : alk. paper) | ISBN 9781438483467 (pbk. : alk. paper) | ISBN 9781438483474 (ebook)
Further information is available at the Library of Congress.

10 9 8 7 6 5 4 3 2 1

Contents

LIST OF TABLES AND FIGURES   vii

ACKNOWLEDGMENTS   xi

CHAPTER 1
Planning, Technology, and Shrinking Cities   1

CHAPTER 2
What Can Data and Technology Do for Shrinking Cities and
Distressed Communities?   33

CHAPTER 3
Three Shrinking Cities: History, Practice, Data, and Technology   65

CHAPTER 4
Data and Modeling Preliminaries: An Application to Fall River,
Massachusetts   121

CHAPTER 5
Shrinking City Data and Decision Modeling: Baltimore, Maryland   145

CHAPTER 6
Technology, Data, and Community-Building Where People Matter   183

CHAPTER 7
Lessons Learned: How Can Data, Models, and Technology
Support Shrinking Cities and Distressed Communities?   207

WORKS CITED	219
ABOUT THE AUTHORS	253
INDEX	255

Tables and Figures

Tables

1.1	U.S. Cities with the Highest Absolute Population Loss, 1950–2010	8
1.2	Candidate U.S. Cities for Shrinkage and Distress Analysis	17
1.3	Changes in Population and Vacancy Measures in Candidate U.S. Cities	19
1.4	Sample Cities Description	22
3.1	Sample Cities: Selected Characteristics	66
3.2	Population Changes, 1900–2016, Sample Cities	67
3.3	Changes in Population & Race/Ethnicity, 1970–2016, Sample Cities	68
3.4	Changes in Housing & Economic Characteristics, 1970–2016, Sample Cities	68
3.5	Population & Race/Ethnicity in Flint: 1970–2016	73
3.6	Flint Housing & Economic Characteristics: 1970–2016	75
3.7	Population & Race/Ethnicity in Baltimore: 1970–2016	86
3.8	Baltimore Housing & Economic Characteristics: 1970–2016	89
3.9	Population & Race/Ethnicity in Fall River: 1970–2016	107
3.10	Fall River Housing & Economic Characteristics: 1970–2016	108

3.11	Comparing Sample Cities: Primary City Goals	116
3.12	Comparing Sample Cities: Primary Decision-Making Systems and Processes	116
3.13	Comparing Sample Cities: Future Uses Considered	118
4.1	"Idea Space" for Data and Tech-Inspired Interventions in Shrinking Cities and Distressed Communities	122
5.1	Vacant Land Planning Model: Criteria for Clusters	165
5.2	Strengths and Weaknesses Identified in City Demolition Cluster Selection Process	175
5.3	Cross-Case Comparison of Process and Outcomes	179
6.1	Benefits and Costs of Big Data/Smart Cities Innovations for Shrinking Cities and Distressed Communities	203

Figures

3.1	Population Change in Flint, 2000–2016	73
3.2	Nonwhite Population in Flint: Nonwhites as Percentage of Population	74
3.3	Housing Vacancy in Flint: Percentage of Housing Units Classified as Other, Vacant	76
3.4	Abandoned Home in Flint	76
3.5	Shuttered Public School in Flint	77
3.6	Typical Row House in Baltimore Next to Vacant Lot	87
3.7	Urban Agriculture Is a Common Use for Large Blocks of Vacant Land in Baltimore	87
3.8	Population Change in Baltimore, 2000–2016	91
3.9	Housing Vacancy in Baltimore: Percentage of Housing Units Classified as Other Vacant	91
3.10	Nonwhite Population in Baltimore: Nonwhites as Percentage of Population	92

3.11	Homegrown Baltimore's Linkage to Baltimore City Initiatives	97
3.12	Typical Residential Neighborhood in Fall River	104
3.13	Street View of Quequechan Mills District in Fall River	104
3.14	Population Change in Fall River, 2000–2016	106
3.15	Housing Vacancy in Fall River, 2016: Percentage of Housing Units Classified as Other, Vacant	109
3.16	Nonwhite Population in Fall River: Nonwhites as Percentage of Population	110
4.1	Neighborhood-Level Planning Model Objective Space Results: Corner Solutions and Two Compromise Solutions	140
4.2	Neighborhood-Level Planning Model Decision Space Results: Two Non-Dominated Solutions	141
4.3	Neighborhood-Level Planning Model Decision Space Results: Compromise Solution—Residential and Non-Residential Investments	143
5.1	Examples of "Demolition Clusters" in the City of Baltimore	148
5.2	Interview Map	151
5.3	Means-Ends Network for Smart Shrinkage Decision Problem	161
5.4	Vacant Land Planning Model Objective Space Results: Value Chart	169
5.5	Vacant Land Planning Model Decision Space Results: Compromise Solutions Associated with Objective Function Weights Suggested by City of Baltimore	171
6.1	Diagram Representing Constructs, Aspects, Premises, and Relations (Arrows) between the Constructs Comprising the Enhanced Adaptive Structuration Theory 2 (EAST2) Framework	198

Acknowledgments

The research in this book was supported by The Abell Foundation, "Decision Modeling Tool for Vacant Structure Demolition and Redevelopment," January 1 to December 31, 2013. We are grateful to the cooperation of the City of Flint Planning Division, Fall River Planning Department, and the Baltimore City Planning Department for ideas, data, interviews, and comments that made our research possible.

Our work benefitted greatly from the contributions of many research assistants over the course of this project: University of Massachusetts Boston students Merritt Hughes (PhD '17), Hyun-Jung Lee (PhD '18), Heather MacLean (MS '21), and Omobukola Usidame (PhD '18), and Tufts University student Jingyu Tu (MS '15). University of Massachusetts Boston Public Policy PhD students Jason Wright, Liz James, Shengli Chu and Jamie Lannon, and Tufts University Urban and Environmental Policy and Planning masters student Sarah Cohen served as editorial assistants.

We appreciate the detailed and thoughtful feedback of anonymous reviewers.

We thank our families, employers, and colleagues for their support and guidance.

CHAPTER 1

Planning, Technology, and Shrinking Cities

1.1 Introduction: Policy, Planning Context, and Book Goals

Municipal decline or urban shrinkage has been the subject of extensive academic research[1] and many recent stories in the popular press.[2] In the United States, a relatively large number of cities and regions have experienced increased distress over the past two decades, according to measures relating to population and economic decline, or vacant and abandoned housing. These changes have significantly reduced the quality of life for residents: extreme examples include severely degraded infrastructure in Flint, Michigan, and social unrest in Baltimore, Maryland. Declining urban centers usually fall into two large categories: the "legacy" cities of the postindustrial regions of New England, the Mid-Atlantic, and the Midwest that have dealt with industrial transition and suburban flight for many decades now (Mallach and Brachman 2013), as well as cities in the Sunbelt that have borne the brunt of the post-2008 foreclosure crisis and related abandonment of housing in suburban and suburban-style subdivisions (Hollander 2011). These trends are not limited to the United States: cities in Europe, Asia, and Africa also confront decline and shrinkage (Stohr 2004).

The reverse of the coin is that many other cities have become increasingly attractive over the past decade, as millennials and baby boomers alike recognize the benefits of easily accessible jobs and cultural amenities associated with urban living (Wieckowski 2010; Frey 2014; Nielson 2014). A recent best-selling book by Fallows and Fallows (2018) has made a highly persuasive case for the social and economic value of smaller cities, even in decline. Recent U.S. Census data is relatively ambiguous, although it seems to indicate a moderate resurgence in suburban population growth rates as compared to traditional cores (Frey 2017). It is thus probably best to not oversell any one storyline regarding central city versus suburban growth, and overall trends of urban growth versus decline (even more so in the wake of the 2020 coronavirus crisis).

Community distress is usually a corollary of the dynamic of shrinking cities (Beauregard 2009). To provide an example, the Economic Innovation Group (2018) measures community distress using an index composed of seven equally weighted components:

1. the percentage of the adult population without a high school diploma;
2. the housing vacancy rate;
3. the percentage of adult nonelderly population not currently employed;
4. the poverty rate;
5. the median household income as a percent of the state's median household income;
6. the percent annual change in the number of jobs; and
7. the percent annual change in the number of business establishments.

By comparing distress measures between 2007 and 2011, the depths of the Great Recession, and 2012 and 2016, an era of sustained economic recovery, the EIG found evidence of migration from distressed zip codes toward more prosperous ones (the bottom and top quintiles according to the Distressed Community Index). For troubled areas, this population shift resulted in a lag in jobs recovery and business creation, higher housing vacancy rates and educational attainment, and a greater proportion of majority-minority communities—in brief, an even more concentrated degree of distress.

Vast and increasing inequality represents another particularly concerning trend in U.S. urban affairs. Studies have documented increasing gaps in income (Institute for Policy Studies 2018a), wealth (Institute for Policy Studies 2018b), household debt (Coibion et al. 2014), access to quality education (Semuels 2016), and life expectancy and other measures of physical, mental, and social well-being (Institute for Policy Studies 2018c; Centers for Disease Control and Prevention 2016). These gaps, which often cut across race, class, gender, and ethnicity lines, present structural barriers to opportunity for many Americans. In fact, a recent book (Harris and Curtis 2018) on the work of the 1968 Kerner Commission, which warned that the United States was "moving toward two societies, one black, one white—separate and unequal," concluded, rather dispiritingly, that the social problems documented fifty years ago remain prevalent today.

> Inequalities of opportunity are highly spatially concentrated, in particular in central city cores, as well as in older suburbs that have seen deindustrialization and large employer decline; very few U.S. cities enjoy both high levels of prosperity and low levels of spatial inequality. When there is some spatial equality, it tends to be at the bottom: shrinking cities tend to be in regions that also score poorly on the Distressed Community Index.

We believe there are opportunities to address municipal decline issues by using tools of planning and policy design that take advantage of recent innovations in data analytics and information technology. In contrast to recent work by one of us (Hollander 2018) that elucidates a research agenda for shrinking cities based on retrospective and exploratory analysis common to applied social sciences, we emphasize here prospective and prescriptive analyses. These are intended to provide stakeholders with specific, evidence-based responses using principles of decision sciences applied to spatial data. These responses are rooted in principles of inclusion, engagement, empowerment, and advocacy with, by, and for localized and traditionally underrepresented communities. Our book describes promising examples of data-driven decision making for shrinking cities and distressed communities, and hints at new applications that can leverage data and technology for greater positive impacts. We argue that decisions informed by qualitative and quantitative data and analytic methods, implemented through accessible and affordable technologies, and based on notions of social impact and social justice, can enable residents to play a leading role in the positive transformation of their distressed communities.

Cities certainly differ according to their ability to rebound from a period of decline; while some may regain population as local housing and labor markets resume growth (sometimes with help from foreclosure response strategies that help stabilize troubled communities), others may require more extensive and coordinated efforts across government, private sector, and nonprofit actors to achieve regeneration. For some cities, "regeneration" may not aim at demographic gains but rather at moderating levels of population decline, new land uses and distributions of existing population, and an acceptance that the city as it evolves may not regain the level of activity and visibility that it had in the past.

The faces of decline, stabilization, and regeneration are quite varied. In Cleveland, researchers explore ways to encourage temporary uses of abandoned buildings and vacant land such as arts programming, recreational events, "pop-up" shops, and community visioning in anticipation of more permanent uses (Schwartz 2014). New Orleans, a city that lost hundreds of thousands of residents in the wake of Hurricane Katrina, has gained many new residents who tend to be whiter and more affluent than those who left (some of whom are unlikely to ever return); the "Big Easy" wrestles with booming housing markets alongside stagnating flood-ravaged neighborhoods (Sayre 2015). In Detroit, bankruptcy and a politically controversial land use plan that limits investments in certain distressed neighborhoods coexists with recent growth in the downtown core (Bradley 2013; Gallagher 2013; Detroit Future City 2012; Kinney 2016). In Baltimore, recent city-led initiatives (notably "Vacants 2 Value" and "Growing Greener") have resulted in revitalized antivacancy actions (Thomas 2016), though popular unrest associated with a case of police violence has complicated its fight against blight (Eversley 2016).

In an exploration of gentrification, Evan Moskowitz (2017) argues that investment strategies driven by the needs of elites in government, non-profits, and for-profit companies may indeed result in overall gains in measures of municipal health, but these gains may mask starkly different levels of municipal services and business growth between certain targeted communities, with white and affluent incomers on one side, and low-income and predominantly minority communities on the other. Regeneration is a dynamic that may be broader than community-level gentrification. Many states have economically booming urban centers surrounded by pockets of postindustrial decay: in Massachusetts, Boston is doing better than ever, relying on its leadership position in the fields of higher education, biotechnology, and pharmaceutics, while on the edges of its metropolitan region, older industrial towns like Lawrence, New Bedford, and Fall River face significant barriers to economic opportunity (Frank 2016a). The median household income for Massachusetts in 2014 was $67,846: but this measure masks wide variations in income (Rocheleau 2015). Boston's suburbs, comprising about a quarter of the state, generally have a median household income of over $100,000, going as high as $201,200 for Weston, while similar figures for Lawrence, New Bedford, and Fall River were $34,496, $36,813, and $33,763, respectively (Rocheleau 2015). The large disparities in such measures of economic health between towns that are thirty to sixty miles away from each other make the notion of a single "region" only a geographic label; its communities represent different socioeconomic universes.

Such patterns recur in many other states across the country. In Ohio, Columbus is booming, while Cleveland, Toledo, and Youngstown are among the nation's fastest shrinking cities. In Illinois, Chicago is gaining population, while Rockford and Decatur continue to lose population; New York City is as wealthy as ever, while upstate New York is struggling to offer jobs, and its population is slowly drifting away. States often have a center that has gained from the transformations of the past two decades, to the detriment of many of their other towns. There are, however, exceptions: Michigan's largest city, Detroit, has lost even more people than its other struggling communities, such as Flint and Dearborn (United States Census Bureau 2015a). Amazon's recent competition among cities to host its second headquarters ("HQ2"; see Kopp 2018) was expected to result in a high-profile industrial siting generating tremendous growth in housing, ancillary businesses, education, and infrastructure in or near a city center. Indeed, the recent choice of Crystal City, in Virginia's Arlington County as the site of HQ2 (Banister 2020) is expected to generate 25,000 jobs in exchange for $573 million in public incentives. But without concerted regional planning, intraregional inequalities may persist or even increase.

Urban shrinkage in its many dimensions cannot be dissociated from the process of globalization and the arrival of the "innovation" economy, resulting in investments shifted at ever-accelerating speed away from spaces seen as marginal for the information society. Urban shrinkage may also be associated with changes in migration patterns resulting from the current COVID-19 pandemic. However, trends associated with shrinkage need not automatically translate into decline: the resilience of various territories can be mitigated or exacerbated by many different urban, social, and economic policies as distinct from traditional large-scale economic development initiatives such as the introduction of a large employer.

This book describes a new approach to citizen-engaged, community-focused planning methods and technologies for cities and regions facing decline, shrinkage, and blight. Our approach, inspired in part by the "big data" and "smart cities" movements, highlights the special role that decision sciences and information technology can play in enabling citizens, especially those in traditionally underserved or distressed communities, to have an active voice in the future of their neighborhoods. Acknowledging the importance of planning support systems in this task, we present a vision of inclusive planning and policy design intended especially to meet the needs of shrinking cities and declining regions that incorporates experiences of community residents, professionals, and researchers across many geographies, disciplines, technologies, and institutional contexts.

Our work is rooted in research investigating the role that data and decision analytics may play in designing flexible and evidence-based planning strategies for shrinking cities (Johnson, Hollander, and Hallulli 2014; Johnson, Hollander, and Davenport Whiteman 2015; Németh et al. 2018). Our analysis reflects recent work in a number of domains. *Community-based analytics* can address contemporary issues in housing, community development, and service delivery in which the role of residents of disadvantaged communities in problem definition, solution, and implementation is given particular weight (Johnson 2012a; Johnson et al. 2015; Johnson and Midgley 2018). *Civic data and immersive planning* enables stakeholders, including residents of distressed communities, to design, collect, and use data for community change, both in traditional analysis and novel playable games (Gordon, Schirra, and Hollander 2011; Gordon and Baldwin-Philippi 2013; Gordon and Mihaildis 2016). *Public participatory geographic information systems* enable residents seeking to solve specific planning problems that involve contested uses of space, both on land and at sea, to use GIS to develop new strategies for local development that reflect multiple conflicting understandings of spaces and uses (Craig, Harris, and Weiner 2002; Sieber 2006; Brown and Kyttä 2014). *Urban analytics* represents a broader focus on the uses of mostly quantitative data from diverse sources—censuses, land uses, sensors, social media, and many others—to enable planners and policy-makers to better respond to citizen needs and to anticipate changes in population, services, and even climate (Singleton, Spielman, and Folch 2017; O'Brien 2018).

We believe that decisions informed by analytic planning models, and planning support systems based on these models, should reflect the perspectives of multiple stakeholders, facilitate active participation across diverse groups, address a wide variety of active and passive land uses, and be rooted in principles of inclusion, engagement, empowerment, and advocacy. Such planning methods and technologies have the potential to transform our notion of what more widely available data and smart cities can do with and for shrinking cities, declining regions, and distressed communities. For shrinking cities to take advantage of these methods, they will need a commitment to community engagement, good governance, and appropriate technical expertise. Goldsmith and Crawford (2014) describe a range of promising applications in a number of large U.S. cities. There are multiple examples of IT-supported participatory planning applications applied outside of the United States (e.g., "Carticipe," http://carticipe.net; "Madam Mayor, I Have an Idea," https://idee.paris.fr; and SeaSketch, https://www.seasketch.org/home.html).

The environment of shrinking cities makes it especially difficult for disadvantaged populations to assert agency over their daily lives, and the central role of planning data, models, and technologies, especially those that use community engagement and critical, policy-focused perspectives, should be to reverse that trend. Specific improvements in communities may enable planning and policy efforts to help mitigate social stresses, reduce structural barriers to opportunity, and increase the desirability of declining regions. Of course, regional and national trends in the political economy often overwhelm more localized planning efforts: in this case, we explore how data, models, and technologies for planning can support responses to these larger dynamics.

Through analysis of specific urban communities in the United States, we study how the current practice of urban planning, policy analysis, and decision sciences generates social benefits, and for whom. Specifically, we are interested in learning whether and how these tools and applications may improve the capacity of planning practitioners, working with community stakeholders and business interests, to identify alternative pathways for development in distressed and declining communities.

Based on interactions with planning practitioners in one large and one small city in the Northeastern United States, we have developed specific decision models to support planning for shrinkage and distress. These models, based on principles and methods of community data analytics, enable planners to identify detailed and localized responses that represent improvements over current practices and technologies. We show that much more can be done to ensure that such data- and technology-driven applications reflect the needs and concerns of diverse communities, as well as those of planners. We argue that data analytics and decision technologies to address shrinkage and blight can achieve even greater impact if they explicitly address concerns of policy impacts and social equity as well as process efficiency and planning effectiveness. However, the importance of our work is not limited to decision modeling. Our core belief is that data, information technology and analytics, as well as decision science, can enable residents of shrinking and disadvantaged communities to play a leading role in determining the uses to which their land is put, and ensure that their neighborhoods increasingly enjoy the opportunities, amenities, and influence that we normally associate with more affluent and gentrifying places.

1.2 Shrinking Cities and Distressed Communities

Shrinking Cities

According to the 2015 United States Census, sixteen of the country's twenty largest cities in 1950 have experienced substantial population decline over the last sixty-five years. This includes many rust-belt cities such as Detroit, Buffalo, Cleveland, Pittsburgh, St. Louis, Baltimore, and Philadelphia. In some of these cities, the population has dropped by more than 50 percent (see table 1.1).

Shrinking cities have been defined by scholars as involving more than population decline—these cities are marked by physical blight and

Table 1.1. U.S. Cities with the Highest Absolute Population Loss, 1950–2010

City	Population in 1950	Population in 2010	Absolute Change	% Change
Detroit	1,849,568	713,777	−1,135,791	−61.4
Chicago	3,620,962	2,695,598	−925,364	−25.6
Philadelphia	2,071,605	1,526,006	−545,599	−26.3
St. Louis	856,796	319,294	−537,502	−62.7
Cleveland	914,808	396,815	−517,993	−56.6
Pittsburgh	676,806	305,704	−371,102	−54.8
Baltimore	949,708	620,961	−328,747	−34.6
Buffalo	580,132	270,240	−309,892	−53.4
Cinncinnati	503,998	296,943	−207,055	−41.1

Source: U.S. Census Bureau 2015.

economic transformation. The Shrinking Cities International Research Network defines a shrinking city as "a densely populated urban area with a minimum population of 10,000 residents that has faced population losses in large parts for more than two years and is undergoing economic transformations with some symptoms of a structural crisis" (Hollander et al. 2009, 6). Other definitions in the literature suggest "increasing levels of vacant and abandoned properties, including blighted residential, commercial and industrial buildings" as characteristics of such cities (Schilling and Logan 2008, 452).

We start by noting that the demographic shift in shrinking cities can be measured in terms of both race and income. Baltimore, Detroit, and St. Louis, to name just three, were majority white in 1950, but by 2000 had shifted to majority African American (U.S. Census; Cohen 2001). Additionally, median income as a percentage of standard metropolitan statistical area median income has decreased significantly over the past sixty-five years (Cohen 2001). This means that wealth has spread to the suburbs, leaving the urban core significantly poorer.

WHY CITIES SHRINK

Shrinking cities are everywhere, but the reasons different cities undergo such transformations can vary enormously. Several suspects include natural disasters (Vale and Campanella 2005), deindustrialization (Bluestone and Harrison 1982; McDonald 2010), suburbanization (Jackson 1985; Clark 1989), globalization (Sassen 1991; Hall 1997), and of course the natural economic cycle of boom and bust (Rust 1975). Beauregard's (2009) analysis of shrinking U.S. cities from 1820 to 2000 argued against such wholesale claims, concluding instead that causes of population decline vary from one historical period to another. A paper produced from an Urban Affairs Association annual meeting affirmed that view; a global group of scholars discouraging a "one-size-fits-all" explanation for why places lose population (Großmann et al. 2013).

Among experts on cities, two models explaining why neighborhoods depopulate tend to emerge as frontrunners: neighborhood life-cycle theory and an alternative, neighborhood change theory.

By viewing neighborhood change in terms of a life cycle, the first theory posits that places grow and die in a way analogous to the human body: "the constant cycle of birth, life, and death is inevitable in both" (U.S. Federal Home Loan Bank Board 1940, 3). Hoover and Vernon (1962) described five stages in a neighborhood's life cycle: new development, transition, downgrading, thinning-out, and renewal. The Real Estate Research Corporation (1975) outlined five similar steps along a continuum: healthy, incipient decline, clearly declining, accelerating decline, and abandoned.

Neighborhood life-cycle theory was developed in an effort to better understand and rationalize the declining city. Many writings on the topic set out to identify planning and policy interventions that might either arrest or reverse this "natural" process (Bradbury, Downs, and Small 1982). The stated goal of policy-makers was to help revitalize devastated places while preventing the future deterioration of existing stable neighborhoods. Neighborhood life-cycle theory has been tremendously influential in U.S. urban policy and planning, but has been subject to insightful critique (see Metzger 2000).

Believing that such policies can arrest the slow death of neighborhoods, Blakely (1994) and others in the economic development tradition draw on neighborhood life-cycle theory in advocating public intervention through investments in vacant land. Described as redevelopment or revitalization, this approach is often top-down in nature and uses forced relocation via eminent domain to achieve its objectives. A notorious example of this approach is the Boston Redevelopment Authority's urban renewal program in the West End of Boston (Gans 1962; Teaford 2000). More recently, the City of New London's Supreme Court victory allowed it to move forward with the condemnation of sixty-four privately owned homes in order to allow the expansion of a large corporation (Langdon 2005; Salzman and Mansnerus 2005). The Kelo v. City of New London, 125 S. Ct. 2655 (2005) case generated a groundswell of popular sentiment against the use of eminent domain for the purposes of economic development and provoked a rash of new state laws and public protests against government seizure of private property for economic development (Egan 2005).

The dominant interpretation of neighborhood life-cycle theory is that public investment is needed to stop an out-of-control process. This view of neighborhood change fails to account for those scenarios in which a city loses population but does so without suffering the expected accompanying blight. Rather than look for ways to manage population loss so that blight may be prevented, the theory only allows for the neighborhood to be seen as growing or declining, alive or dead (Hollander et al. 2009).

According to Metzger (2000), the future of a city depends not on its stage in a "natural" life cycle, "but on whether residents had access to financial resources within an environment of community control" (7).

Metzger draws on a body of critical theory that rejects the modernist notions of advance and retreat, of growth and decline. Beauregard (2003) also explores this dialectic in examining the discourse of urban decline. He finds that urban decline was incorporated into a socially constructed story of the rise of suburbia and the fall of the city—a fictional account reified into the public consciousness through oral and written communication.

Critics such as Dear and Flusty (1998) advance a postmodern notion of neighborhood change that escapes this grand narrative and allows the details of each city, each neighborhood, and each block to speak for itself. Mitchell (2002) contributes to this alternative theory in his account of planning in Egypt. He shows how the "informal, clandestine, and unreported" activities of society determined planning outcomes, not the "fabricated" script developed by Western colonizers. An understanding of urban decline as a disaggregated, finely complex phenomenon is possible under this alternative theoretical framework. This alternate theory of neighborhood change allows planners to be cognizant of urban problems while avoiding the inevitability embedded in the discourse of urban decline. Such an unshackling from the structures of urban decline opens up the possibility for city leaders to work toward proactively managing depopulation.

A planner or policy analyst drawing on this alternative theoretical framework may attempt creative intervention as described above, or may avoid action altogether. Hoch (1996) suggests that a consequence of postmodern planning practice is that a sense of hopelessness may infect the planner because all interventions are somehow intertwined with the forces of power. The planner who embraces alternative neighborhood change theories may be reluctant to label her city as "in decline," or might be timid about her own ability to manipulate power relations in an affected neighborhood.

Indeed, we can attribute much of the success of community development professionals in general, and community development corporations (CDCs) in particular, to their grounding in this alternative neighborhood change theory. For decades, CDCs and grassroots organizations have fought for a higher quality of life for residents of some of the poorest neighborhoods in America. For the most part, CDCs reject conventional views of neighborhood death and dying and instead promote new building and growth, often through the construction of new, affordable housing. New movements are underfoot, however, that recognize a certain inevitability of decline but plan for these demographic and socioeconomic shifts in proactive ways.

Race, Ethnicity, Shrinkage, and Distress

Shrinking cities tend to become more homogenous as they get smaller, in terms of percentage of the population in poverty, and in terms of race (Wilson and Taub 2007; Sugrue 2005; Logan and Stults 2011). Many of the largest shrinking cities in the United States are in some of the most highly segregated metro areas—Detroit; Gary, Indiana; Pittsburgh; Baltimore—leading Logan and Stults (2011) to coin the term "Ghetto Belt" to describe such areas across the Northeast and Midwest.

The concentration of African American and Latino populations in shrinking urban areas attracts the attention of critics who contend that past discriminatory practices are alive and well. Researchers studying hazardous waste facility siting in the 1980s noted a high correlation between the location of those facilities and the presence of poor and nonwhite populations, suggesting an environmental injustice (Bullard and Wright 1990; O'Hare, Bacow, and Sanderson 1983). Much attention followed, leading to the birth of an entire field of environmental justice, which is concerned with how disadvantaged groups too often bear the unfair burdens of community decline, disinvestment, pollution, and waste (Bullard 1994; Agyeman 2005; Schlosberg and Rinfret 2008).

In shrinking cities, the shifting racial make-up of emptying neighborhoods tends to create racialized ghettos, making local government intervention in these areas subject to increased scrutiny. The Massachusetts State Government has classified hundreds of neighborhoods throughout the state as "environmental justice communities" based on demographic characteristics like race, income, and environmental exposures. For these designated communities, the acute problems of shrinkage are required to be addressed through direct engagement that acknowledges roles of race, ethnicity, and language (Commonwealth of Massachusetts 2018).

We use the notion of "distress" to represent adverse social and physical characteristics of communities associated with racial, ethnic, and class residential segregation and structural barriers to opportunity. Shrinkage and decline have complicated relationships with community distress; to capture these distinct but complementary concepts, we refer to "shrinking" or "declining" cities and "distressed communities" throughout the book, but do not treat these terms as synonymous.

Scholars such as Henry Taylor have deeply explored the impacts of race, ethnicity, and class in declining cities and distressed communities, focusing particularly on the intersections of systematic structural racism, market-based approaches to urban development, and the knowledge-based neoliberal economy (Todd 2018). While Dr. Taylor is pessimistic about the current level of influence of marginalized communities in urban change, he looks to recent public opposition to police violence and the Movement for Black Lives, as well as Black Lives Matter, as potential catalysts to a new movement to empower these communities based on principles of Lefebvre's Right to the City (Lefebvre 1996; Shields 2013).

Social Justice, Equity, and Shrinkage

Scholarship and practice on smart decline has faced criticism that such interventions reflect values and result in behaviors consistent with discredited notions of urban renewal, or are inappropriate strategies for saving cities (Gratz 2011; Florida 2011). Foundational work on smart decline (Németh and Hollander 2011) presented a number of propositions based on notions of equity and social justice. The goal of these propositions was to be able to test notions of procedural and distributive justice in practice. Recently, these authors (Németh et al. 2018) tested these propositions using the example of the city of Baltimore (a city we will discuss in detail throughout this book). They found that, since 2000, through multiple planning, demolition, and redevelopment initiatives intended to address blight, vacancy, and abandonment, the city has made only modest progress toward ensuring that citizens have a high level of knowledge of, engagement with, and ownership of neighborhood-level strategies.

Vacancy and Abandonment

With some context on why places depopulate, which people are most often directly impacted, and the implications of these impacts for social justice and equity, we now turn to the most well-known outcome of decline: vacancy and abandonment. As there is no universally agreed-on definition of vacant property, legal definitions vary by city. Many cities use length of vacancy and structural conditions of the unit as primary criteria (Cohen 2001). As defined by the National Vacant Properties Campaign, vacant properties are:

> vacant residential, commercial, and industrial buildings and lots that threaten public safety and/or have been subject to the neglect of fundamental duties of property ownership. Neglect of ownership duty includes failure to pay taxes or utility bills, mortgage default, and failure to pay liens on the property. (Schilling 2008, 463)

The vicious cycle of disinvestment that Schilling highlights, wherein landlords fail to make necessary repairs and stop paying property taxes, leads to declining property values, often resulting in foreclosures and abandonment. This, in turn, only further depresses the housing market (Cohen 2001).

Vacancy has arisen largely as a result of shrinking populations—the U.S. cities with the largest number of abandoned housing units are also the cities with the most dramatic population decline (Cohen 2001). More recently, however, the subprime mortgage crisis and subsequent rampant foreclosures have contributed to widespread vacancy. Baltimore alone had more than 33,000 home foreclosures between 2000 and 2009 (Role of the Lending Industry 2009). Baltimore's long history of minorities being denied access to credit and of racially segregated living patterns make the city particularly susceptible to predatory lending (Role of the Lending Industry 2009). This, along with the mortgage crisis, contributed to a disproportionate number of foreclosures in black neighborhoods in the city (Blessett 2011).

Vacant and abandoned properties can be expensive for cities, in terms of both economic and social costs. A recent study in Baltimore found that each additional vacant building costs the city $1,472 per year—largely in additional police and emergency response costs (Winthrop and Herr 2009). Vacant buildings have also been linked to higher rates of fire, injury, crime, and illegal activity including prostitution, violence, and drug sales and use (Schachterle et al. 2012; Garvin et al. 2013; Gomez and Muntaner 2005). Research supports the linkage between vacancy and increased rates of poor health outcomes such as HIV/AIDs, STDs, premature mortality, diabetes, and suicide (Garvin 2013; Gomez and Muntaner 2005).

The physical impact of vacancy and abandonment on an urban landscape, which includes not just empty buildings and lots but also broken windows, trash, and drug paraphernalia, constitutes in part what is often referred to as "physical neighborhood disorder." Physical disorder is defined as "visible cues in the environment that indicate lack of control over neighborhood conditions" (Garvin et al. 2013). Research has shown physical disorder to be associated with crime, fear, and social isolation, resulting in further physical and social decline (Garvin et al. 2013). Disorder has also been linked to poor health outcomes such as cardiovascular disease, obesity, and mental illness (Robert Wood Johnson Foundation 2008; Dulin-Keita et al. 2013; Chang, Hillier and Mehta 2009).

The fear and social isolation associated with neighborhood disorder can reduce people's perception of safety and social interactions in their neighborhood, which can lead to such adverse changes in behavior as reduced physical activity. If people are scared to go outside, or if the physical environment is not conducive to exercise or play because of glass, needles, or damaged sidewalks, physical disorder can be a significant deterrent to physical activity. Just as physical disorder can deter outdoor activities, presence of quality features in the built environment, such as enjoyable scenery, is strongly associated with increased physical activity (Chang, Hillier, and Mehta 2009). Parks, walkability, and street connectivity are also associated with physical activity—attributes often lacking in neighborhoods with a high degree of disorder (Dulin-Keita et al. 2013).

Physical disorder can also lead to poor health and social outcomes such as chronic stress and risky behavior. In addition, social ties, collective efficacy, and social capital, all of which are associated with positive health outcomes, are all reduced as a result of the social isolation resulting from neighborhood disorder (Garvin et al. 2013). Garvin and colleagues note that "physical disorder is theorized to lead to negative health outcomes by promoting chronic stress and attendant maladaptive physiologic responses, encouraging risky behavior, and eroding resident social interaction" (413). A 2008 systematic review of the relevant literature found consistent associations between social cohesion and physical health (Kawachi, Subramanian, and Kim 2008). The presence of social capital was found to decrease rates of obesity, diabetes, cardiovascular disease, and all-cause mortality and to increase self-rated health.

This link between social capital and health outcomes is made via various mechanisms. Social cohesion has been shown to cause positive psychosocial effects and to foster network-based resources (Eicher and Kawachi 2011). Additionally, collective efficacy, found to be a strong determinant in health behaviors, is developed in communities where there is an ability to mobilize for collective action (Glanz, Rimer, and Viswanath 2008; Eicher and Kawachi 2011). Informal social control or other behaviorally mediated mechanisms can also improve health outcomes in communities with strong social capital (Eicher and Kawachi 2011).

The built environment can influence the level of social capital by providing spaces for formal and informal interactions and promoting shared investment in physical spaces (Eicher and Kawachi 2011). Just as parks are associated with increased physical activity, they are also linked to higher levels of collective efficacy, which can in turn facilitate more pedestrian travel and promote social interactions. All of these types of social interactions, however, are jeopardized in neighborhoods with high levels of vacancy and disorder.

Changes to the built environment are not always positive. Redevelopment efforts, while intended to improve neighborhoods, often cause disruption and displacement, both of which have been linked in many studies to increased levels of stress, feelings of hopelessness, and associated negative health outcomes (Gomez 2005). According to Gomez and Muntaner (2005), "[When] redevelopment results in the displacement of residents without assurance of adequate shelter, the health of community residents suffers through mental disorder, exacerbation of chronic illness and subsequently premature death" (99). Being uprooted from one's home is a source of stress, as is lack of influence and the ability to make choices about the fate of one's home or neighborhood (Gomez 2012; Fullilove 2001).

An extensive community investigation in East Baltimore, where large-scale redevelopment efforts have been focused in recent decades, found that the neighborhood lacks communitarian and institutional social capital due to disruption and distrustful relationships with developers, institutions, and government (Gomez and Muntaner 2005). This leaves the community without much strength for organizing in the face of redevelopment efforts. Themes from the study suggested both insufficient bonding relationships among community organizations as well as insufficient bridging relationships between the community and external institutional networks. This lack of social capital reveals a community with very little perceived control over redevelopment efforts, and thus very little perceived influence over the health outcomes of the neighborhood.

1.3 Sample Cities for This Book

This book is motivated by our desire to generate planning and policy insights for shrinking and declining cities and regions, and for distressed and blighted communities. However, for ease of analysis, we focus here on central cities, understanding that different approaches can generate different insights associated with different kinds of study areas. In order to learn how cities can respond to shrinkage, distress, and blight through the lens of data and decision analytics, we will examine multiple central cities that vary along a number of dimensions. While there is a well-developed theory of case study research (Yin 2018), this book will not pursue a formal case study design. Instead, we have selected a convenience sample of cites based on our experience with each, proximity, and access to local officials. This choice was made in consideration of a variety of historical, demographic, geographical, and socioeconomic dimensions.

In order to situate these three cities and ensure they were somewhat representative across a variety of characteristics, we began by considering three categories of cities. The first category is "Massachusetts Gateway Cities," smaller, postindustrial cities in Massachusetts, the state in which two of us (Johnson and Hollander) have conducted extensive research, that are the focus of regional development policy (MassInc 2012). The second category is "Great Cities," thirty cities with population ranking more than 500,000 habitants in 2010 (U.S. Census 2016). The third category is cities of various sizes considered by scholars to be of special interest because of declines in population, economic activity, or quality of life (Beauregard 2009; Hollander 2011; Silverman et al. 2016). Table 1.2 lists sixty-one cities across these three categories.

Table 1.2. Candidate U.S. Cities for Shrinkage and Distress Analysis

30 cities with largest population in 2016		Cities of particular interest to scholars of shrinkage and decline	Massachusetts Gateway cities
Austin, TX	Los Angeles, CA	Ashland, KY	Brockton
Baltimore, MD	Memphis, TN	Birmingham, AL	Fall River
Boston, MA	Milwaukee, WI	Buffalo, NY	Fitchburg
Charlotte, NC	Nashville, TN	Camden, NJ	Haverill
Chicago, IL	New York, NY	Cleveland, OH	Holyoke
Columbus, OH	Oklahoma City, OK	Dayton, OH	Lawrence
Dallas, TX	Philadelphia, PA	East St. Louis, IL	Lowell
Denver, CO	Phoenix, AZ	Flint, MI	New Bedford
Detroit, MI	Portland, OR	Jackson, MS	Pittsfield
El Paso, TX	San Antonio, TX	Memphis, TN	Springfield
Fort Worth, TX	San Diego, CA	New Orleans, LA	Worcester
Houston, TX	San Francisco, CA	Norfolk, VA	
Indianapolis, IN	San Jose, CA	Pittsburgh, PA	
Jacksonville, FL	Seattle, WA	Reading, PA	
Las Vegas, NV	Washington, DC	Richmond, VA	
		Rochester, NY	
		Syracuse, NY	
		Trenton, NJ	
		Wheeling, WV	
		Youngstown, OH	

We believe that insights regarding responses to shrinkage and distress through data and decision analytics are likely to vary according to city type. For this research, we selected a city from each category: one Massachusetts Gateway city, one Great City, and one city of special interest to scholars of shrinkage and distress. As these categories of cities differ by population size, we chose cities across three population sizes: small (less than 100,000 population), medium (100,000 to 500,000 population), and large (greater than 500,000 population).

The causes and nature of shrinkage and distress differ according to histories and traditions of economic and social development that vary across geographies, so our choice of three sample cities reflects different U.S. regions. Social scholarship has traditionally distinguished between U.S. regions based on "physical characteristics, cultures, politics and history of the states" (TheClassroom.com, 2018); we refer to nine divisions grouped into regions as Northeast (New England and Mid-Atlantic), Midwest (East North Central and West North Central), South (South Atlantic, East South Central, and West South Central) and West (Mountain and Pacific) (U.S. Census Bureau 2013). Our sample of cities reflects the New England, Mid-Atlantic, and East North Central regions.

Insights regarding responses to shrinkage and distress by U.S. central cities will vary according to the nature and intensity of shrinkage and distress. Multiple studies have proposed and quantified measures of shrinkage, distress, and blight (e.g., see Ganning and Teague 2018; Manville and Kuhlmann 2016; Hollander 2018). Metrics used by researchers include single-dimensional measures such as population change, housing vacancy, unemployment, poverty, education attainment, prevalence of single female–headed households; derived measures such as segregation based on residential location, school enrollment, poverty and wealth, and composite measures such as the Weaver Index (Weaver et al. 2017), defined as the geometric mean of population percent nonwhite, percent persons who have not graduated high school, percent of households that are female-headed, percent of population that is below poverty, and unemployment rate. We will not create a comprehensive database according to consensus measures and rank cities. Instead, we show that certain of the cities listed in table 1.1 have particularly high levels of population change, both overall and by nonwhite persons, as well as housing vacancy change, associated with shrinkage and distress (table 1.3).

Finally, our work in this book draws from our previous published research on shrinking cities (Johnson, Hollander, and Hallulli 2014; Johnson, Hollander, and Davenport Whiteman 2015).

Table 1.3. Changes in Population and Vacancy Measures in Candidate U.S. Cities

City [Region]	Population Percentage Change, 2000–2016	Population Percentage Nonwhite Change, 2000–2016	Housing Vacancy Rate Change, 2000–2015
Ashland, KY	−3.97	1.50	−0.30
Austin, TX	41.00	−20.05	−4.80
Baltimore, MD	−5.24	5.65	8.50
Birmingham, AL	−12.35	1.79	7.40
Boston, MA	14.02	6.45	−3.00
Brockton, MA	3.07	61.82	0.00
Buffalo, NY	−12.08	15.79	3.40
Camden, NJ	−6.72	−4.77	4.00
Charlotte, NC	47.69	26.69	−4.20
Chicago, IL	−6.60	−4.90	4.60
Cleveland, OH	−19.05	6.36	4.90
Columbus, OH	20.13	22.81	−2.30
Dallas, TX	10.66	−8.89	−2.60
Dayton, OH	−15.27	3.74	9.60
Denver, CO	24.63	−25.11	−6.90
Detroit, MI	−28.83	1.52	18.60
East St. Louis, IL	−14.69	−0.87	9.80
El Paso, TX	20.94	−26.92	−5.10
Fall River, MA	−4.13	158.88	−3.20
Fitchburg, MA	−3.01	−8.11	−4.40
Flint, MI	−21.93	−0.08	11.60
Fort Worth, TX	56.43	−3.24	−5.40
Haverhill, MA	23.06	1.30	−8.90
Holyoke, MA	−7.84	−32.01	1.0
Houston, TX	16.43	−7.41	−0.50
Indianapolis, IN	10.55	23.96	3.00
Jackson, MS	−8.70	24.78	3.70
Jacksonville, FL	19.55	16.65	2.80
Las Vegas, NV	30.64	32.55	0.70
Lawrence, MA	14.59	−35.48	−5.00

continued on next page

Table 1.3. Continued.

City [Region]	Population Percentage Change, 2000–2016	Population Percentage Nonwhite Change, 2000–2016	Housing Vacancy Rate Change, 2000–2015
Los Angeles, CA	7.34	−5.37	−6.40
Lowell, MA	6.89	42.29	−6.70
Memphis, TN	−5.43	15.55	4.20
Milwaukee, WI	−0.34	22.35	−2.00
Nashville-Davidson metro, TN	25.37	11.94	−2.80
New Bedford, MA	−3.50	57.93	−9.60
New Orleans, LA	−19.06	−5.88	7.20
New York, NY	6.53	7.31	−0.90
Norfolk, VA	4.62	−0.09	−4.60
Oklahoma City, OK	25.77	11.81	−5.00
Philadelphia, PA	3.57	9.73	2.20
Phoenix, AZ	21.61	18.70	−1.40
Pittsburgh, PA	−9.01	3.72	0.90
Pittsfield, MA	−12.19	2.22	−5.60
Portland, OR	20.75	7.47	−8.60
Reading, PA	7.71	13.42	−1.30
Richmond, VA	12.86	−3.89	1.70
Rochester, NY	−4.83	3.86	−4.40
San Antonio, TX	28.26	−30.09	−4.60
San Diego, CA	14.67	−8.16	−7.60
San Francisco, CA	12.03	16.66	−3.10
San Jose, CA	13.44	26.76	−9.50
Seattle, WA	24.86	15.97	−7.30
Springfield, MA	−1.84	−26.30	1.00
Spokane, WA	9.24	30.32	0.75
Syracuse, NY	−1.84	18.38	−1.10
Trenton, NJ	−1.58	−5.32	10.80
Washington, D.C.	19.14	−13.56	−1.30
Wheeling, WV	−12.52	−2.43	−0.40

City [Region]	Population Percentage Change, 2000–2016	Population Percentage Nonwhite Change, 2000–2016	Housing Vacancy Rate Change, 2000–2015
Worcester, MA	8.77	47.82	−2.70
Youngstown, OH	−21.30	2.41	4.30
Minimum	−28.83	−35.48	−9.60
Maximum	56.43	158.88	18.60
Mean	5.95	8.52	−0.44
Standard deviation	17.45	27.91	5.78

Note: For racial demographics, different measures were used in 2000 vs 2016, because 2000 is a census year, whereas 2016 data comes from an American Community Survey 5-year estimate: "VD-01 Total population in occupied housing units–White only" for 2000, "HC01_VC49 2012–2016 Estimates; RACE: One race–White" for 2016.

Source: U.S. Census Bureau; for population data, American Community Survey, 2011–2016, American Community Survey 5-Year Estimates, Tables CP05 and H011I; and Profile of General Demographic Characteristics: 2000, Table DP-1; for vacancy status, American Community Survey 1-Year Estimates, 2015, Table DP04, and Profile of Selected Housing Characteristics: 2000, Census 2000 Summary File 3 (SF 3), Table DP-4. Generated by George Chichirau; using American FactFinder; <http://factfinder2.census.gov> (June 26, 2019).

Our three cities chosen for detailed analysis are Fall River, Massachusetts; Flint, Michigan; and Baltimore, Maryland. These cities show variation across size, geography, population change, and vacancy change (table 1.4 on page 22). This variation means that the choice of these three cities can offer a sense of the diversity of circumstances and responses to shrinkage and decline.

1.4 Policy and Planning Technologies

We now introduce some technologies, applications, and analytic methods we will examine in more detail throughout this book. Our viewpoint is mostly prescriptive; we are interested in in the ways that these disciplines, models, and tools can be used to address current concerns of quality of life as well as ways to improve the physical and social environment of

Table 1.4. Sample Cities Description

City	Size (2016) population)	Region (Division)	Population Percentage Change, 2000–2016	Population Percentage Nonwhite Change, 2000–2016	Housing Vacancy Rate Change, 2000–2015
Baltimore, MD	Large (621,849)	Northeast (Mid-Atlantic)	-5.24	5.65	8.50
Fall River, MA	Small (88,930)	Northeast (New England)	-4.13	158.88	-3.20
Flint, MI	Small (97,386)	Midwest (East North Central)	-21.93	N/A	11.60

Source: U.S. Census Bureau; for population data, American Community Survey, 2011–2016, American Community Survey 5-Year Estimates, Tables CP05 and H01I1; and Profile of General Demographic Characteristics: 2000, Table DP-1; for vacancy status, American Community Survey 1-Year Estimates, 2015, Table DP04, and Profile of Selected Housing Characteristics: 2000, Census 2000 Summary File 3 (SF 3), Table DP-4. Generated by George Chichirau using American FactFinder; <http://factfinder2.census.gov> (June 26 2019).

shrinking cities and distressed communities. While multiple groups of people play a role in adapting and using these tools, such as residents, visitors, and for-profit businesses and government and nonprofit organizations, our primary focus is on residents, who are most affected by measures of local quality of life, and who often have the least ability to change their local environment.

SMART CITIES

The city has traditionally been seen as an agglomeration of physical infrastructure, but the arrival of communication technologies has added an invisible layer of information on top of the material world. Many of us already live in a state of augmented reality, and the shift is accelerating: yesterday we became accustomed to checking traffic on our smartphones, today we are in contact with the city hall through e-government apps, and tomorrow the internet of things might well incorporate every vehicle, traffic light, and security camera in our vicinity.

While smart city scholarship is developing at a tremendous pace, new studies tend to fall under an established taxonomy, usually emphasizing one dimension of human development (technological, business, environmental, etc.) and most often operating within the confines of a one or two subdisciplines. In Staffans and Horelli's (2014) opinion, a corporate-institutional approach to smart cities, characterized by a technocratic, top-down approach, is dominating the current debate. In their view, the idea of community empowerment is falling by the sideline, and community informatics are marginalized as powerful corporations are competing on a market worth as much as $1.5 trillion over the next 10 years (Staffans and Horelli 2014). But the understanding of "smart cities" as marketable products does not help shrinking cities and distressed communities, since their relative lack of financial resources means that large corporations are unlikely to design tools for their specific needs.

Pro bono programmers working on projects stemming from a participatory philosophy are unlikely to be able to match the sophistication and power of IBM's or Cisco's urban operations centers, sold wholesale to governments the world over. This is a problem since not only are participation and democratization worthy goals in themselves, they also enhance the quality of governance. In a wide-ranging metastudy of existing smart city models, Kim and Steenkamp (2013) state that current proposals "lack a holistic and integrated approach to city development, and neglect human factors" (638). Their innovative approach was based on four simple questions regarding the surveyed models: how would an existing "smart city" model handle a major recession, a public health crisis, a period of population shrinking, and a period of rapid growth. They suggest that smart cities should do much more than improve investor opportunities and make life for the middle class a little more convenient. However, networks that significantly improve community resilience must rely by necessity on a large degree of community engagement and support, a component that Kim and Steenkamp found lacking.

Depending on whose interests go into designing the technology, a smart city is as likely to perpetuate injustice and inequality as it is to improve citizen participation and opportunities. Imagine having discount coupons for chain stores automatically beamed to your cellphone as you walk by, or benches that rotate and eject sitters who sit for longer than five minutes (in order to discourage homeless users) (Shepard 2011). Such changes would be logical technical upgrades for already present phenomena—our daily bombardment with coupons, and the resorting of city managers to metal spikes and slanted benches to drive away the homeless—but little by little they would turn cities into threatening and unpleasant places for less-privileged residents. An alternative vision for smart cities that will enable all of its residents to enjoy more satisfying and productive lives must incorporate values of inclusion, equity, and democracy. We will show in this book that use of data, models, and technologies to design novel interventions for shrinking cities and distressed communities with people at the center can broaden our notion of what a "smart city" could be, and for whom.

Big Data

The recent uses of big data in urban science have made its potential clear: Glaeser and colleagues (2015) think the computerization of society has triggered a truly fundamental change in city management, because we are now able to measure far more variables at much finer resolution and at far less expense than ever before. In New York City, the adoption of highly local and digitalized measurements of activity is believed to have contributed very significantly to the large decline of crime over the past decade (Goldsmith and Crawford 2014). The future, however, will rely far more on data extracted from automated sensing networks as opposed to humans who manually input information. In Boston, drivers now have the option of activating a mobile app called "Street Bump," which uses the phone's accelerometer and GPS to record the severity of bumps and automatically transmit their location—with the hope that eventually most cars will communicate directly with the city's department of public works (Glaeser et al. 2015).

Social sensing (or crowd sensing) for urban planning is still in its beginning stages, but the engagement of citizens for the acquisition of localized, human-interpreted data is now seen as irreplaceable. Tisma and colleagues (2015) surveyed the social sensing landscape and proposed a general framework of twelve criteria for mobile apps that gather citizen data to meet (such as reliability, accuracy, continuity, spatial resolution, etc.) Their theoretical exercise has been inspired by recent large-scale experiments with crowd sourcing in a number of cities around the world: the largest implementation to date has been in Paris, where the city hall allocated €500 million over five years to projects proposed by citizens by means of a web-based cartographic tool (Saunders and Baeck 2015).

With the appearance of academic research centers dedicated exclusively to studying how real-time data impact urban planning, there is no shortage of technical discussion on modeling, optimization, and improving visualization. One of the more visually striking studies to come out of the MIT-based SENSEable City Lab shows how human activity as seen through the clustering of online sources and phone data does not take into account "outdated" state borders and local government divisions. This research design choice implies that government remains geographically organized for an industrial economy, even though today we live mostly in a knowledge economy (Offenhuber and Ratti 2014). But this wealth of knowledge is unlikely to make a difference unless old-style community organizing takes advantage of it in order to trigger meaningful political change. The end goal is to remake American cities into "responsive cities," where ideas circulate from the bottom up as often as they come from the top on down: but for all the optimism apparent in recent surveys of e-government in America (e.g. Goldsmith and Crawford, 2014), most of the work remains to be done. The data we will use in this book to design interventions for shrinking cities and distressed communities is generally not as large as the sorts of repositories associated with real-time monitoring or the Internet of Things. However, these data represent metrics that are more sophisticated than those routinely collected by cities. We will show in this book that lessons learned from data- and model-driven responses to shrinkage and decline may influence the kind of measures collected in "big data" repositories and deployed in new applications.

Planning Support Systems

The field of planning support systems (PSS) has been well defined for over three decades, ever since its distinctions from both GIS (Geographic Information Systems) and SDSS (Spatial Decision Support Systems) have become widely accepted. Unlike its cousins, PSS focuses on use of spatial data and decision modeling methods (about which more below) to aid specific professional planning tasks, in a long-term, strategic fashion (Geertman et al. 2015, 3). However, as most things technology-driven, PSS evolves at a remarkable pace, with continuing implications for both theory and practice.

In recent years, PSS practitioners have energetically tackled the issue of public engagement: Raghothama and Meijer (2015) have attempted to bridge the gap between the group of technical-rational planners, with roots in mathematical modeling and systems engineering, and qualitative researchers, who emphasize participation, narratives, and values. Their innovative answer is based on developing an integrated framework of PSS modeling and collaborative processes through gaming simulations, and two initial case studies have shown encouraging results. Lieske and colleagues (2015) have examined how PSS can help mitigate the problem of top-down inaction on climate change by putting visualization and analysis tools in the hands of local communities. After assessing multiple methods, they discovered that the most effective path to both improve PSS usability and engage the public lies in the area of 3D visualization. Jutraz and Zupancic (2015) took gaming and 3D rendering a step further, and investigated how well virtual worlds can function as support tools in urban planning. Their exploration of user opinions through semistructured interviews revealed that the experience of immersion greatly improves presentation, communication, and citizen participation.

Critiques have followed hand in hand with the excitement brought by recent professional developments: Minner (2015) looked at the use by Austin (Texas) city planners of "Envision Tomorrow," an award-winning open source planning support tool. While the audience was delighted by the ability of quickly designing scenarios, participation was extremely limited by the fact that deployment took place at work stations one had to physically travel to. Even if the tool were to be deployed online, Minner points out that planning took place with a complete lack of equity indicators and green infrastructure: a reminder that the usefulness of PSS is directly proportional to the quality of work done in terms of criterion selection. It is important to realize that mediocre participatory PSS design can give audiences the impression of transparency while limiting planning options to fewer options than ideal (e.g., simulating different scenarios of road placement but not of road width). We will show in this book that planning support systems that put people and communities at the center of data collection, functionality design, and routine use for planning and development can provide tools that empower stakeholders committed to inclusive responses to shrinkage and distress.

Data Analytics and Decision Science

Methods and applications for acquiring, organizing, and analyzing data to identify trends and patterns, estimate future values of important variables, and create policy and planning prescriptions in the short, medium, and long term are referred to variously as "data analytics," "operations research and management science," and "decision science." These complementary disciplines enable practitioners and researchers to solve challenging problems in business and public affairs in multiple ways: by articulating values that undergird methods to identify decision opportunities and quantify performance metrics (Keeney 2007), applying statistical and forecasting methods for management and operations (Albright and Winston 2015), developing simulation models that represent operations of actual or imagined organizations and systems to generate insights for design and practice (Desai 2012), and building prescriptive models that support decisions related to domains such as facility location and scheduling (Eiselt and Sandblom 2004), service design and management (Fitzsimmons, Fitzsimmons, and Bordoloi 2014), and logistics and supply chain management (Christopher 2016).

Though data analytics and decision science are most often understood to be tools for business, health care, and engineering, there is a long tradition of public- and nonprofit sector applications of decision science and analytics in areas such as urban transportation, environment, the military, energy policy and politics (Pollock, Rothkopf, and Barnett 1994), and urban service delivery and emergency management (Larson and Odoni 2007). Moreover, while common notions of data analytics and decision sciences assume the use of quantitative data and analytic methods within centralized organizations or individual practitioners, there is a different conception of the field, called community operational research (Johnson and Midgley 2018; Midgley and Ochoa-Arias 2004) and community-based operations research (Johnson 2012a), that uses a variety of qualitative as well as quantitative analytic methods and inclusive and participatory engagement methods with community partners. These newer domains are referred to collectively by Johnson (2018a) as "community-engaged operations research."

Within the subfields of public-sector decision modeling, there is an extensive literature on housing and community development (Johnson 2011, 2012b). Work in this area encompasses descriptive research in economic, simulation, and agent-based analyses, prescriptive research for policy design in housing search, provision, and management, and decision-support applications for property management, resource allocation, and housing mobility. Recent research in this area includes models for community-based responses to foreclosed housing (Johnson et al. 2015), development of affordable housing in a formerly distressed community to improve informal social controls (Fabusuyi 2018), and location of affordable housing to ensure transit access to areas of job growth (Zhong et al. 2019). The efficacy of decision-modeling applications in housing and community development relies on most-current social science evidence on the nature of the phenomenon and descriptions of classes of promising responses; in the case of shrinking cities and distressed communities, contemporary work such as Heim LaFrambois and colleagues (2019), Manville and Kuhlmann (2016), and Galster (2017) are important in this regard as they address specific planning responses, indicators of shrinking cities, and theory-building regarding shrinking city dynamics.

Another perspective on the role of decision sciences can play in urban planning is in clarifying the relationship between analysis motivated primarily by the nature of data generated by organizations and processes (the "data-driven" approach often associated with Big Data) and analysis motivated primarily by the nature of the problem to be solved, or the intervention to be designed (the "problem-driven" approach often associated with Smart Cities and decision sciences). Analytics, defined as the "scientific process of transforming data into insights for making better decisions" (INFORMS 2019; Liberatore and Luo 2010), embraces descriptive, predictive, and prescriptive inquiry and thus data-driven and problem-driven analysis, and is the conceptual foundation for the analysis in this book. We will show in this book that community-engaged operations research, connecting knowledge acquisition and theory-building regarding the nature of municipal shrinkage and community distress (evidence) and design of local interventions, based on community input, that optimize multiple social objectives (action), embodies a promising frame for responses to shrinking cities and distressed communities. In particular, we see a strong connection between understanding how residents of shrinking cities articulate their goals and visions about the future, and how they make decisions to achieve them, and exploring specific ways that data analytics and decision modeling can generate productive responses to shrinkage and blight.

In the chapter to follow, we will examine in more detail the pros and cons of a variety of technologies, including Big Data, Smart Cities, and analytics. Our discussion will clarify how these technologies can enhance our understanding of shrinking cities and distressed communities, as well as the potential impacts of interventions rooted in data, models, and technology.

1.5 The Roadmap for the Book

This chapter has provided a rationale for a research and practice focus on the ways in which data and technology can support shrinking cities. It has also described current research and best practices related to shrinking cities as well as information technologies and decision modeling relevant to shrinking cities. The second chapter will argue for the value of data and technology responses to shrinking cities and distressed communities, and discuss barriers to the application of such responses in shrinking cities. We will make two opposing arguments. First, data and technologies can support sustainable and equitable urban planning through community engagement and democratic participation. However, there are serious obstacles to the use of data- and technology-infused planning in lower-income and minority communities, such as political disengagement and social isolation of minority and distressed communities, unequal access to planning technologies by geography, class, and caste, and a bias of planning support technologies toward more-privileged communities.

Chapter 3 reviews how three U.S. cities—Fall River, Massachusetts; Flint, Michigan; and Baltimore, Maryland—do, and do not, make best use of data and technology to address challenges to sustained growth and improved quality of life. These cases will review the recent history of these cities, particularly their understanding of and responses to shrinkage and decline, to learn what kind of data analytics and decision support might be most appropriate for cities of varying sizes, population compositions, and economic characteristics.

The fourth chapter introduces notions of data analytics and decision modeling for shrinkage. We apply these concepts to identify neighborhood-level investments to address blight and decline with a case study of Fall River, Massachusetts. We describe two types of neighborhood-level investments: traditional, focused on housing and economic development, and nontraditional, encompassing passive uses and warehousing. Our findings regarding a portfolio of potential policy and planning directions that correspond to different neighborhood-level investment strategies serve as a preview of the empirical work we do in the next chapter.

Chapter 5 is a case study of shrinkage decision analytics for the city of Baltimore. After describing how planners and analysts use data and analytics to address decline, we show how planners engaged with new models for planning and policy design to develop new responses to blight and decline in one portion of their city. We also use responses by planners to hypothetical planning contexts based on real-life neighborhood data to identify a collection of values that can serve as the basis for a decision modeling and decision support approach that more fully accounts for multiple stakeholders, community engagement, social as well as physical, land-based modeling outcomes, and an explicit focus on equity and social justice.

In chapter 6 we apply lessons learned from previous chapters to develop principles regarding the purpose, requirements, and potential uses of a community-engaged and technology-infused planning support system for resident-led community change. We provide an argument for development of new planning support technologies that can address a wider range of social concerns than those applications that have been developed to date. Such systems can fulfill the promise of on-demand, widely available applications that are accessible to diverse urban populations and enable them to engage in a substantive way with government agencies and nonprofit organizations whose development decisions have significant long-term impacts on the sustainability of their communities.

Chapter 7, our concluding chapter, explores how our case studies help us understand what has and has not worked for big data, smart cities, and planning support for shrinking cities and declining regions.

Our assessment will address recent events in Baltimore and Flint, and most recently, the COVID-19 pandemic, that lay bare trends in inequality and structural barriers to opportunity and basic needs—and prompt a reflection on the most productive role of planning support technologies in such distressed and contentious environments.

Notes

1. Key references include Dewar and Manning Thomas (2012), Galster (2017), Ganning and Teaghe (2018), Heim LaFrambois et al. (2019), Hollander and Németh (2011), Manning and Kuhlmann (2016), Németh et al. (2018), Oswalt (2006), Popper and Popper (2002), Ryan (2012), Weaver et al. (2017), Wiechmann (2008), and Wolff (2010).

2. Recent news articles include Catsaros (2015), El Nasser (2011), Fernández Campbell (2016), Gallagher (2013), Glink (2015), Swope (2006), *The Economist* (2015), Picchi (2017), Thomas (2016), and Tortorello (2011).

CHAPTER 2

What Can Data and Technology Do for Shrinking Cities and Distressed Communities?

Communities and regions facing persistent declines in population, economic activity, and quality of life can benefit from a variety of interventions. Our belief, developed in the first chapter, is that in many shrinking cities and distressed communities it is most important to find ways to provide for needs of current residents and maintain quality of life, without making growth a primary goal. This is the domain of community and city planning and economic development. However, community residents, local institutions, experts, and decision makers may be able to design and implement these interventions more effectively using well-chosen tools and methods from data analysis, information technology, and decision sciences. In other words, data analysis, information technology, and decision sciences are a means to an end. To use these methods productively and creatively, it is important to understand how planners conceive of community interventions, and ways in which data analysis, IT, and decision sciences could affect—positively and negatively—the quality of life and the development trajectory of shrinking and distressed communities. We hope that this chapter will provide residents, planners, service providers, and other professionals ways to make sense of the sometimes overly enthusiastic promises of advocates for various models, technologies, products, or services. We start by reviewing a number of schools of thought in planning that set the stage for data, modeling, and tech for community redevelopment.

2.1 Planning Preliminaries

Participation by community members is an important way of distinguishing between alternative planning approaches, from traditional hierarchical models to contemporary negotiated planning. Fainstein (2000) places urban planners into six categories: three major ones (communicative/collaborative, neotraditionalist, equity-oriented) and three minor ones (traditional rationalist, incrementalist, and Corbusian modernist). Levels of participation are important for major approaches, especially collaborative planners.

Traditional Rationalists

The first steps of urbanism were defined by a philosophy of enlightenment, rationality, and progress. At the turn of the twentieth century, sanitation, water management, insalubrity, and the question of how to assist the needs of slum dwellers were the key preoccupations of the new science; urban reform, carried out in the name of a general interest enunciated by science and guaranteed by the public authority, accompanied the construction of a wage society. Urban values and ideal representations of the city were enunciated formally but the assumptions behind them rarely questioned: the age of rationalist planning was an age extolling technical knowledge placed at the service of a grand political design (Cullingworth and Caves 2003, 34–40).

Rationalist planning arguably both peaked and ran out of steam during the postwar years (up through the 1960s), when planning practices became widely structured around a model of global planning (master plans at all levels of a territory). This period was characterized by interventionism and an activist government that produced major planning operations, including the production of large neighborhoods (Fainstein 2003, 452–453). Federal involvement was widespread in the United States, reflected in the implementation of major highway programs, decisive in the development of suburbs and urban renewal operations for inner cities. But all this activity also resulted in a contestation of this centralized power, of the forms of urbanism thus produced and of spatial inequalities (Fainstein 2000, 453)

Decision-making models under the traditional rationalist approach assume that planners have adequate information, in terms of quality, quantity, and accuracy, and rely heavily on mathematical tools to optimize city planning.

Corbusian Modernists

The twentieth-century planner Le Corbusier led a school of thought that was basically rationalist, but had a deep commitment to mass production and aesthetics centered on the use of unadorned concrete. However, Le Corbusier's interest in democracy may have been more self-proclaimed than aligned with specific actions. Through urban planning, Corbusian modernists also claim to create a scientifically rational and comprehensive solution to urban problems, but they distinguish themselves from "simple" rationalists through an idealized perspective on technology and considerable faith in modernity's ability to deliver progress and social improvement: a modernity centered on a certain design aesthetic (minimal or no ornamentation, repetitive units, high rise towers, and separation of use zoning) (Jacob 1984).

Corbusian modernists support "total" city planning: their vision is distinguished by hugeness, hierarchy, and planning at both the micro and macro levels, ranging from room size and ideal room layout, to building-level elements and streets, to neighborhoods and cities.

Incrementalists

Early critiques of the rationalist model resulted in adopting incrementalism as urban policy. Incrementalism's supporters argued that decisions in complex systems are generally characterized by a high degree of uncertainty, in the sense that future system states are very difficult to predict (Innes and Booher 2010). Policy-makers almost never have all the information they need; by restricting the number of options considered and the information used to evaluate them, one cannot anticipate all possible future developments. As a result, the rationalist ideal appears to be poorly adapted to the challenges of solving complex problems, given the cost of synoptic analysis (in terms of time and resources). If planning cannot be rational for a complex system, then the best course of action is to take a step in what appears to be the right direction and adapt accordingly (a policy of small steps based on the prescriptions of neoclassical economics) (Fainstein 2000, 452).

NEO-TRADITIONALISTS/NEW URBANISTS

New urbanism arose in opposition to modern rationalist designs, which favored car use toward destinations spread out over large areas, and a reliance on international architectural styles that often did not reflect local cultures. New urbanists are essentially defined by a relentless opposition to nearly all characteristics of the uniform residential areas rapidly built in the postwar period. Their aim is to build cities around pedestrians, which implies changing the density of the city in order to "re-humanize" city spaces; they are also attempting to make cities *less* systematic: new urbanists favor neighborhoods where houses are different from each other, though of roughly the same size and assembled in functionally coherent neighborhoods (Fainstein 2000, 461–463). One of the goals of the movement is also to make the population of all social categories live together by offering several types of housing in the same neighborhood (Corburn 2003).

Planners subscribing to this approach stress the substance of their ideas and are relatively uninterested in the political struggle (i.e., how to achieve them). New urbanism, is a design-oriented approach that aims to make all daily needs of life "accessible within a five minute-walk" (Kunstler 1996, 117).

"Just City" Proponents

The past two decades have seen increased support for developing an urban theory of justice. For "just city" proponents, justice should be "the first evaluative criterion used in policy making" (Fainstein 2010, 6). Debates between these proponents is centered on the relationship between democratic processes and just—and efficient—outcomes. Theorists fall into two camps: radical democrats, who take public participation to the furthest possible extent, and political economists interested in making values explicit who believe that democratic processes are insufficient in the absence of relative material equality.

"Just city" theorists are interested in "total planning" as much as Corbusian modernists, but whereas Corbusian planners referred to material things, "just city" theorists wish to use human habitats to remake social life. Fainstein (2010) lists seventeen principles to be followed in pursuit of justice, which she sees as resting on the pillars of diversity and democracy. Important principles include the following among others: make low-income housing part of all new housing development; keep affordable units at current price levels in perpetuity; keep regional transit fares high and in-city fares low, and use affirmative action for housing. This approach is not consistent in all respects; for example, Fainstein insists on both desegregation at all levels and on consulting local populations as to the extent and kind of land use (2010, 18).

Communicative/Collaborative Paradigm

Some planners adhere to a communicative conception of rationality: according to this view, people are not subjects with constant preferences who use logic and science to guide their own actions, but rather they continuously develop views through dialogue (Cullingworth and Caves 2003, 67–71). Given the great diversity of interests and expectations in the public sphere, not only material, but also social and symbolic, good urban planning must begin by tapping as many different sources as possible to establish broad knowledge of the urban space. From this perspective, the planner is best seen as a negotiator or an intermediary among various stakeholders, and planning is first and foremost an effort of social interaction (Fainstein 2014, 14).

Contemporary Trends

Starting in the late 1970s, American planning professionals began to note the limitations of the traditional rationalist planning model, especially its excessive use of mathematical models in the design phase, the linearity of the process, and an oversimplifying framework of analysis (Fainstein 2000). Other critiques were directed at zoning practices, most notably formulated by Jane Jacobs in a widely quoted book on modern cities (Jacobs 1984). Above all, claims of objectivity and political neutrality were widely questioned: urban planning began to be understood as a value-laden process, and the role of the planner refashioned. Could planners escape politics? In a context in which many scholars were beginning to answer in the negative, new methodologies emerged in order to overcome the limits of the rationalist model and trigger new social dynamics (Alexander 2000).

The questioning of the rationalist model has led to the construction of a "new orthodoxy" (Rydin 2007, 53). The profession now views its main task as an interactive political process in which the issue of participation is central and decisive, rather than based on an objective and instrumental rationality (Fisher et al. 1993). Collaborative approaches feature dialogue to define common values and to promote exchanges among stakeholders (Alterman, Stay, and Healey 1999). Planners can facilitate negotiations between citizens and organizations of all levels of economic and political power to support collective learning (Forester 1999). They do this by developing strategies to facilitate dialogue and resolve conflicts. This strategy development helps anticipate the concerns of stakeholders in advance of negotiation. In neighborhood revitalization, for example, planners can lead processes that balance efforts to change the built environment, to address social needs and emotions of residents, and to engage internal stakeholders (e.g., residents and business owners) as well as external stakeholders (governments, nonprofits, and financial institutions). Interactions among these four domains can generate a rich set of strategies (Morckel 2014).

Planners attempt to adopt a neutral attitude between the parties in conflict; they draw attention to specific problems, propose solutions, and offer different points of view and arguments; they seek to build trust between the parties and to reconcile divergent interests—in brief, they act as negotiators, facilitators, and mediators (Forester 1999, 5–12). What, then, is the difference today between collaborative practitioners, neotraditionalists, and "just city" proponents?

The debate turns on what weight the planner's voice should have at the public table. Almost five decades ago Sherry Arnstein had already identified eight different degrees of public participation, ranging from none to full managerial power (Arnstein 1969); earlier than that, Davidoff (1965) asserted the right for planners to advocate for underserved and underrepresented populations. Most modern planners would agree that the public needs to be consulted; but while neotraditionalists are happy to emphasize transparency in decision making and little more, collaborative theorists stress the value of education—not only the education of the public by the agency but also of the agency by the public (Innes and Booher 2004, 426). In other words, city planning should be based on a model of coproduction of knowledge (Corburn 2003). Neotraditionalists and just city proponents, however, tend to deny the practical feasibility of this ideal: in their view, citizens should be consulted on the issues, but only selectively placated, because they almost always have a view narrower than that of professional planners (Campanella 2011, 147).

There are multiple critiques of the collaborative approach, however. The neotraditionalist approach, represented by Campanella (2011), sees no reason why planners should give up the prerogatives that come with expertise. After all, goes the critique, doctors don't rely on patients' knowledge of medicine before they diagnose, and economists don't hold community meetings to decide the course of fiscal policy (Campanella 2011, 147). Fainstein dismisses the communicative planning paradigm as procedures "without substantive content" (Fainstein 2000, 472) and devotes an entire book to proposing a different paradigm, that of the "just city" (Fainstein 2010). In her view, deliberative planning is not only insufficient for overcoming structural inequalities, but also impossible to fix; she goes on to propose an urban theory of justice based on Amartya Sen's capabilities approach, in order to constrain urban planners into benevolence. Her views (Fainstein 2010) follow a fairly long tradition of proponents of planners as enlightened despots (see for instance Beauregard 1984).

Controversy continues regarding the merits of communicative planning theory, with its most often cited fundamental weakness being an expectation that disadvantaged communities could gain meaningful representation from their presence at the table alone. Planners subscribing to other schools point out that ability to participate means little without access to expertise and good organization, two features unlikely to emerge organically from the ranks of everyday citizens (Rydin 2007). Collaborative planners, however, have attempted to incorporate their opponents' critiques into improved versions of their practices, drawing heavily on a growing literature on best practices in citizen engagement (Innes and Booher 2004; Lane 2005; Ansell and Gash 2008).

WHERE DO DATA, MODELS, AND TECHNOLOGY COME IN?

Though there may be a contemporary consensus that planning approaches that emphasize collaboration and engagement are most likely to provide a better quality of life through procedural and substantive methods that emphasize voice, values, and equity, implementing these approaches in practice can be challenging. Electronic data, analytic models, and information technology have become ubiquitous in most domains of modern life, but they are not always well incorporated into planning practice (Innes and Booher 2010). Moreover, as discussed above, many planning movements represent a reaction to an overreliance on a rationalist view of planning rooted in quantitative data and modeling. Is it possible, however, that the concern with data, models, and technology is really that they are not often used in ways that can support collaboration and engagement with community members? Or that we have an overly restrictive notion of what data, models, and technology can mean?

The subject of data, models, and technology in planning continues to be an active area of research—see for example the triennial Computers in Urban Planning and Urban Management (CUPUM) conferences over the past twenty years, or the presence of academic journals and tracks at conferences that emphasize data, models, and technology. The emerging field of geodesign (Goodchild 2010; Steinitz 2012) represents an innovative conception of design that crosses scales (local to regional), disciplines (cartography, GIS, physical design, landscape architecture, information technology, and decision sciences), participants (residents, planning practitioners, technologists, and researchers), and processes (representation, evaluation, forecasting, and decision modeling). However, many planning programs do not emphasize data analytics, decision modeling, or information technology at the level of other data- and analytics-intensive graduate professional programs, and many planning organizations do not extensively use data, models, or technology as ways to engage or collaborate with community members. Such a deficit in use of this knowledge in the field appears especially acute in shrinking cities and distressed communities, where technical capacity and financial resources are most limited—a point we will elaborate on in chapter 3.

In the next two sections we will explore the ways in which data, modeling, and technologies can advance the mission of community-engaged planning *and* impede progress toward a community-engaged planning ideal, especially in shrinking cities and distressed communities. We'll then synthesize our findings to make the case for certain kinds of analytic and tech approaches that appear to be promising candidates to support the planning needs of community members as co-equal collaborators with professionals where the usual goals of planning—planning for more uses, more growth, more people—may not reflect the reality of certain communities, cities, or regions.

2.2 The Glass Is Half-Full: How Data and Technologies Can Support Sustainable and Equitable Urban Planning

If one thinks about the wide variety of services and products delivered by the internet, or made possible by the internet, or accessed through our smartphones, the opportunities for data, models, and technologies to improve urban life may seem limitless. The view for planning seems equally promising: computerized applications such as geographic information systems, planning support systems, and spatial decision support systems have been studied and used in the field for over thirty years (Timmermans 1997; Mantaay and Ziegler 2006; Brail 2008; Geertman et al. 2015). Surely this abundance of scholarship, applications, and practice could be adapted to meet the needs of neighborhoods, cities, and regions seeking ways to regenerate, to advocate for more equitable allocations of resources, and to plan for less. We'll discuss eleven areas in which this might be possible.

Quality of Life

Big data, and analytic methods used with big data, have the potential to improve urban life, first by helping answer a variety of questions relevant to urban social science to support more effective and efficient services and interventions, and to improve city management, resulting in higher-quality urban services (Glaeser et al. 2015). Questions that big data could answer include (1) How does urban development influence the economy? (2) How does the physical city interact with social outcomes? (3) How much do people value urban amenities? and (4) How can public policy improve the quality of physical space? For example, Glaeser and colleagues demonstrate that visual recognition techniques applied to Google Street View imagery could predict values of wealth and poverty and residential segregation or show changes in these values over time. It might also be possible to use complaints on TripAdvisor or Yelp to guide public inspections via predictive algorithms.

Advanced analytic methods, combined with metrics that can be generated by big data, can also be used to compute new measures of quality of life. Rankings such as Huffington Post's "Most Livable Cities" (Abbey-Lambertz 2016) and *New York Times*' "Most Livable Neighborhoods" (Buckley 2010) are representative of many livability indices that can be viewed as weighted sums of quality-of-life indicator scores, which are qualitative (e.g., surveys or subjective measures) or quantitative (administrative data) measures. The decision of what input measures and what weights to use are subjective, which is why there are so many livability indices. Geers and Economou (2014) use machine learning methods to compute a general and consistent livability index based on many different objective quality-of-life measures that can support a wide variety of planning and operational investment decisions.

One could collect a variety of quality of life indicators for a particular city to enable residents to better understand future trends, and consider alternative living patterns, and to engage more closely with planners. In Japan, the aging population makes it likely that cities will become more compact, resulting in significant changes in cities' footprints. In this case, an application called "My City Forecast" (Hasegawa et al. 2015) simulates a variety of values related to demographics, access to local amenities, environmental resources, safety, and finance under allowing for a transition to a more compact city, as well as no changes in underlying demographic trends ("business as usual"). This application allows residents to understand how population loss on different streets will affect their daily lives. With the increasing use of open data and city-specific datasets, these applications can help residents collaborate with planners on potentially controversial decisions regarding future land uses.

Technology-Enhanced Community Engagement

We commonly use information technology to communicate, manage relationships, and build community. But how can data, models, and IT enable residents of neighborhoods to work together to imagine, and to then design, better communities? This is likely to require more than discussions on social media and online meetings. The My City Forecast application described above has the potential to support community engagement, but other applications go even further in providing tools for citizens to build deep knowledge about their neighborhoods and to work with planners to design new interventions. Perhaps the most widely used tool for community data sharing and engagement is the 311 system (Goodyear 2018). Deployed in many cities, this system allows residents to phone in requests for all manner of public services—from maintenance to emergency services to reporting public dangers—and is an example of an application that allows residents to take ownership of public spaces where they live. Services such as 311 also generate rich data that can be linked with many others to better understand a wide range of descriptive, explanatory, predictive, and prescriptive analytic questions. CityEye (Lee et al. 2015) is a proposed platform that brings together operations, sensor, and citizen feedback data through a web-based dashboard and a service-based mobile application. Designed for citizens as well as city workers and service providers, it serves as a sort of next-generation 311 system. For certain operations, such as garbage pick-up, citizens could monitor services, check environmental conditions, and submit accident reports, and workers could monitor individual and aggregate demands for service and engage citizens. Designed for two Spanish cities, Barcelona and Santander, the authors note that it is not yet deployed in the field.

An application that extends real-time, location-aware comments like the 311 and City Eye applications to community planning is the ChangeExplorer service (Wilson, Tewdwr-Jones, and Comber 2019). This smart watch program, linked to a mobile phone, enables citizens to respond to requests for comments about proposed changes in defined areas; these responses could consist of categories selected on the smart watch, or more detailed comments entered on a mobile phone. This pilot project demonstrates the potential for information technology to allow citizens to participate in local planning processes without the need for detailed technical knowledge or attending formal meetings. This technology also enables citizens to have a deeper connection with their local environment and to identify problems they may not have noticed before and opportunities for improvements.

Another approach to data visualization for community engagement is three-dimensional modeling. Jutraž and Zupančič (2015) explore the potential of the "Terf" virtual world that incorporates multiple actors, multiple analytic methods, and multiple software tools as part of an urban-planning and urban design process. By evaluating this tool among planners and the general public, they determine how important different features of navigation are within the virtual space to different groups. They use these results to test a decision-making process in which priorities placed on various features allow for ranking of defined design alternatives. This kind of work is promising because it demonstrates an interest in philosophical assumptions and presentation related to software use beyond features of a specific package.

An alternative to an immersive 3-D experience is "augmented reality," in which 3-D objects are superimposed onto photographic representations of spaces. Reinwald and colleagues (2014) present the "ways2gether" augmented reality mobile phone application to learn whether groups who do not traditionally participate in planning processes, such as those who are not interested (teenagers) or who have little time to take part (caregivers), might find special value in this application. By comparing participation with the new AR application to 3D renderings and traditional 2D plans, the authors find that AR has the potential to make planning efforts more inviting, understandable, and supportive of communication as compared to conventional methods. *Carticipe* ("*Debatomap*") (http://carticipe.net) is a web-based application that supports online and in-person community discussions about proposed changes to local infrastructure, with features to allow map-based visualization of proposed community changes and summary reports.

Earlier we discussed the role that 311 services play in community data sharing and engagement. A more expansive view on 311 services is provided by O'Brien (2018), who argues that 311 services are provided to shared public spaces called the "urban commons," and that the process of asserting responsibility for and collective maintenance of this shared ownership space is called "stewardship." The 311-type services provide a way to learn how community members contribute to the maintenance of their neighborhoods, how they collectively build knowledge about their neighborhoods, and how generally they help government provide important services through coproduction via civic technology. By treating residents as partners rather than clients, 311-type systems can enable a more robust notion of citizenship and a more responsive notion of government services.

Web-Supported Democratic Participation

Data and tech have the potential not only to facilitate citizen engagement with planning processes but to provide platforms for them to speak directly with each other and with elected officials and other public servants regarding the configuration of their neighborhoods. One application that makes this possible is *Better Reykjavik* (https://betrireykjavik.is), a website that enables residents of the Icelandic city of Reykjavik to review and vote on ten to fifteen top priorities of the Reykjavik City Council. Seventy thousand people have participated out of a population of 120,000 since the site opened; 257 ideas have been formally reviewed and 165 accepted since 2011. The site *Madame Mayor, I Have an Idea* (https://idee.paris.fr) enables residents of Paris, France, to propose their own ideas for community improvement and to receive government support for certain projects. Between 2014 and 2020 the Paris city government has awarded over €500 million to projects proposed by citizens, the largest exercise of its kind in the world. One particularly innovative citizen-inspired project has been vertical gardens.

UrbanData2Decide (http://www.urbandata2decide.eu/) is a European Union project intended to provide data visualization and decision support for difficult urban problems using open data and social media for inputs, and expert panels for assessments. A case study in Malmö, Sweden, focuses on urban safety and security, relating to how decisions are made on a proactive and operational level. Another case study in Copenhagen, Denmark, focuses on municipal spatial planning, including information on how decisions are made for a longer period of time in collaboration with the citizens. In Austria, this project has been applied in Vienna to ten ongoing and future urban planning projects.

Analytics and Decision Modeling

A different approach to quantitative urban planning with a focus on sustainability and shrinking and distressed cities and communities is based on descriptive, predictive, and prescriptive analytic methods applied to large datasets. Appel and colleagues (2014) built a computer model based on machine learning and data mining to classify neighborhoods in the city of Syracuse, New York, into four categories based on recorded vacancy rate and regression-estimated risk for vacancy. These categories—distressed, transitional, bubble, and stable—provide support for planners to design interventions for property acquisition and redevelopment that is systematic and predictive rather than reactive and transactional (often the case for even well-intentioned and experienced local planners and community development professionals). McLarty and associates (2014) used mathematical modeling to generate measures of suitability for assigning pairs of cities to pursue "sister city" relationships based on synergies associated with common interests in water, energy, food, agriculture, social and environmental welfare, and waste collection and recycling, plus a measure of general amicability. The resulting PAIRS metric can be used to identify partnerships between cities that offer the greatest amount of mutual benefit as a function of the level of heterogeneity across these five sectors. Morckel (2016) used suitability analysis to create an index by which candidate properties for demolition could be ranked and thereby support a decision model for demolition planning.

A different application of analytics is the question of what sort of sensing can enable planners to assess the variation in strength of citizens' preferences for various local environments. Social sensing is a developing field, based on the marriage of mobile devices, accelerometers, and location sensors. Tisma and colleagues (2015) established a framework for what constitutes "good sensing" and presented a set of requirements for mobile apps for landscape and urban planning. Their proposed "Landscapiness" mobile phone app solicits data from users regarding their perceptions of the environment they are located in, and aggregates this data to show how certain indexes, such as perception of pleasure, may vary over space. This information can enable researchers, urban planners, and users to collaborate on targeted policies for improving communities and natural resources.

The CityNexus data analytics tool, developed by students at Massachusetts Institute of Technology and piloted in a number of Massachusetts cities, enables multiple datasets related to blight, abandonment, and community development to be combined to support analysis, mapping, and rapid response (Larson 2016). The Boston Data Portal, hosted by the Boston Area Research Initiative, combines data and documentation on Boston neighborhoods (The Boston Data Library) with interactive neighborhood maps that support user input (BostonMap) (Boston Area Research Initiative 2018).

Civic Games and Simulations

Conventional modes of data collection and analysis to support planning-type interventions can be time consuming, administratively burdensome, and cognitively demanding. Researchers can appear more enthusiastic about the willingness of non-expert residents to commit time and energy to planning exercises than are the participants themselves. This can be especially true for residents of neighborhoods and cities facing social, physical, and economic symptoms of decline and distress. In response, researchers have adapted notions from creative play, game-making, and simulations to enable planning process participants to bring to the exercise their own perspectives and problem-solving skills, without expectations that participants engage in potentially stressful or distressing analysis.

Raghothama and Meijer (2015) argue that analysis and design of urban systems can be classified into two groups: systems engineering and politics and process. The former can be viewed by ordinary participants as too mathematical, and the latter can be critiqued by researchers as not sufficiently engaged with scientific facts. Their solution is to create gaming simulations, which combine computer simulations with collaborative processes using qualitative and quantitative analytic methods. Given the enormous popularity of gaming for recreation—an estimated 2.3 billion gamers around the globe generated $137.9 billion in gaming revenues in 2018 (Wijman 2018)—this approach seems well aligned with preferences of many people. However, it is technically demanding and expensive to create realistic simulations of real-world planning environments: major games have budgets in the hundreds of millions of dollars. The authors present a framework for designing games that incorporate multiple simulations and multiple stakeholder perspectives in order for participants to explore scenarios and achieve goals. Examples of gaming simulations applied to pedestrian and traffic congestion related to university students traveling between classes in Stockholm, Sweden, and managing security at sports stadia in Paris. While early results of these simulations are promising, much work needs to be done to create realistic gaming environments and stimulating communities of design practice.

Another approach to gaming and play is focused less on the technological challenges of creating realistic and immersive gaming environments using information technology than on understanding how people conceive of problem solving as playful versus resembling work. Gordon and Walter (2016) critique the notion of efficiency usually associated with industrial and technical "work" as "defined by cost-effectiveness, speed, and market distribution" (244). Next, they interrogate the notion implicit in smart cities and government 2.0 applications that a "good user" denotes a persons who acts within specific and well-defined abstract procedures, such as attending meetings or submitting complaints. In response, they define a notion of "meaningful inefficiency" in which users gain value from taking extra time to reflect and engage in a spirit of play, in which, problem solving generates its own intrinsic value. This notion is represented in an experimental game called Community PlanIt, which is intended to make planning less efficient yet more effective. This can be done because researchers and participants engage with "the messy data of deliberation, the playful competition, and the creative story-telling" (261). Another example of creating gaming for community change is the game "@Stake," in which participants take on roles of community stakeholders trying to solve a common problem by engaging common conflicts in motivations and goals. This game originated as a card-playing activity and is now available as a smartphone app (https://elab.emerson.edu/projects/atstake).

Social Media

Like gaming, social media are ubiquitous in today's internet-connected age. As computer-based and online games adapt the spirit of in-person and analog games to a new environment, social media adapt traditional modes of face-to-face and telephone contact to build relationships across space, time, and multiple communities via communication technologies. Social media support social networks, groups of persons related by work, friendship, families, and interests for sociability, support, and control (Hampton and Wellman 2003). While most readers have firsthand experience with social media like Facebook and Twitter, and the communities and networks associated with these applications, their relevance to planning is less certain. Can social media use by community groups result in productive efforts by a social network of community members to engage in a planning process?

Williamson and Ruming (2015) explore the use of Twitter by five community groups in Sydney, Australia, that are opposed to changes in local planning procedures. The current land uses of interest to the community groups vary widely (horse racing, vacant lots, tennis courts) as do the sizes (2,230 square meters to 105,000 square meters). Using Social Network Analysis, they discover that there is limited participation by group members in planning-related discussions: the groups are led "by a small number of active people, which do not attract large numbers of friends and followers on Twitter and key stakeholders play a passive listening role in the networks." Though we can't generalize from these case studies in a prosperous, growing region to shrinking cities and distressed communities, we should be cautious about the ability of social media to support inclusive community engagement for local change.

Geographic Information Systems, Participatory GIS, and Extensions

Geographic information systems can be understood as information about the real world represented in a simplified and abstract way in computerized databases which, when combined with specialized hardware, software, and skilled analysts, can produce data to solve problems of a spatial nature (Mantaay and Ziegler 2006). GIS technologies can support mapping projects that involve community members as well as experts, but these technologies have been long criticized for exploiting marginalized communities and exacerbating local and regional conflicts (Sieber 2006). In response, public participatory GIS provide a way for the public to be actively engaged, not just consulted, in spatial problem solving. PPGIS can allow non-expert participants to map out their values and understanding of the local environment; such efforts to increase stakeholder engagement and diversity while accounting for multiple social identities can improve project outcomes (Brown 2012).

Among the many research projects related to PPGIS, Carver (2003) reviews technological approaches to improving public participation that emphasizes the effects of space, place, and locality. Cultural and institutional dimensions that may affect participation in PPGIS efforts are particularly important: size and density of communities, developed versus less-developed country environments, European Union versus North America environments, and regions with fixed versus shifting borders, among others. However, evidence that PPGIS processes lead to greater public participation, empowerment, and conflict resolution is limited (Sieber 2006; Brown 2012; Cuppen 2012). One perspective on use of GIS and spatial data in the field is provided by Chorianopoulos (2014), who explores the mismatch between the represented (on Google Maps) and the experienced image of the city. The author proposes the design of dynamically crowd-sourced mobile map applications, where (for instance) the most frequently used streets will be illustrated according to user feedback. SeaSketch (Goldberg et al. 2018) and CommunityViz (Aggett and McColl 2006) are examples of PPGIS applications in active use throughout the United States and internationally.

A recent extension of PPGIS called community geography (Robinson et al. 2016) addresses well-documented concerns that human, financial, and technical resource constraints, limited data, and lack of long-term commitments between experts and communities reduced the impact of community-engaged spatial analysis. Community geography integrates human actors, referred to as "chauffeurs" or "facilitators," who can translate technology to community residents, a willingness to build partnerships based on local capacity-building going beyond strictly spatial data acquisition and analysis, and a commitment to long-term relationships based on reciprocity, co-learning, and cultural competence.

Community-Based Research and Technology Design

There is a long tradition of methods to work closely with members of a community, or with organizations and institutions that employ members of a community, or are owned, directed, or responsible to community organizations in order to build knowledge, technical capacity, and voice for advocacy and social change. These methods go by many names, but are referred to here as "community-based participatory research" (CBPR; Pant 2008). In a community-based participatory research process, community members take a co-equal role with trained researchers and professionals in four ways. First, they identify and define a research question to be studied. Next, they define values and principles that distinguish one way of knowing about the question from another. They also generate characteristics of the research question that allow identification of alternative courses of action and attributes by which to assess progress toward an improved state. Finally, they define criteria by which one might determine that a new way of doing things generates, or is likely to generate, outcomes that represent an improvement over the status quo. It is especially desirable for community stakeholders, with researchers, to be able to generate one or more new states of affairs that are likely to be, or are guaranteed to be, the best possible new outcomes as compared to the status quo.

CBPR in the context of technology-based approaches to community change is referred to as participatory action design research (PADR). PADR is challenging because it requires a critical perspective of imbalances of power and influence between poor and affluent, between communities of color and majority populations and the need for research aimed for social justice (Lykes and Mallona 2008; Torre 2009), as well as a deep understanding of technologies and processes used to create new applications for active use in urban environments that reflect social and cultural contexts of users (Bilandzic and Venable 2011). It can be best understood as technology-infused data collection and analysis for community problem solving (Johnson 2015a). Mayorga (2014) describes how PADR is used in the field for public education and community development, and emphasizes the challenges associated with building online plus in-person communities for local change. Community geography (Robinson et al. 2016), introduced previously as an extension of public participatory GIS, shares values, analytic methods, and outcomes quite consistent with CBPR and PADR, though of course rooted in spatial data and analysis.

Community-Engaged Operations Research and Community Data Analytics

Operations research is an interdisciplinary field devoted to empirical problem solving using models that abstract from real-world organizations, systems and processes, and analytic methods that aspire to identify optimal, or most-preferred, solutions. As mentioned earlier, analytics describes a collection of approaches to learning about the world through data, encompassing what is known about the world, or what has occurred (descriptive analytics), what could occur in the future (predictive analytics), and defined directions for operations and strategy based on well-articulated values and objectives (prescriptive analytics) (Albright and Winston 2015).

An adaptation of OR to the needs of community members and community-based organizations, called community-engaged OR (Johnson 2018a), recognizes that solutions to problems of a localized nature, affecting disadvantaged or marginalized communities, require meaningful engagement with these organizations, yielding co-creation of models and solution (community-based OR; see Johnson 2012) or meaningful engagement with community members themselves (community OR; see Johnson, Midgley, and Chichirau 2018). The collection of these approaches has yielded many examples of researchers working in and with communities to address important social problems such as housing and community development (Johnson 2005; Johnson et al. 2016) and urban planning, youth development, post-disaster response, and many others (Johnson and Midgley 2018).

A related area of inquiry is focused on ways in which researchers and community representatives use community-based participatory processes to learn about local problems and systems using a mix of primary and secondary data and qualitative and quantitative methods. Called community data analytics (Johnson 2015b), this effort emphasizes the role of non-expert community members to define data elements, to collect them using local knowledge, and to use the data to generate knowledge for empowerment and local impact. One example of this work is the efforts of youth in a low-income community in Boston to collect data on attitudes and knowledge of their peers regarding searching for and acquiring jobs that contradicted much common knowledge by established service providers (Gardner, Snyder, and Zuguy 2019).

Geodesign

In response to a desire for the fields of design (urban planning and landscape architecture) and geographic information science (geographic information systems, spatial science, and information systems) to work more closely together, researchers in the first decade of the 2000s convened multiple workshops and conferences that produced the new domain of geodesign. Geodesign integrates multiple processes, analytic methods, and technologies to produce solutions to problems in the built and natural environments that range from small-scale (a single structure) to large-scale (a metropolitan area, watershed, or ecosystem), are rooted in interdisciplinary and transdisciplinary collaborations based on the scientific method, and integrate the sometimes-competing perspectives and roles of residents, scientists, engineers, practitioners, and technologists (Goodchild 2010). Geodesign is a way of practice that uses systems thinking to understand how challenging environmental problems represent multiple dynamic systems that respond to human interventions and require an iterative, flexible approach to problem solving. This approach consists of *representation models*, which determine how the study area can be described; *process models*, which provide base-line knowledge about the operation of the study area; *evaluation models*, which assess the current quality of the study area; *change models*, which generate a range of potential alterations to the study area; *impact models*, which identify outcomes associated with specified changes to the environment, and *decision models*, which determine how the study area should be changed (Steinitz 2016). These models are applied sequentially in the order presented above to identify the scope of the study, then in reverse order to specify the particular methods needed for the study, and finally again in original order to perform the actual geodesign study. During this last stage, stakeholder input and review is essential to determine if and how the project should be continued, or redesigned (Steinitz 2012). Geodesign includes traditional design disciplines, geographic information sciences, and data and decision analytics as special cases, each of which is limited by their disciplinary understandings of problems to be identified, formulated, solved, and implemented. Software and technology for geodesign is available via well-established applications such as ESRI's ArcGIS, a multitude of spatial decision support systems, and newer applications supporting real-time "sketching" in GIS like ArcSketch, and the Geodesignhub software service (https://www.geodesignhub.com) for strategy design and conflict resolution in a spatial context. Geodesign's greatest contribution may be its potential to support ways of designing that are "robust, resilient, flexible [and] adaptable" and that allow traditionally marginalized stakeholders to counter powerful interests using collaboration and science (Steinitz and Pinheiro 2018).

New Models for Researcher-Community Collaborations

Learning about and creating solutions to problems of interest to traditionally underresourced and underrepresented urban communities, such as those in shrinking cities and distressed neighborhoods is difficult; doing so in an authentically collaborative and engaged manner is even more challenging and requires new models for working with communities. One such model is the Boston Area Research Initiative (BARI; https://cssh.northeastern.edu/bostonarearesearchinitiative). BARI is a collaboration between Boston-area universities, the city of Boston's Mayor's Office of New Urban Mechanics (MONUM; https://www.boston.gov/departments/new-urban-mechanics), for-profit companies, and other city and state agencies. This collaboration has yielded multiple high-impact projects that defy the usual academic model of researcher-dictated agendas and results that are neither timely nor of great interest to community partners. One example is the Boston 311 study presented by O'Brien (2018) and discussed above.

Another model for researcher-community collaborations is less focused on large datasets and advanced quantitative analytic methods and instead places its emphasis on relationship building between researchers and individual community members and community-based organizations for organizing, engaged research, and advocacy for social change. One organization that spearheads this model is called the Urban Research-Based Action Network (URBAN; http://urbanresearchnetwork.org). URBAN has generated collections of researchers and community members across geography (city "nodes") and disciplines (education, sociology, and urban planning). Knowledge generated has ranged from the role of youth in making their schools more responsive to their concerns, to documenting the nature of unaffordable housing in California, to evidence-based advocacy by communities of color in New York City against "broken-windows" policing. The BARI or URBAN model, or a combination of the two, may be well suited to meeting the planning and policy needs of shrinking cities and distressed communities, where local voice and immediate impact are critical to successful interventions.

2.3 The Glass Is Half-Empty: Limits to the Benefits of Data and Technologies in Urban Areas

It's not surprising that there are so many dimensions along which data, models, and information technology can benefit cities and communities, including those at high risk for declines in population, economic activity, and quality of life. There really are many ways in which technological progress can benefit the wider society. However, American society is riven with structural barriers to equality of opportunity, disparities in social outcomes, and institutional racism, among other structural flaws. It should be equally obvious that data, models, and information technology, on their own, cannot possibly be a remedy to larger institutional flaws in civic life. Nevertheless, it is instructive to consider the ways in which our unequal society generates specific barriers to opportunities for many persons and communities to benefit from the Big Data and Smart Cities movements.

Political Disengagement, Social Isolation, and Unequal Technology Access of Minority and Underserved Communities

America's neighborhoods are highly segregated by race, ethnicity, and income (Logan 2013; Do et al. 2017, Bischoff and Reardon 2014). The consequences of this fact are manifold and long present in American life. Physical and social isolation of minority and low-income communities is associated with low socioeconomic status that in turn is associated with poorer health outcomes (Popescu et al. 2018) and higher levels of violent crime (Krivo, Peterson, and Kuhl 2009), among many other measures of individual and neighborhood distress. But racial residential segregation is also associated with race-based inequalities in measures associated with resources that might reduce levels of distress. For example, civic-sector associations, which can build social capital and support social and economic advancement, are more likely to dissolve when located in predominately minority communities than in than white communities (Garrow 2015). Minority communities have lower levels and lower quality of local service provision and reduced regional political influence than white communities (Troustine 2018). Minority communities have lower levels of information technology infrastructure, including internet access generally (Hargittai and Hennant 2008) and certain social media (Cranshaw et al. 2010).

These characteristics of minority and low-income communities mean that there are real limits to the benefits that data, models, and information technology may provide. For example, Baibarac (2014) has documented innovative spatial representations of urban communities using residents' lived experiences on the "Urban Spacebook" participatory urban planning platform. Such rich visualizations of communities are likely associated with high levels of community efficacy.

However, as Teixeira (2016) has shown in her study of youth mapping using community-based participatory research, residents of distressed communities may have fears of criminal victimization and feelings of anger and frustration at the level of blight and abandonment in their neighborhoods. Therefore, technologies that could empower residents to highlight "hidden gems" of their neighborhoods or suggest areas for improvements that build on identified strengths rather than weaknesses may not be especially relevant to those who are fearful of abandoned houses, withdraw from dangerous surroundings, and believe they have no control over the future of their neighborhoods. In addition, residents of communities in which they feel themselves to be vulnerable may be less likely to routinely share personal information about themselves, such as GPS coordinates in the case of the Urban Spacebook study, than are more-advantaged persons or those in more affluent communities. The training, expertise, and resources that could enable residents to co-create knowledge of their environments and enrich their daily experiences in communities would have to be augmented with awareness of social justice issues to enable residents in distressed communities to express positive views of their surroundings, investments that are less necessary in more-advantaged communities.

We have described in the previous section a study by Raghothama and Meijer (2015) on gaming simulations that offer the possibility of immersive experiences that bridge the gap between engineering-based planning interventions and process-based approaches that rely on subjective impressions. However, development of actual applications is very expensive; it is less likely that residents and representatives of economically disadvantaged communities would advocate for such large investments in planning-related services when so many basic needs—shelter, health, education, and more—are unmet.

One assumption of community engagement and democratic participation in neighborhoods is that residents have common understandings of where and how to engage in discussions and deliberations that can determine the future of a community. Balassiano and Seeger (2014), in their study of community informatics, urban planning, and newcomer integration in local governance rural American towns, use community-based participatory mapping to show that white and Latino residents have systematically different conceptions of acceptable places to have informal discussions about community affairs. While both groups use recreation centers, high schools, grocery stores, and libraries, the groups tend to cluster in similar types of facilities in different locations. In addition, males, especially white males, tend to use local city or town halls as central locations for decision making and discussions about public affairs, while women use community-based locations for more informal discussions related to daily activities. As a result, data and technology interventions for community participation that rely on computer-mediated group discussions must accommodate a diversity of locations to reflect a diversity of needs and perspectives on acceptable and welcoming places for civic discussions.

Lack of Recognition of Privilege, Inequity, and Community Exclusion in Planning Support Technologies

A study of people's conceptions of "smart cities" that uses communicative and deliberative planning principles to tell a story about smart cities that seeks a sustainable and livable community through principles such as "smart people," "smart living," and "smart environment" (Staffans and Horelli 2014) is a welcome corrective to corporatized notions of the ways that automation and ubiquitous data can improve residents' lives. Indeed, a study with university students in a planning class at a university in the northwest area of Italy to identify novel interpretations of smart cities yielded promising themes including "responsible and responsive community with active citizens," "participation and democracy brings forth the smart city," and "the smart city recognizes the need to manage change." However, the lack of social and economic variation in the study participants leads one to wonder whether less-privileged, less-educated, or older participants may have had different notions of what a smart city could be.

A study of planning reforms in the New South Wales region of Australia by Piracha (2015), dubbed "ePlanning," intended to increase use of computer technology revealed that the overwhelming emphasis of new technologies was to improve administrative efficiency for day-to-day planning, rather than engaging community stakeholders. Planning decision makers have increasingly reflected policy preferences of a politically conservative party that recently gained control of the state government. As a result, planning reforms have emphasized "fast-tracking" projects and limiting local input into approvals, and computer applications have focused on improving customer service, delivering improved user experiences and making it easier for businesses to identify investment opportunities. This imbalance in planning priorities disadvantages less-influential and nonprofit/third-sector stakeholders.

In contrast to many trends in planning toward strategic visualization, brainstorming, and alternatives identification and selection using information technology (Wyatt 1999; Klosterman 2001; Pamuk 2006), Piracha shows that there have been few efforts in Australia, and in New South Wales particularly, to incorporate computerized tools to engage stakeholders in collaborative policy-making. In other areas outside of Australia where neoliberal trends toward efficiency gains reflect concerns of housing and other corporate interests rather than local communities and environmental organizations, investments in data and technology may not improve social outcomes of residents, especially in distressed and inner-city communities where housing profits can be greatest (Desmond 2016).

Envision Tomorrow is an award-winning open source planning support tool to support large-scale planning in Austin, Texas, through scenario design and simulations. A review of the tool (Minner 2015) revealed a complete lack of equity indicators and green infrastructure. Indeed, nothing in the tool required public input or participation. This is not unusual; a sample of public agencies by Göçmen and Ventura (2010) showed that GIS tended to be used for simple mapping or accessing basic information rather than modeling or spatial analysis. In addition, Bartholomew's (2007) review of transportation planning has documented a lack of meaningful citizen participation, development scenarios based on political or business agendas and showing limited variation and limited adoption of effective implementation strategies.

Lack of Trust

Use of information technology by citizens, and acceptance of data collection on citizens by authorities, requires trust that the data they share will not be used against them, and that the data collected about them is done in a fair and equitable fashion and used for administrative and law enforcement tasks that do not result in discrimination or disparities in processes or outcomes. Unfortunately, citizen trust in these two aspects of data collection can be undermined by government actions. Schuck (2015), in a study of factors associated with levels of surveillance camera use in law enforcement, finds that higher-crime and higher-inequality areas, and areas that are more politically conservative, tend to have more in-car cameras; similar trends were observed for use of mobile cameras. This may indicate that in liberal areas where there is less trust and confidence in the police, initiatives such as cameras that can increase perceptions of legitimacy may be less effective; in contrast, higher-crime and higher-inequality areas may have residents who have less influence to object to cameras.

A study by Ali (2006) of police surveillance of Muslim communities in New York City after the terrorist attacks of 2001 demonstrated widespread use of informants and surveillance of all types of Muslims: those who were politically engaged as well as those who were not, those who were religiously active as well as those who were not, young versus old, and so on. The effect of this pervasive profiling on the young Muslims who are the subject of this study is increased mistrust of other community members, reduced solidarity, self-censorship, and limited engagement in public activities. Shuck's study on surveillance camera use in law enforcement generates a number of provocative questions—implicit in Ali's study of Muslims in New York City—that have received less attention in smart cities and big data studies, especially as they relate to minority and lower-income communities: (1) Who should have input in deciding how advanced surveillance technologies should be implemented in a community? (2) Who should be subjected to higher levels of camera surveillance, and higher levels of generalized surveillance? (3) How much discretion should law enforcement and government have in deploying surveillance technologies and human data gatherers? (4) Who benefits from increased surveillance? The answers to these questions could determine the level of acceptance, especially within minority and disadvantaged communities, of data gathering and surveillance methods and technologies presented as measures to improve public safety.

Unclear Beneficiaries of Big Data and Smart Cities

Among the many definitions of smart cities, one that captures the optimism of technology providers comes from an article produced by Deloitte Consulting:

> "Smart cities" consist of investments in human and social capital, traditional infrastructure, and disruptive technologies that fuel sustainable economic growth and a high quality of life with the wise management of natural resources through participatory governance." (Hamilton and Zhu 2017, 4)

This is a general-enough concept that it seems no city could be opposed to smart cities. Yet, in practice, "smart city" has become a tool more for marketing a city's potential for economic growth, to attract companies that will employ educated workers and to provide opportunities for technology providers, than a city that will, according to the conception by Staffans and Horelli (2014), use information and computer technologies to enhance quality of life, environment, economy, mobility, governance, and social and human capital. Illustrating this concept, Wiig (2016) shows how the city of Philadelphia, in its efforts to benefit from participation in IBM's Smarter Cities Challenge, promoted a new concept called "Digital On-Ramps" intended to enable youth from underserved areas to use on-demand and mobile learning to increase access to jobs in the information and knowledge economy. Unfortunately, this project was poorly designed (the youth gained training for mostly entry-level, low-skill jobs that used technology), poorly executed (the software did not work well and did not engage youth to support independent learning), and had no measurable outcomes at the end of the project. This case study shows that, in many cases, the term "smart city" is more a rhetorical construct, a marketing tool, a signifier of cities who wish to welcome capital and higher-SES residents, than a concept by which opportunity can be made more broadly accessible and social and physical infrastructure be made more sustainable, through the use of data and ICTs.

Another aspect of the beneficiaries of big data and smart cities is related to the nature of data at the center of this movement: is the movement "data-driven," that is, motivated primarily by the technology, where people are originators or conduits, or "data-engaged," where people take a central role in what data are relevant to their lives, and how the data can be used to improve their communities? While the 311 movement, to take an example, puts people at the center of data that can be viewed as inputs to a process of civic stewardship (O'Brien 2018), it is not obvious that current and potential 311 users actually have a say over what problems most salient to them they could report to 311 (vacant houses, fear of criminal victimization, poor quality of local schools—complex and longstanding problems involving multiple city agencies) as opposed to the ones that 311 has been understood to be best positioned to solve (abandoned cars, fallen trees, potholes, and the like—the province of the Division of Inspectional Services or the Department of Public Works). Indeed, Steinitz and Pinheiro (2018) use the framework of geodesign, in which models, technology, and methods are deployed for the end goal of productive change in the environment, to critique the Big Data and Smart Cities movements. They assert that vast amounts of data are generated and collected with no clear goal, and urban technologies are developed that can marginalize communities.

Third Spaces Are Not Available to All

In an economy and social environment that increasingly revolves around mobile technology, people use such technology everywhere: at home, during recreational activities, while traveling, and of course at work. One common place to use technology is "third spaces"—places that are neither work nor home, where people gather to relax, discuss topics, eat, drink, and check their mobile phones. Examples include coffee shops, bars, barber shops, and plazas. As mobile technology becomes ubiquitous and people's jobs are increasingly contingent, part-time, and unconnected to traditional offices, third spaces are increasingly important for people to engage with digital life. Thus, there is an opportunity to learn about how technology changes the experience of third spaces and the characteristics of these locations. Memarovic and colleagues (2014) study how third spaces have changed and new types of third spaces have emerged, as well as how mobile phone applications could improve the lived experience of third spaces. This is all very good, for those who feel comfortable in such spaces and who can take advantage of the opportunity to relax, network, and recharge (usually with free Wi-Fi). Unfortunately, for many members of minority or stigmatized groups, this is not the case. As widely reported in 2018, two African American men waiting to meet a potential business client at a Starbucks coffee shop in Philadelphia were arrested when the shop's manager became convinced the men were a potential threat to other customers. The experience of being evicted from, or heavily scrutinized at, or prevented from using, third spaces is a common experience for communities of color and those who may not confirm to white, middle-class standards, such as homeless people (Dias, Eligon, and Oppel 2018). For these groups, the benefits of third spaces in which to contribute to or benefit from the many dimensions of smart cities and big data are highly compromised. And, in disadvantaged and underserved communities, like the Homewood neighborhood of Pittsburgh that was the subject of Teixeira's (2016) study, there may be no safe and high-amenity third spaces to use at all.

Excessive Costs

Designing and implementing big data and smart city initiatives is expensive and technically challenging. The distinction between "financing" ("the time-shifting of costs through which a borrower (for example, a city) can defer costs incurred for capital projects until a future point in time (such as the loan maturity date)" and "funding" ("the means by which project costs are repaid by the city through mechanisms such as property taxes") is critical for more- versus less-affluent cities and regions (Hamilton and Zhu 2017, 7). Those cities (growing, gentrifying) with robust tax bases are more likely to implement large tech initiatives through funding, while other cities that are shrinking, stagnant, or blighted are more likely to rely on financing, which can compromise a city's long-term financial health. In addition, fiscal incentives like tax abatements, public-private partnerships, and qualified infrastructure bonds are more likely to be feasible options for healthy cities than those that are shrinking or distressed.

The process of starting a smart city or big data initiative can be administratively burdensome as well. According to a conversation with a staffer at the Mayor's Office of New Urban Mechanics at the city of Boston (Lucas 2018), key tasks for a city's chief data officer in developing a data portal include:

- Building data analytics team
- Purchasing/assembling hardware infrastructure
- Upgrading data portal
- Rolling out data portal, for example to libraries

In the short term, it could cost between $5 and $10 million to open a public-facing data portal or data repository, especially since a city would have to offer salaries competitive with tech companies and engage in procurement and development activities it may be unfamiliar with. In the long term, such an operation could be directed by two staff members, one of whom serves the public while the other works with city, state, and federal government offices and agencies, at a cost of about $500,000 per year.

Some of these costs could be offset through conventional funding and financing mechanisms. In addition, novel approaches exist by which the private sector may support tech initiatives as an initial investment that may incur losses in the short term, but only if there is the promise of more-profitable investment opportunities in the future. Unfortunately, some cities may compromise their long-term technology strategy or promises to citizens to guard their privacy out of a need to acquire otherwise unavailable financial support for new technology initiatives. An example of these concerns is the LinkNYC initiative by which branded kiosks providing mobile device charging, Wi-Fi, and other digital services have been built throughout New York City in exchange for access to resident data by CityBridge, the consortium of companies providing the kiosks (DeLessio 2018). Another example is Philadelphia's Digital On-Ramp, developed via IBM's Smarter Cities Challenge, described above. It may also be possible for smaller or less-prosperous cities to acquire philanthropic funds and government grants to pursue big data and smart city initiatives, but such opportunities are limited.

Limited Resources and Technical Capacity

Many cities, or communities within cities, have limited technical and financial capacity to make productive use of large datasets and high-tech products. Johnson (2015b) describes the challenges faced by community-based organizations to attract and retain skilled staff to develop and use technology for data collection and analysis, as well as the challenges they face to determine what their data needs are, and how to meet those needs through a combination of visualization, database-oriented, and analytic technologies. Community-based organizations especially, but smaller cities as well, tend to be distinguished from city governments and for-profit organizations according to size of data used, type of technology deployed, capacity to apply theory to practice, and type of mission. Overall, there are "substantial gaps between needs for data and analytics knowledge and the resources available to NPOs and especially CBOs to acquire, analyze and deploy such knowledge in practice. In particular, a lack of standardized measures for needed data, and training to collect such data are significant barriers to CBO engagement with data and analytics" (81).

2.4 Can Data and Technology Do More Good than Harm for Shrinking Cities and Distressed Communities?

The case for investments in big data and smart city–related technologies is by no means air tight, especially for smaller cities, shrinking cities, and cities with substantial areas that are distressed. While planning trends increasingly point toward methods and tools that support community engagement, active participation, and inductive learning according to coproduction of knowledge, recent research and practice appears to demonstrate that principles of widely accessible technologies in support of broader access to social and economic opportunity, more sustainable human and physical infrastructure, reduced levels of inequality, and increased quality of life are more aspirational than achieved. Authentic public participation, flexibility in response to public criticism or increased understanding of best practices, ample access to human, financial, and technical resources, and a thoroughgoing commitment to equity, inclusion, and diversity are more often observed in the United States in the breach than in routine practice. We hope, however, that the results we describe later in the book regarding planning data, models, and technologies specifically designed for the needs of shrinking cities and distressed communities demonstrate that the benefits of big data and smart city initiatives, properly conceived, communicated, and implemented, can exceed the costs.

In the next chapter we set the context for discussion of these innovations by describing Baltimore, Flint, and Fall River, three cities that are shrinking, declining, or distressed and that could benefit from the technical innovations we have developed.

CHAPTER 3

Three Shrinking Cities

History, Practice, Data, and Technology

3.1 Rationale for Selecting Cities

Our goal in this chapter is to learn about the experiences of a small but diverse set of cities that are responding to shrinkage, decline, and distress, using a range of tools and methods drawn from urban planning, public policy and public management, and information technology and decision science. By doing so, we can define a framework for understanding how certain cities have set goals for responses to decline and distress, and how they have acted to meet these goals, with a particular focus on the role that information technology and decision science play in supporting these responses. This will provide a basis for our presentation of decision modeling–inspired analyses in two cities, in chapters 4 and 5.

We believe our study will be enriched if the cities we study show interesting variation with regard to size, urban form, region, and level of shrinkage and distress. We have thus chosen the following three cities for closer examination: Baltimore, Maryland; Fall River, Massachusetts; and Flint, Michigan. As shown in table 3.1, these three cities represent small (less than 100,000) and large (more than 500,000) populations; multiple geographic regions (Mid-Atlantic, New England, and East North Central) and demographic and housing measures consistent with shrinkage. Baltimore and Flint have received substantial popular-press attention in recent years for events related, we believe, to long-term underlying indicators of decline and distress, while Fall River is known locally as an example of the

Table 3.1. Sample Cities: Selected Characteristics

City	Size (2016) population	Region (Division)	Population Percentage Change, 2000–2016	Population Percentage Nonwhite Change, 2000–2016	Housing Vacancy Rate Change, 2000–2015
Baltimore, MD	Large (621,849)	Northeast (Mid-Atlantic)	-5.24	5.65	8.50
Fall River, MA	Small (88,930)	Northeast (New England)	-4.13	158.88	-3.20
Flint, MI	Small (97,386)	Midwest (East North Central)	-21.93	N/A	11.60

Source: U.S. Census Bureau; for population data, American Community Survey, 2011–2016, American Community Survey 5-Year Estimates, Tables CP05 and H011I; and Profile of General Demographic Characteristics: 2000, Table DP-1; for vacancy status, American Community Survey 1-Year Estimates, 2015, Table DP04, and Profile of Selected Housing Characteristics: 2000, Census 2000 Summary File 3 (SF 3), Table DP-4. Generated by George Chichirau; using American FactFinder; <http://factfinder2.census.gov>; (June 26 2019).

challenges and promise of smaller postindustrial cities seeking renewed growth and prosperity.

While these three cities have all experienced measures of decline, they offer very different narratives with regard to intensity of blight, economic distress, and urban revitalization. While Baltimore has been a focus for scholars and journalists for over two decades, Flint has received less attention, at least until the lead water contamination crisis, which received national coverage starting in 2015. In contrast, Fall River has been less studied, and thus represents a novel perspective on depopulation. For each city, we interviewed planning professionals to learn about their hands-on experiences responding to shrinkage and distress.

Tables 3.2, 3.3, and 3.4 offer side-by-side views of the cities, contrasting their population changes, urban form, and geography. Table 3.2

Table 3.2. Population Changes, 1900–2016, Sample Cities

Population Year	Baltimore, MD	Fall River, MA	Flint, MI
1900	508,957	104,863	13,103 *
1910	558,485	119,295	38,550 *
1920	733,826	120,485	91,599 *
1930	804,874	115,274	156,492 *
1940	859,100	115,428	151,543 *
1950	949,708	111,963	163,143 *
1960	939,024	99,942	196,940 **
1970	905,759	96,898	193,317 **
1980	786,775	92,574	159,611 **
1990	736,014	92,472	140,761 +
2000	651,154	91,938	124,943 ++
2010	620,961	88,857	102,434 +++
2016	621,849	88,930	97,386 ++++

Data sources:
* 1950 Census of Population Volume 1: Number of Inhabitants
** 1980 Census of Population U. S. Summary Chapter A-B
+ 1990 Census of Population Social and Economic Characteristics: Urbanized Areas Section 1 of 6
++ 2000 Census of Population and Housing, United States Summary, Population and Housing Unit Counts Part 1
+++ Social Explorer Tables (SE), Census 2010, Social Explorer & U.S. Census Bureau
++++ Social Explorer Tables (SE), American Community Survey 2016 5-year estimates, Social Explorer & U.S. Census Bureau

Table 3.3. Changes in Population & Race/Ethnicity, 1970–2016, Sample Cities

City	Population	White	Black/African-American	Hispanic/Spanish
Baltimore	−31.34%	−22.82%	+16.52%	+3.82%
Fall River	−8.22%	−16.34%	+4.34%	+9.91%
Flint	−49.62%	−30.62%	+27.14%	+2.25%

Data sources:
1970 Social Explorer, Census 1970 (T13: Race; T13: Spanish Origin or Descent Indicator)
2016 Social Explorer, ACS 2016 5-year estimates (T13: Race; T14: Hispanic or Latino by Race)

Table 3.4. Changes in Housing & Economic Characteristics, 1970–2016, Sample Cities

City	Total Housing Units	Other Vacant	Unemployment Rate	Total Employed	% Below Poverty Level
Baltimore	−2.8%	+345.0%	+147.8%	−22.1%	+65.0%
Fall River	+25.3%	+160.3%	+136.5%	−6.00%	+101.8%
Flint	−20.1%	+536.1%	+295.0%	−57.5%	+341.1%

Data sources:
1970 Social Explorer, Census 1970 (T107: Housing Units; T111: Vacant Housing Units by Type of Vacancy for Year-Round Housing Units; T88: Poverty Status for Families; T56: Unemployment Rate)
2016 Social Explorer, ACS 2016 5-year estimates (T95: Occupancy Status; T96: Vacancy Status by Type of Vacancy; T33: Employment Status for Total Population 16 Years and Over; T37: Unemployment Rate for Civilian Population in Labor Force 16 Years and Over; T114: Poverty Status in 2010 for Children Under 18; T115: Poverty Status in 2010 for Population Age 18 to 64; T116: Poverty Status in 2010 for Population Age 65 and Over)

shows that Baltimore and Flint both peaked in population during the post–World War II industrial economic boom of the 1950s through '70s, while Fall River's population peaked in the early twentieth century, when its industrial mainstay of textile production moved outside of New England. Fall River, the smallest of the sample cities, has experienced the smallest amount of decline between 1970 and 2016, with only 8 percent population loss during this time, and, unlike Flint and Baltimore, a sizable increase in the number of housing units in the city (25%). Overall, Fall River has less pronounced trends than the other two sample cities according to increase in nonwhite population, vacant housing units,[1] unemployment, and poverty rates. Flint stands out among the group of sample cities as a leader in most indicators of distress: population decline, white flight, drop in housing units, increase in vacant housing units, decrease in total employment, and increase in unemployment and poverty rates. Baltimore had the biggest growth in unemployment among the group, but was otherwise typical in the other indicators. It is notable that Baltimore's and Fall River's populations have shown recent signs of stabilization and modest increase since 2010, the period of a sustained national recovery from the Great Recession of 2007 to 2009.

Shrinking cities may draw upon a number of strategies when responding to demographic and land use changes. Before we move to the city studies, and in order to provide context for our deeper analysis of each city, we offer a short overview of the conventional and alternative ("smart shrinkage") policy responses cities may use to combat depopulation.

Themes of Sample Cities

For each sample city, we will begin by providing historical and demographic context as an orientation to the reader about the place.[2] Each city grew, peaked in population, and then shrank; evidence of stabilization or growth is tentative where it exists. Each section will tell the city's story: why it grew, why it declined, what impacts that decline had, and how the city responded and continues to respond today. While there are many ways to focus on that last piece—the governmental and nongovernmental policies and plans to address decline—we take a particular stand on what really matters most. This book is about how shrinking cities and distressed communities articulate their goals and visions about the future, how they make decisions (in light of those goals), and what outcomes result from those decisions.

There are many ways that cities consider (1) their goals when approaching depopulation, (2) the ways they make decisions, and (3) potential future uses for vacant and abandoned property. As a way to organize the city studies, we offer here a short introduction to each of these three dimensions.

The Goal of a Shrinking City. Shrinking cities, like any city, will seek to enhance themselves. Some will measure betterment by rising populations, others by higher incomes or increased property values. Some cities prefer to use quality of life as their aim, operationalized as happiness or life satisfaction. Key policy goals for a city may include an equitable distribution of resources across neighborhoods or an efficient expenditure of public funds. Equity is an important consideration because in an environment of reduced resources, all populations, especially those that have been traditionally marginalized, want to ensure they are treated fairly. Shrinking cities tend to measure success by goals such as reducing blight or stabilizing population levels. The goals (whether implicit or explicit) are grounded in the values of those who set these goals—typically planners and other city officials. This brings us to the question of how cities make decisions.

How Cities Make Decisions. Scholars love to ponder the question of how cities make decisions. Are cities rational? Do they weigh all the considerations? Or, as Logan and Molotch (1987) argue, do city officials seek simply to advance the growth machine or their own political ambition? As we review the experiences of three cities, all facing depopulation, we seek to answer a number of questions. Is decision making concentrated in the Mayor's office, or does it seep up from the grassroots level? When decisions about what to do with vacant and abandoned property arise, who is in charge? How are neighbors consulted or not consulted? What future uses are considered? How explicitly are values and objectives discussed as part of decision making? Through a review of the literature and conversations with city officials, we attempt to identify some of the inner workings of the decision-making process in each of our sample cities.

Considering Future Uses. For a shrinking city with a financial windfall, the first thing one can expect is the arrival of wrecking crews to take down abandoned buildings. While that may seem intuitive, how does that same city consider the future uses of the land left behind? Future uses can include low-maintenance grasses or clover, which essentially amounts to keeping a lot ready for some future, undetermined use. A city might also plan to use this land for urban agriculture, energy production, stormwater management, parks, or nature preserves. In the following examination of sample cities, we will pay close attention to the kinds of future uses each city identifies and plans for.

3.2 Flint

The houses on Orange and Beech Street are the ones beyond repair. Nobody is going to go in there and fix them up and sell them. At this point all they do is cause other problems for the neighborhood. (Flint resident, Cheryl, as quoted in Johansen et al. 2015, 3063)

My two little grandsons were here from Atlanta and my husband wanted to take them to the park so he took them to that one up the street there because it's the one with the playground. Right there in the middle of broad daylight someone started shooting! My husband had to pluck up my little grandsons, up by their shirts. . . . It's a damn shame, when you can't even take your grandbabies to the park. (Flint resident, John, as quoted in Johansen et al. 2015)

Crime, polluted water, financial insolvency, and abandoned homes have made Flint, Michigan, infamous. Dubbed the murder capital of the United States and the most dangerous city in America (LeDuff 2011; Harris 2011; Johansen et al. 2015; Sterbenz and Fuchs 2013), the city has been in precarious condition over the last fifty years, losing more than half its population. A scandal associated with a change in the source of tap water for Flint's homes in 2015 led to unsafe levels of lead in children's blood samples, and ten deaths from Legionnaire's disease associated with the contaminated water (Clark 2018). This public health crisis is generally seen as arising from decisions made by an emergency manager for Flint and his leadership team intended primarily to save money by switching the city's water source from Lake Huron to the Flint River, and subsequently choosing not to treat the water with corrosion-control chemicals, resulting in lead and other chemicals entering the water supply (Morckel and Terzano 2018).

First settled in 1818, Flint is located sixty miles northwest of Detroit along the Flint River. The city depended largely on the timber industry until General Motors was founded there in 1908; this event turned the city into a world capital of the automobile industry in just three decades (May 1965; Edsforth 1982; Matthews 1997). Flint became known as Vehicle City, where residents' lives were inextricably tied to the fate of G.M.:

Over the years, Flint became the quintessential company town. Most people worked for G.M. Your house was built by G.M.'s construction company, and G.M. held the mortgage. You bought your car from G.M., and the company held that mortgage, too.

General Motors, the saying went, would take care of your every need, from womb to tomb. (Moore 1987, n.p.)

As General Motors and the American automobile industry shrunk their workforces in the 1970s, so too went Flint's fortunes. Unemployment and reduced taxes translated to a reduction in city services, causing many firefighters and police officers to be laid off (Matthews 1997). City officials responded with hundreds of millions of dollars in tax abatements and redevelopment financing in the 1980s and 1990s in an effort to encourage new industrial development, bolster the city's central business district, and market the city as a tourist center (Matthews 1997). At the same time, the U.S. government and the State of Michigan invested tens of millions of dollars in grants and loans, while local philanthropists pushed vast sums of money into rebuilding downtown Flint (Gilman 1997). In his review of fourteen redevelopment projects executed in Flint from 1970 to 1992, costing $568.5 million total, Gilman (1997) found that all but one of these initiatives were explicitly intended to foster greater economic growth. Others have shined an even harsher light on these renewal projects, charging city leaders with creating "a renewal program that valued short-term industrial growth and ghetto containment over housing equity" (Highsmith 2009, 348).

Demographics and Continuing Shrinkage in Flint

While the city and its residents saw some benefits as a result of the redevelopment projects described here, the overwhelming evidence available shows that these efforts largely failed to reverse the city's continuing economic decline and may have exacerbated the ghettoization of the city's African American population (Matthews 1997; Gilman 1997; Highsmith 2009). Table 3.5 and figures 3.1 and 3.2 illustrate the effect of Flint's white flight: while Flint's total population fell by nearly 50 percent over the last half-century, dropping from 193,317 in 1970 to 97,386 in 2016, and the city's African American population grew from 28 percent in 1970 to 55 percent in 2016, nearly all of these changes resulted from a dramatic decrease in the white population during this time (Census 1970, 2016). This has resulted in high levels of racial segregation in the city's neighborhoods. According to Highsmith (2009), "unregulated pollution, discriminatory appraisal practices, racial steering by realtors and relocation offices, segregated public housing, federal non-enforcement of civil

Table 3.5. Population & Race/Ethnicity in Flint: 1970–2016

Year	Total Population	White Population	%	Black/African-American Population	%	Hispanic/Spanish Population	%
1970	193,317	138,565	71.7	54,250	28.1	3,322	1.7
1980	159,611	89,647	51.2	66,124	41.4	3,974	2.5
1990	140,761	69,788	49.6	67,485	47.9	4,014	2.9
2000	124,943	51,710	41.4	66,560	53.3	3,742	3.0
2010	102,434	38,328	37.4	57,939	56.6	3,976	3.9
2016	97,386	39,988	41.1	53,757	55.2	3,869	4.0

Data sources:
1970 Social Explorer, Census 1970 (T13: Race; T13: Spanish Origin or Descent Indicator [15%])
1980 Social Explorer, Census 1980 (T13: Race; T13: Race by Spanish Origin Status)
1990 Social Explorer, Census 1990 (T13: Race; T13: Hispanic or Origin by Race)
2000 Social Explorer, Census 2000 (T14: Race; T15: Hispanic or Latino by Race)
2010 Social Explorer, Census 2010 (T54: Race; T55: Hispanic or Latino Origin by Race)
2016 Social Explorer, ACS 2016 5-year estimates (T13: Race; T14: Hispanic or Latino by Race)

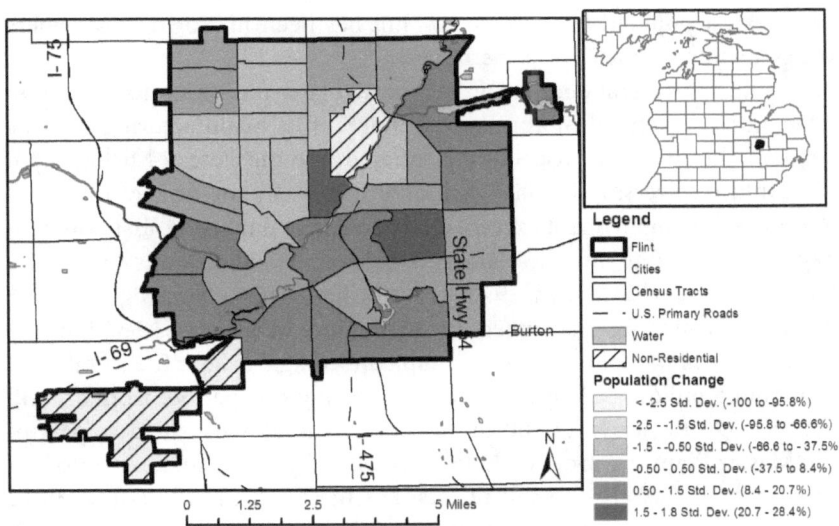

Figure 3.1. Population Change in Flint, 2000–2016.

74 | Supporting Shrinkage

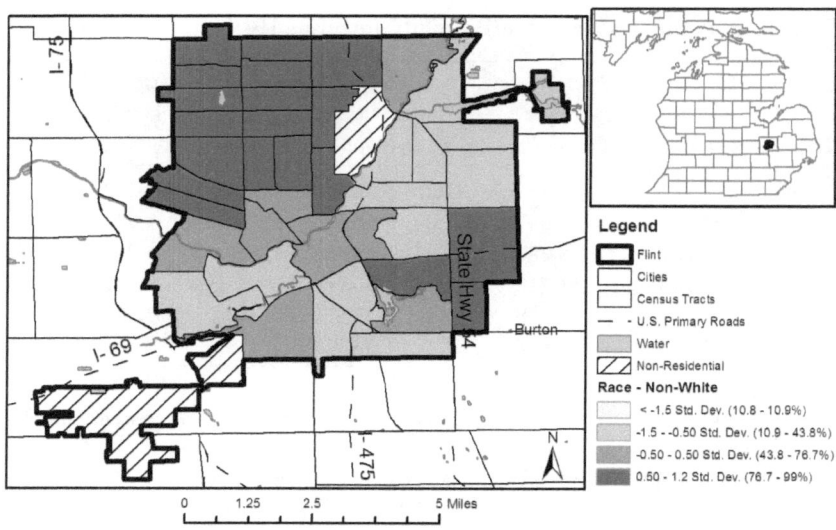

Figure 3.2. Nonwhite Population in Flint: Nonwhites as Percentage of Population.

rights laws, and white violence all combined to maintain state-sanctioned residential apartheid in the Vehicle City" (362). These figures show that the greatest population decrease in Flint has been in North Flint, where the nonwhite population is the largest.

The last several decades proved particularly punishing for Flint (see table 3.6). As General Motors moved much of its manufacturing into the suburbs, the city's basic fiscal health suffered, and the State of Michigan put Flint into receivership in 2002 (Schindler 2013). By the time of the Great Recession, unemployment exceeded 20 percent, and housing abandonment began to seep into middle-class and affluent neighborhoods (Schindler 2013; Hollander 2011). In 1970, the city had 64,265 housing units, 95 percent of which were occupied. By 2016, there were only 53,554 housing units, and only 79 percent were occupied (see figure 3.3). The number of abandoned buildings, likewise, exploded during this period, from around 900 in 1970 to nearly 11,500 in 2016. In a survey performed as part of the Master Planning process, 52,095 residential parcels were examined; of those, 11,333 (22%) were vacant lots. For the lots with a building, 5,614 were determined to be either poor or substandard (Imagine Flint 2013a).

Table 3.6. Flint Housing & Economic Characteristics: 1970–2016

Year	Total Housing Units	Other Vacant	Unemployment Rate	Total Employed	% Below Poverty Level
1970	64,265	919	6.0%	69,909	9.5%
1980	60,910	1,279	18.2%	54,180	16.9%
1990	58,724	2,365	18.3%	47,016	30.6%
2000	55,464	2,889	12.9%	45,885	26.4%
2010	51,321	5,846	21.7%	32,323	36.6%
2016	53,554	11,450	23.7%	29,681	41.9%

Data sources:
1970   Social Explorer, Census 1970 (T107: Housing Units; T111: Vacant Housing Units by Type of Vacancy for Year-Round Housing Units; T88: Poverty Status for Families; T56: Unemployment Rate)
1980   Social Explorer, Census 1980 (T80: Year-Round Housing Units; T83: Vacancy Status; T40: Unemployment Rate for Civilian Population; T100: Poverty Status In 1979 [short version])
1990   Social Explorer, Census 1990 (T72: Housing Units; T75: Vacancy Status by Type of Vacancy; T29: Unemployment Rate for Total Population 16 Years and Over; T99: Poverty Status in 1989 by Race)
2000   Social Explorer, Census 2000 (T155: Housing Units; T158: Vacancy Status; T73: Unemployment Rate for Civilian Population in Labor Force 16 Years and Over; T183. Poverty Status by Sex)
2010   Social Explorer, Census 2010 (T68: Housing Units; T71: Vacancy Status]; ACS 2010 5-year estimates; T37: Unemployment Rate for Civilian Population in Labor Force 16 Years and Over; T114: Poverty Status in 2010 for Children Under 18; T115: Poverty Status in 2010 for Population Age 18 to 64; T116: Poverty Status in 2010 for Population Age 65 and Over
2016   Social Explorer - ACS 2016 5-year estimates [T95: Occupancy Status; T96: Vacancy Status by Type of Vacancy; T33: Employment Status for Total Population 16 Years and Over; T37: Unemployment Rate for Civilian Population in Labor Force 16 Years and Over; T114: Poverty Status in 2010 for Children Under 18; T115: Poverty Status in 2010 for Population Age 18 to 64; T116: Poverty Status in 2010 for Population Age 65 and Over]

One city official put it bluntly: "We do have a tremendous problem with vacant properties in Flint." Figures 3.4 and 3.5 illustrate the nature of abandoned private and public spaces in Flint: homes, schools, factories, stores, and other places, often leaving vacant land in its place.

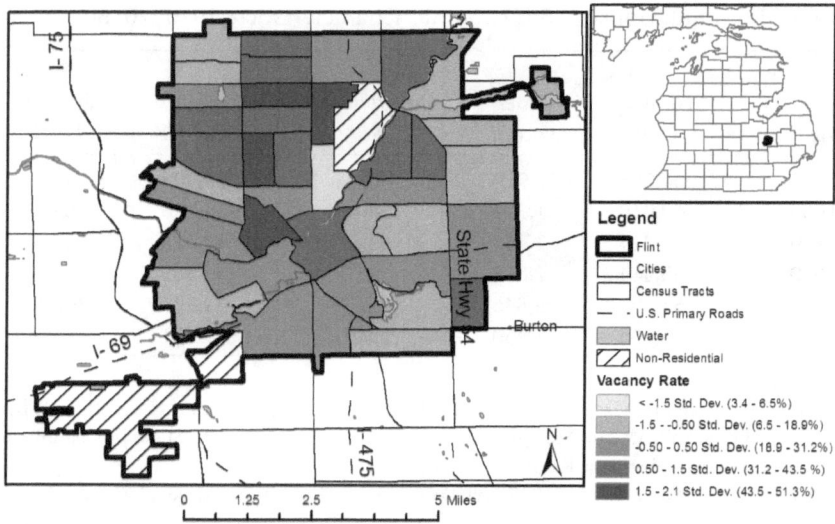

Figure 3.3. Housing Vacancy in Flint: Percentage of Housing Units Classified as Other, Vacant.

Figure 3.4. Abandoned Home in Flint.

Figure 3.5. Shuttered Public School in Flint.

With abandoned and foreclosed homes everywhere, employment down, and tax revenues to the city plummeting, fears began to grow in 2013 that Flint would follow Detroit's fall into bankruptcy:

> That Flint might follow Detroit . . . isn't surprising, given their shared circumstances. Both were once boomtowns brimming with auto jobs for collars white and blue. General Motors employed about 80,000 in the area in the early 1970s. Fewer than 8,000 GM jobs remain. (Karoub 2014, n.p.)

But Flint is hardly a rusting relic: the city's extreme automobile wealth from the mid–twentieth century continues to endow an impressive cultural hub, including the Whiting Auditorium, the Sloan Museum, and the Bower Theater, as well as four colleges and universities (Kettering; University of Michigan, Flint; Mott Community College; and Baker College). Additionally, recent real estate prices appear to be on the rise. Though the median price per square foot in Flint is $39, as compared to $107 in the Flint metropolitan area, and the median rent price in Flint is $650, as compared to the metropolitan area value of $750, Flint home values increased by 3.2 percent between 2018 and 2019 (Zillow.com 2019). A slightly earlier review of real estate prices in Genesee County indicated increases in property values in commercial, industrial, and residential properties in Flint as well as most other communities (Raymer 2017).

With regard to the bigger picture, Flint still has many of the geographic attributes that made it desirable enough for General Motors to maintain its global headquarters there for decades: it is situated at the intersection of three interstate highways (I-69, I-75, and I-475) and is positioned in close proximity to an international border with Canada. The city is a regional employment hub, attracting over 30,000 commuters on a daily basis (Imagine Flint 2013a). According to the Flint's recent master plan, agriculture is on the rise in the city: as of 2013, there were over 200 active farms and gardens in the city.

Shrinkage Responses and Policy

Rather than grow for the sake of growth, Flint has recently responded to its predicament with a focus on improving the quality of life for those residents remaining in the city. The city's primary policy goals today center on right-sizing the physical form of the city to better match a smaller population. According to one city official: "[We're] not envisioning ourselves as a city of 250,000. Just because we accept the reality that we're smaller doesn't mean that we have to be a lesser community. We can be a very vibrant community. We have embraced that and planned for that."

Land Bank. Beginning in 2002, Genesee County formed a land bank that has received acclaim and global recognition (Alexander 2005; Schindler 2014). Led by then County Treasurer Dan Kildee, the Land Bank reversed the standard practice of letting tax-foreclosed abandoned homes languish in shrinking cities. Kildee stated: "We have a 35-year history of letting so-called market forces deal with the problem of abandonment in cities, and we all know how well that worked out" (Young 2010). Kildee succeeded in changing that, banking almost 80 percent of all properties that came his way, selling some new abutters and others to real estate developers. The Land Bank maintains most properties (with some help) through semiregular mowing.

What is remarkable about the Land Bank is that it is taking so much of the city's land off the market, which, in theory, pushes up the value of the rest of the city's land. One city official explained: "In Flint, the Land Bank owns 20% of the property and they are totally on the board. I really think we're going to be on the cutting edge of cities." The Land

Bank appears to be committed to partner with the city on development and nondevelopment, according to its new Master Plan.

The Land Bank's primary goals are demolition and simple maintenance of vacant lots, something that further supports the goal of improving the quality of life for residents by removing blighted buildings and unmanaged lots. Because the Land Bank maintains possession of so many of its lots, it's hard to assess the decision-making process it uses—except for the case of blight bundling. Like Detroit and a few other cities, the Land Bank will bundle the worst-off buildings with more attractive ones when it does public auctions. The result is always that nobody bids on these bundles and the Land Bank gets to keep the good with the bad. It is the aim of the Land Bank to be sure not to be stuck with only the least desirable properties, but to maintain a cache of valuable sites and buildings as well.

Imagine Flint Master Plan. It was in 1960 when the City of Flint last adopted a Master Plan,[3] that is, a written document outlining the city's vision for the future and the basis for zoning and other policy decisions. In 1960, Flint was near its peak of almost 200,000 persons, and the Master Plan at that time projected even greater growth. The aim of the plan was to prepare for and manage the growth projected to take place over the coming decades. Instead, the plan was rendered a useless document as the city faced five consecutive decades of population decline, and its primary land use policy tool instead reified a certain misplaced optimism about the future. But in 2010, with funding from the U.S. Department of Housing and Community Development and several local foundations and organizations, Flint embarked on a new Master Plan: Imagine Flint (www.imagineflint.com; Imagine Flint 2013a, 2013b).

This plan was grounded in an awareness of a half-century of decline and, while optimistic about improving quality of life, the environment, transportation, and arts and culture, the plan has a decidedly pragmatic viewpoint on future demographics. "It is projected that the City will lose approximately 20,000 individuals between 2010 and 2020" (Imagine Flint 2013a, 16). Much of the rest of the document accounts for that prognosis, with one of the seven pillars of the plan an "Adapting to Change" vision: "We imagine Flint as a city that . . . adapts to change by reshaping our physical environment to be greener and more efficient for a smaller population" (Imagine Flint 2013a, 274). This bold and unusual statement for an American master plan is presented among seven standard tropes about a growing and diverse economy, providing for clean air and water, ensuring safe neighborhoods, and other benefits—all the niceties a plan of this nature tends to seek out. But Flint is following in the footsteps of Youngstown's famed Youngstown 2020 plan in calling for a smaller, better city.

The plan's authors and city officials we interviewed state that this vision, this pragmatism, was borne out of a massive public participation process. The plan itself reports the involvement of more than 5,000 residents over two years of meeting, workshops, and charrettes. One official put it this way:

> I've never seen a more involved community effort in the master planning process as what happened with Imagine Flint. Had 5,000 plus people involved—over 200 people drafting language for the plan. We have done a tremendous job of getting people to believe and buy into the plan as a draft for the future. People in the city are aware of the plan and telling their politicians to follow it.

Indeed, this process has resulted in a website, www.imagineflint.com, that is an impressive repository of planning documents that link city- and neighborhood-level efforts. Imagine Flint represents much more than good outreach; it has successfully wrestled with many of the daunting problems faced by shrinking cities. The conceptual approach to rethinking the city's land use was to orient planning around places instead of uses.

The plan creates twelve categories of places: "Each place type consists of a combination of primary and complementary land uses, development scales, and character" (38). These place types provide a key framework for the city to adjust to a smaller population. The exact mechanism of the distribution of these place types was developed through extensive public conversation and debate, as well as a surprising alignment of history with the present.

The City's first Master Plan was adopted in 1920. This is also the last decade during which the City of Flint had a population comparable to that of today—102,000 according to the 2010 Census. The city is using that 1920 map as a foundation for today's decision making. The planners looked at the neighborhoods with the most decline and decided they were not likely to be repopulated anytime soon. A city official explained the design process with the community: "So we told them they cannot be a traditional neighborhood, but they can be anything else from the other place types—what should they be?" From this interactive, iterative, years-long process, a final map was drawn up assigning neighborhoods to the twelve place types.

The master plan was built around three important goals for addressing vacancy and abandonment: "Repurpose and reinvent under-populated areas; Encourage homeowners to assemble property for larger lots in high-vacancy areas; Activate vacant property for productive and innovative uses such as urban agriculture and green infrastructure" (Imagine Flint 2013a, p. 28).

Blight Elimination Framework. One of the most significant implementation actions stemming from the city's Master Plan was the Blight Elimination Framework, adopted by the Flint Planning Commission in 2015 (Pruett 2015). Taking the place types introduced in the Master Plan, the Framework went into detail on a key goal of the plan: to eliminate blight.

Blight elimination is a contested, ambiguous topic. The city's planners developed a comprehensive definition of blight that includes (1) structures classified by the city as being in "poor" or "substandard" condition (nearly 5,500 in the city today) and (2) vacant lots (over 14,000 in the city today). The Framework treats all of the city's vacant lots as blights, though many are well maintained, and some are even being re-used for passive green space or gardens.

As with the Master Plan, the Framework relied on extensive public participation in shaping its topical areas of focus and priorities. The Framework's author, Natalie Pruett, explains that the key values in the report are drawn from the Master Plan and from the sixteen engagement sessions she ran with Flint stakeholders. She offers the example of the participatory budgeting workshops in each of the city's wards that were conducted by the Framework team. According to the report, 230 residents in nine separate sessions allocated funding predominately to demolition (compared with code enforcement, vacant lot re-use, rehab and redevelopment, waste removal, and mowing and boarding). The participatory budgeting process went like this:

> residents individually allocated ten blight tokens (tenths of a given budget) among the seven Blight Elimination Activities. At the end of the exercise emerged a collective budget that combined the individual allocations of all participants. . . . One noticeably consistent theme was the prioritization of demolition. Demolition received the greatest allocation at eight of the nine workshops. . . . Clearly, Flint residents allocated more in demolition than any other activity. (Pruett 2015, 26)

Through the active involvement of residents, planners were able to gauge general attitudes about which areas of investment were considered more important than others. Within each activity, the Framework also outlines priorities based on a tiered system that designates neighborhood stabilization as the first and most significant goal in the blight elimination. As a result, for demolition, the first-tier priorities are to demolish vacant structures in neighborhood and neighborhood-supporting place types, denoted as Neighborhood Centers, Traditional Neighborhoods, Green Neighborhoods, Mixed Residential, University Avenue Corridor, and City Corridor (six of the twelve place types). The report goes on to explain that "demolition eligibility depends on property condition, value, and place type location" (Pruett 2015, 44). Here, the City is making its goals perfectly clear: demolition should occur in those six place-types because they are intended to host much of the city's residential population in the future, and then further prioritization will occur based on the condition of properties and their value. Presumably, high-value areas will receive attention before low-value areas (though the report is not explicit on this).

While this tiered system is impressive and unusual among shrinking U.S. cities, it has very ambitious goals about the suitability of parcels for future uses and is not explicit about its incorporation of equity or cost effectiveness in the decision framework. This may be due in part to the Framework's extremely aggressive goal of eliminating all blight in Flint within five years, which, if realized, would nullify the need for an explicit decision-making process. If unable to meet this goal, the City will be forced to make strategic choices about which properties to demolish—it is here that the Framework uses the neighborhood stabilization goal as its guide. Designated future uses, including those classified as nonresidential, are implicit in the definition of each place type. Within residential areas, vacant lots in particular are prioritized for re-use as explained by the report: "Reuse contiguous vacant lots by converting them into low-maintenance sites that provide environmental and social benefits" (Pruett 2014, 55). The report identifies "Green Innovation" and community open space uses as a second-tier priority. Uses that complement redevelopment are the third-tier priority.

The scale of the Framework is startling: over the course of five years, if the funding allows, Flint hopes to eliminate blight within city walls, which the Framework estimates would translate to the demolition of 5,000 structures. One city official explained that two-thirds of the remaining blighted structures are in private ownership and the City plans to use code enforcement to get owners to carry out demolition.

Assessment

Throughout the Master Plan and during our interviews with city officials, we learned a great deal about a particularly strong, persistent quality of the city's response to shrinkage: the prioritization of social equity. One official explained:

> Social equity is really important to our community. What we try to balance is not doing the peanut butter approach of spreading your resources too thin, but recognizing that there were racially motivated factors that resulted in the way the vacancy has been distributed across the city and it is not fair to walk away just because those communities suffer from vacancy. We were very cognizant that we needed to balance how we did investment.

Where one city might seek to spread resources equitably throughout the city (what the above official described as the "peanut butter approach"), Flint appears to be putting more emphasis and resources into the most impoverished or neglected neighborhoods under the banner of equity. These contrasting definitions of equity are illustrative of how difficult it can be to generate a common vision in a community around a goal or value. Political scientist Deborah Stone (2011) has written about the multitude of ways to define equity, including using the metaphor of equitable ways to cut a pizza into slices for a college classroom. She also writes extensively about ambiguity and how the lack of clear definitions is precisely what enables political institutions to get anything done. In other words, it's easy for Flint to call for social equity, but it's a lot harder for the city to define it and get all parties on board with one unified definition.

Likewise, the definitions the city uses for blight provided earlier present real challenges to the on-the-ground work of making decisions about which houses are demolished and what will become of the land afterward. With an abandoned building problem of extraordinary scope for a city of its size, however, the work going on in Flint does call for some level of optimism:

> Every day I'm a little bit more impressed. More structures are going down and I can see the light of day. With all this abandonment it's hard to see the future. Now people are seeing the future. People believe that we can start tackling the problems. (A city official in 2014)

> It's amazing how good things look in light of how many vacant properties we have. (A city official in 2014)

Recently, community residents, working through neighborhood associations, have taken the lead in redeveloping local vacant lots leased from the Genesee County Land Bank into neighborhood green spaces, using funding from the Community Foundation of Greater Flint (Atkinson 2017a). Community residents across fifty local organizations have also worked with professional planners to take inventory of residential and commercial properties; this work has helped secure federal and local funding for targeted demolitions (Atkinson 2017b). A local pastor is spearheading an effort to develop a food co-op in the North Flint neighborhood with support from the Grocery Stores Initiative, a project of Flint's Economic Recovery Task Force (Atkinson 2017c). In 2014, the Flint Farmers' Market moved half a mile from an isolated location next to downtown to a more accessible location in the central district, resulting in substantial increases in patronage and revenue, as well as increased access to food across the metropolitan area, including for residents in low food access census tracts (Morckel 2017a, 2018).

With the transition of financial control of Flint from the Receivership Transition Advisory Board back to local elected government (Dovey 2018), new funding from the settlement of a lawsuit brought against the state of Michigan by a Flint resident and three nonprofit groups to replace water service lines that had been leaching lead into city water (McCambridge 2017), strong support for downtown development strategies that will attract visitors as well as new residents (Morckel and Rybarczyk 2015), and robust and responsive planning and blight elimination initiatives, there are indeed grounds for optimism in Flint.

3.3 Baltimore

Like Flint, Baltimore has multiple identities relevant to a discussion of shrinkage and distress. Before 2015, Baltimore was well known in planning circles for its large number of vacant properties, its ambivalence regarding an identity as a shrinking city, and its multiple rounds of housing demolitions and planning initiatives (Williams 2013). The death of Freddie Gray in police custody on April 19, 2015, and subsequent demonstrations, violence, and community teach-ins (Gay Stolberg 2015; Chin 2015) have placed renewed attention on many structural factors associated with conventional measures of shrinkage and decline. Among these are racial health disparities (Dubb 2017), a legacy of residential segregation and unequal access to housing finance (Williams and Holt 2017), a skills gap between job seekers and job opportunities (Stanley 2015), and inadequate transportation linking poor neighborhoods to areas of opportunity (Lipsitz Flippin 2018). All of these factors are heavily linked with structural racism and require a commitment to social justice and community engagement that infuses all manner of planning-focused interventions (Williams and Holt 2017). It is in this context that Baltimore may develop new strategies to embrace shrinkage where necessary and to pursue growth where possible.

Here we describe how Baltimore exploded in growth to a city of almost one million in 1950 and has steadily lost population nearly every decade since. We discuss the key reasons for this depopulation and how the city has responded, what its key goals and values were, and how it makes decisions. We conclude with some reflections on what can be learned from Baltimore.

Demographics in Baltimore

Located near the top of the Chesapeake Bay, Baltimore has been a port city since its founding in 1729. The city's early preeminence as a site for industry and shipping, and particularly the distribution of flour to Irish markets, bolstered its population and size (City of Baltimore 2009). Baltimore grew rapidly in the nineteenth century, more than tripling in size between 1850 and 1900. Historical accounts of industry from the period depict a shoreline dotted with shipyards, brick kilns, copper and iron works, glass factories, as well as more than 100 flour, paper, saw, and powder mills (City of Baltimore 2009). The prosperity and industrial boom of Baltimore were not sustained during the twentieth century, and population declined by more than one-third between its peak in 1950 and 2010 (see table 3.2). A large part of this decline has been attributed to the loss of manufacturing jobs in the city, particularly from the downsizing of the Bethlehem Steel plant in the 1970s. Between 1950 and 1990, two-thirds of the city's manufacturing jobs were lost (Friedman 2003) and comprised merely 12 percent of the city's jobs by 1985 (Rosenblatt 2011). But the city's troubles cannot be pinned on the decline of manufacturing alone: the population continued to decline even after the demise of the manufacturing industry, losing more than 115,000 people from 1990 to 2010 (table 3.7).

A modest rebound in the city's population since 2010 has been attributed to an increased focus on immigration (Next City 2014) and gentrification (Goldkamp 2016) as a source of new residents.

According to the city's internal records, as of 2013 the city had 30,000 vacant properties: 16,000 vacant buildings and 14,000 vacant lots (Baltimore City Planning Commission 2013) (see figures 3.6 and 3.7). Of these vacant properties, 40 percent are city-owned. As in other cities, Baltimore's vacant property difficulties can be blamed on federal housing policy that supported (primarily white) out-migration to the suburbs, as well as racially restrictive private lending and real estate covenants that led to disinvestment and neighborhood decline (Cohen 2001). The late 2000s subprime mortgage crisis caused a dramatic surge in vacant and abandoned properties in urban areas, particularly in communities of color. Between 2000 and 2009, Baltimore experienced more than 33,000

Table 3.7. Population & Race/Ethnicity in Baltimore: 1970–2016

Year	Total Population	White Population	%	Black/African-American Population	%	Hispanic/Spanish Population	%
1970	905,979	480,377	53.0	420,147	46.4	8,435	0.9
1980	786,775	345,113	43.9	431,151	54.8	7,638	1.0
1990	736,014	287,753	39.1	435,768	59.2	7,602	1.0
2000	651,154	205,982	31.6	418,951	64.3	11,061	1.7
2010	620,961	183,830	29.6	395,781	63.7	25,960	4.2
2016	621,849	187,894	30.2	391,160	62.9	29,537	4.8

Data sources:
1970   Social Explorer, Census 1970 (T13: Race; T13: Spanish Origin or Descent Indicator [15%])
1980   Social Explorer, Census 1970 (T13: Race; T13: Race by Spanish Origin Status)
1990   Social Explorer, Census 1970 (T13: Race; T13: Hispanic or Origin by Race)
2000   Social Explorer, Census 1970 (T14: Race; T15: Hispanic or Latino by Race)
2000   Social Explorer, Census 1970 (T54: Race; T55: Hispanic or Latino Origin by Race)
2016   Social Explorer, ACS 2016 5-year estimates (T13: Race; T14: Hispanic or Latino by Race)

Figure 3.6. Typical Row House in Baltimore Next to Vacant Lot.

Figure 3.7. Urban Agriculture Is a Common Use for Large Blocks of Vacant Land in Baltimore.

foreclosures, two-thirds of which were in census tracts greater than 60 percent African American (Role of the Lending Industry 2009).

Today, the region's biggest employment sectors are government, education, and health care, all of which rely on federal funding and could be threatened in times of budget cuts and sequesters (GBSRR 2011). Fluctuations in labor force rankings over the years illustrate the challenge the region has faced in transitioning from an industrial labor force to one largely dominated by service- and knowledge-based sectors (GBSRR 2011). Total employment in Baltimore has been slowly edging down, while the unemployment rate has remained quite high, hovering around double digits since 1980 (see table 3.8). The impacts have been severe: since 1980, one in five households has been living in poverty.

Housing Segregation in Baltimore

There exists a long history of housing segregation in Baltimore, as in many other U.S. cities. In 1910, the Mayor signed into law the first housing segregation ordinance in the country (Farquhar 2012). This ordinance prohibited blacks from moving onto a block where more than half the residents were white, and vice versa (Power 1983). While this ordinance and other segregation ordinances were struck down in 1916 in the U.S. Supreme Court case *Buchanan v. Warley* as being unconstitutional (on the basis of interfering with property rights), segregation remained a characteristic theme in the Baltimore housing market for many decades to come (Farquhar 2012). Among these policies were restrictive housing covenants in which the deed specifically forbade selling the property to blacks; redlining of black neighborhoods, meaning these neighborhoods were systematically marked as unstable or risky, making them unattractive to investors; denial of Federal Housing Administration support in neighborhoods with "inharmonious racial groups"; and blockbusting, wherein brokers bought houses at distressed prices from nervous whites and resold them at a premium to blacks (Pietila 2010). Discrimination against blacks by mortgage lenders was commonplace, as were professional sanctions against real estate brokers who sold to blacks (Pietila 2010). Highway construction in the city was frequently routed through black neighborhoods, physically dividing these areas and making them unstable (Blesset 2011; Gioielli 2011).

All of these restrictions meant that housing for black families was limited, leading to housing in poorer conditions and rent at higher rates

Table 3.8. Baltimore Housing & Economic Characteristics: 1970–2016

Year	Total Housing Units	Other Vacant	Unemployment Rate	Total Employed	% Below Poverty Level
1970	305,161	5,100	4.6%	352,700	14.0
1980	302,465	10,974	10.8%	306,248	22.9
1990	303,706	12,774	9.2%	314,688	21.9
2000	300,477	27,153	10.7%	256,036	22.9
2010	296,685	22,795	11.5%	274,033	21.3
2016	296,923	37,744	11.4%	274,906	23.1

Data sources:
1970   Social Explorer, Census 1970 (T107: Housing Units; T111: Vacant Housing Units by Type of Vacancy for Year-Round Housing Units; T88: Poverty Status for Families; T56: Unemployment Rate)
1980   Social Explorer, Census 1980 (T80: Year-Round Housing Units; T83: Vacancy Status; T40: Unemployment Rate for Civilian Population; T100: Poverty Status In 1979 [short version])
1990   Social Explorer, Census 1990 (T72: Housing Units; T75: Vacancy Status by Type of Vacancy; T29: Unemployment Rate for Total Population 16 Years and Over; T99: Poverty Status in 1989 by Race)
2000   Social Explorer, Census 2000 (T155: Housing Units; T158: Vacancy Status; T73: Unemployment Rate for Civilian Population in Labor Force 16 Years and Over; T183. Poverty Status by Sex)
2010   Social Explorer, Census 2010 (T68: Housing Units; T71: Vacancy Status); ACS 2010 5-year estimates (T37: Unemployment Rate for Civilian Population in Labor Force 16 Years and Over; T114: Poverty Status in 2010 for Children Under 18; T115: Poverty Status in 2010 for Population Age 18 to 64; T116: Poverty Status in 2010 for Population Age 65 and Over)
2016   Social Explorer, ACS 2016 5-year estimates (T95: Occupancy Status; T96: Vacancy Status by Type of Vacancy; T33: Employment Status for Total Population 16 Years and Over; T37: Unemployment Rate for Civilian Population in Labor Force 16 Years and Over; T114: Poverty Status in 2010 for Children Under 18; T115: Poverty Status in 2010 for Population Age 18 to 64; T116: Poverty Status in 2010 for Population Age 65 and Over)

in black neighborhoods due to high demand, low supply, and a lack of political or market pressure for landlords to make necessary improvements (Farquhar 2012).

Because of these dynamics, and because black bodies and black neighborhoods were considered the genesis of infectious diseases and social problems, social reformers began to target the conditions of black housing at the very beginning of the twentieth century (Farquhar 2012, 2).

Widespread urban renewal efforts in black neighborhoods became popular in Baltimore in the 1940s under the argument that "slum clearance" was necessary to clear these excessively dangerous and overcrowded areas (Farquhar 2012).

In 1968, the U.S. Supreme Court Case *Jones v. Mayer* ruled housing discrimination unconstitutional in both public and private settings (Cohen 2001). While this may have formally ended the practice of housing segregation in Baltimore, some have argued that land use, housing, and urban renewal policies in the city have continued to systematically prioritize the white elite, while underfunding black neighborhoods (Blesset 2011; Gomez 2012). Blesset exposes the use of federal funds from Community Development Block Grant (CDBG), Urban Development Action Grant, Section 8, and Hope VI for urban renewal projects in wealthier parts of the city, particularly the Inner Harbor project, rather than investment into African American neighborhoods.

> [Both] the Section 8 and the CDBG programs represented an opportunity to improve the living and neighborhood conditions that afflicted the poor in central cities. Instead, Section 8 vouchers still concentrated African Americans in minority and highly impoverished areas and diverted significant proportions of CDBG funds from these communities to support commercial and industrial development. From highway construction to historic preservation to slum clearance, African Americans experienced the worst of redevelopment. (Blesset 2011, 132)

These forms of housing discrimination are less obvious than prior legally sanctioned forms of segregation, but their impact on the housing landscape and the black community of Baltimore is still significant.

Today, the city remains highly residentially segregated by race, with the black and Hispanic population shares on the rise since 1970 (see table 3.7 and figures 3.8, 3.9, and 3.10), though with some moderating trends evident since 2010. Baltimore also has a higher concentration of vacant housing in both neighborhoods that are majority black and neighborhoods below the median income (Ransome 2007) (see figures 3.9 and 3.10). Data from the 2000 Census revealed that neighborhoods with a black population of greater than 50 percent accounted for more than 80 percent of vacancy notices in the city, while neighborhoods with a white population of greater than 50 percent accounted for less than 16 percent of vacancy notices in the city.

Three Shrinking Cities | 91

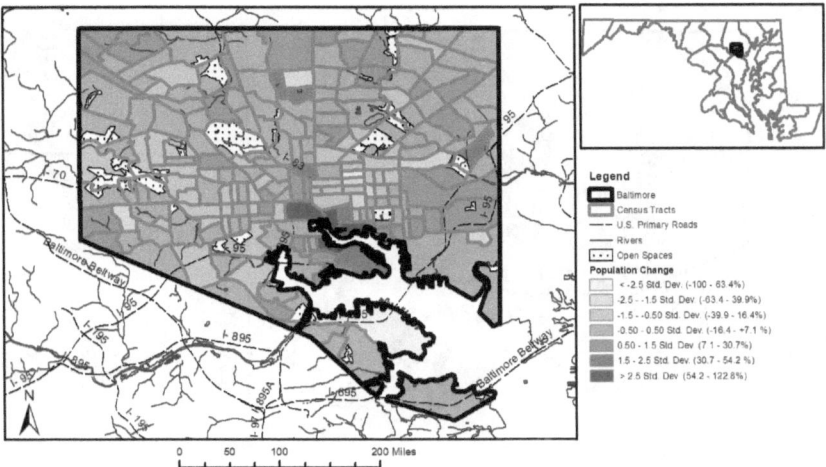

Figure 3.8. Population Change in Baltimore, 2000–2016.

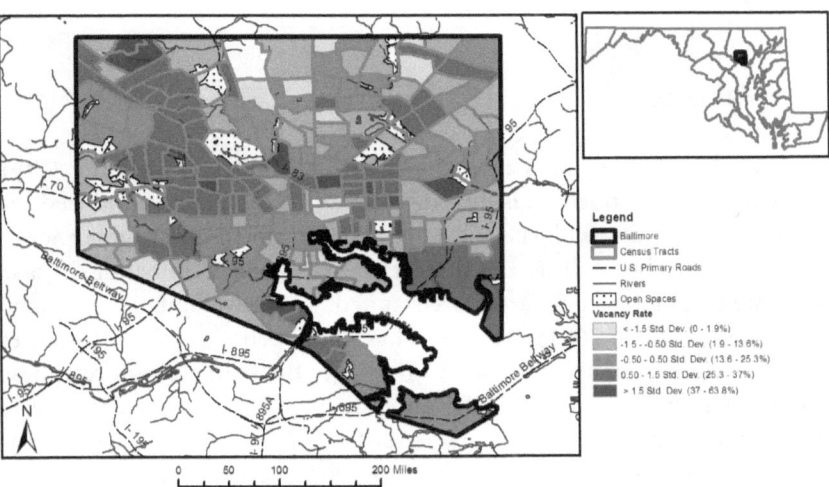

Figure 3.9. Housing Vacancy in Baltimore: Percentage of Housing Units Classified as Other Vacant.

As in Flint, the areas with the greatest population loss, including East and North Baltimore, are also the areas with the greatest nonwhite population and the highest number of vacant units.

92 | Supporting Shrinkage

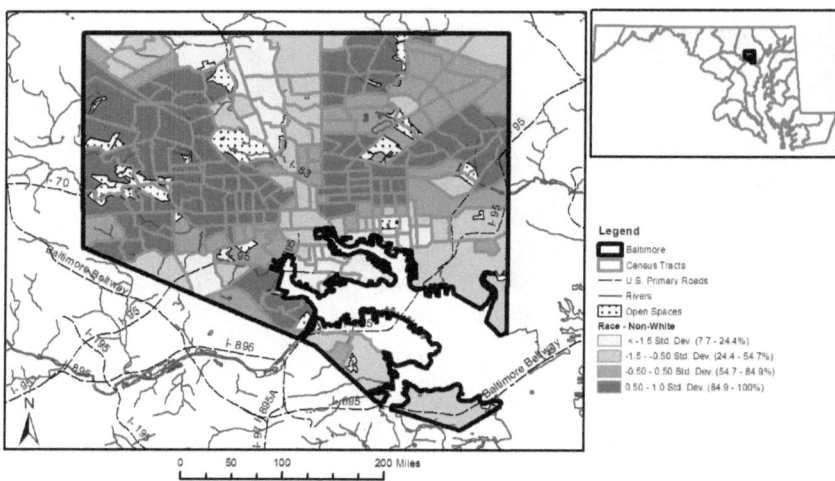

Figure 3.10. Nonwhite Population in Baltimore: Nonwhites as Percentage of Population.

Policy Responses

PlanBaltimore!, the City's master plan from 2000, outlined the City's approach to abandoned housing (Kromer 2002). The plan emphasized the necessity of working with specific neighborhoods to design neighborhood-level strategies, as well as the importance of blight elimination. It also suggested demolition in areas well suited to redevelopment and land assemblage (Cohen 2001). Baltimore has developed a number of policies for addressing vacancy and abandonment over the years that address these goals. Interventions have focused on code enforcement, streamlining of property acquisition, and homebuyer supports, as well as targeted demolition, reinvestment, and rehabilitation. More recently, urban greening initiatives such as urban agriculture and environmental management strategies have been employed.

Homebuyer Supports. Starting in the 1970s as a response to the "urban crisis" of crime, arson, and abandonment being experienced by many U.S. cities, Baltimore promoted vacant-housing ownership under the dual theory that federal disinvestment was the root cause of the strife and that homeownership would serve as a preventative measure against further urban decay (Lieb 2010). As one senator put it: "People won't burn down houses that they own." This initiative was strongly linked to the 1968 Federal Housing Act, which promoted "Home Ownership for the Poor." Well-intentioned in its directive, this campaign in Baltimore often resulted in sloppy rehabilitations of vacant houses and rampant predatory lending in poor, black neighborhoods, which only exacerbated the problem of vacancy and disinvestment (Lieb 2010).

Other creative homebuyer support strategies, such as the Dollar House Program and Rehab Express from the 1970s and 1980s, offered an elite class of potential homeowners very inexpensive prices on vacant homes coupled with low-interest construction loans (Hinds 1986; Lieb 2010). These programs were designed to preserve the city's housing stock, stabilize neighborhoods, and attract people back to the city from the suburbs (Hinds 1986). While this form of urban homesteading assistance was popular, it required significant city subsidies and therefore was not considered a long-term, sustainable solution to abandonment. Homebuyer supports still exist today, both as part of comprehensive vacancy management programs and as a component of private real estate development incentives.

Property Acquisition & Code Enforcement. Acquisition of vacant properties often confronts the twin difficulties of tracking ownership and limited city staffing (Cohen 2001). To combat these obstacles, a strong theme is evident in Baltimore of designing policy that grants the City more authority for the acquisition of abandoned properties. For example, in 1999 the "quick-take authority" in the City was expanded, effectively allowing the municipality to file a petition in district court seeking condemnation and possession of an "abandoned property"[4] (Clagett 2003). In 2003, this authority was expanded again by House Bill 424, which authorized the city to condemn and take immediate possession of any "distressed property"[5] (Clagett 2003).

In 2002, then-Mayor Martin O'Malley launched Project 5000 (United States Conference of Mayors 2006; Krohe 2011). The goal of this plan was to acquire 5,000 vacant and abandoned properties in two years. The plan included the aggressive pursuance of tax sale foreclosures, quick-takes, and traditional acquisitions; transfer of surplus vacant properties owned by the City; and use of law firms, title companies, and others to help clear titles. Project 5000 had four primary steps: (1) strategic identification of properties; (2) strategic partnerships (primarily to provide free and reduced-rate legal and litigation services); (3) building new infrastructure in the form of new legal manuals, new staff, and a more uniform process; and (4) moving beyond acquisitions, which included public-private partnerships for property disposition and heightened code enforcement (United States Conference of Mayors 2006). By 2006, the program had acquired

6,000 abandoned properties with clear titles, returned 1,000 properties to private ownership, and designated an additional 2,000 properties for specific development outcomes (United States Conference of Mayors 2006).

In 2005, the Housing Authority launched TEVO (Targeted Enforcement toward Visible Outcomes). The program was designed to identify and pursue negligent homeowners and enforce either sale or necessary repairs to bring vacant properties into compliance with housing code. TEVO targeted blocks where the pressure of prosecution or the community would be likely to spur homeowners to take action (Ransome 2007). At its inception, TEVO identified 6,000 vacant properties.

Demolition. Given the scope of the vacancy problem in the city, one of the primary strategies for addressing vacancy in the city has been demolition. Former Housing Commissioner Daniel P. Henson aimed to eliminate 11,000 of the worst units by 2003, which led to more than 4,000 houses being demolished between 1996 and 1999 (Cohen 2001). Due to scattered demolitions across the city that left gaps in some blocks and caused adjacent buildings to collapse, this plan was criticized for being "unsystematic and counterproductive" in its approach (Cohen 2001). Additional critiques pointed out that there was often no plan for re-use and many of the cleared lots became public health and safety nuisances (Cohen 2001).

In 2000, as a response to these criticisms, Housing Commissioner Patricia Payne declared a moratorium on demolitions, except in emergencies. Starting in 2001, the City allocated $2 million annually for demolitions, which was sufficient funding for 300 houses. The new plan prioritized houses that posed imminent danger to residents, followed by a focus on areas with highest vacancy concentrations, with overall poor block conditions, and where demolition could help protect future redevelopment efforts (Cohen 2001). An attempt was made to pursue whole-block demolitions, as well, rather than the "snaggle-tooth" approach used in the past. In 2016, Maryland governor Larry Hogan and Baltimore mayor Stephanie Rawlings-Blake introduced a nearly $700 million initiative, called Project C.O.R.E., to support expanded demolitions ($94 million in direct funding) and new development ($600 million in incentives) (Thomas 2016).

Development Revitalization and Relocation

In the 1960s, the idea was hatched to revitalize Baltimore's inner harbor area into a public space incorporating commercial and cultural establishments.

This development plan came to fruition in the late 1970s, when Baltimore planning officials reached out to developer James Rouse (known for developing Faneuil Hall in Boston), who agreed to aid in the construction of a social space along the waterfront consisting of dining and shopping opportunities (Rosenblatt 2011). Baltimore's "harbor renaissance" brought in more than $160 million in local property tax revenue, dramatically increased tourism in the area, and was soon replicated in cities around the world, including Long Beach, California, and Sydney, Australia (Rosenblatt 2011).

Despite the success of the Inner Harbor district and several other notable revitalization projects in the city, and with more investments in the Inner Harbor under development (Bradley 2013, Mirabella 2018), Baltimore's "resource-poor, weak-market" economy has necessitated heavier reliance on local foundations and "med and ed" revitalization efforts rather than on the more traditional commercial real estate and development market (Stone et al. 2008). One such redevelopment project, the East Baltimore Development Inc. (EBDI), is a revitalization, housing, and biotech park project started in 2000 and linked to the Johns Hopkins campus in East Baltimore. In order to clear the land deemed necessary for the redevelopment, EBDI relocated 700 East Baltimore families, 98 percent of whom were black (Farquhar 2012). While EBDI deemed this "responsible relocation" because residents were given some choices in the relocation, the process has been criticized as being a contemporary form of urban renewal. Farquhar found evidence to support this critique:

> Despite policymakers' protestations that EBDI and urban renewal were vastly different, their relocation policies and their effects were remarkably similar . . . EBDI's program of responsible relocation sought to define East Baltimore residents as people without choices and to define relocation as an intervention that transformed and empowered residents by providing choice. (Farquhar 2012, iii)

EBDI defends this involuntary relocation on the grounds that, first, by providing choice in the process, they lessened the negative impacts of relocation and, second, the only solution for the level of blight and deterioration in some neighborhoods was to remove residents, demolish, and start fresh.

Urban Greening and Sustainability Efforts

In addition to strategies specifically related to demolition and rehabilitation, the City has attempted a number of urban greening and sustainability efforts on vacant lots. Currently, the Office of Sustainability is pursuing an initiative called "Growing Green," the goal of which is to employ innovative, sustainable, and cost-effective methods for reusing vacant lots and mitigating the negative impacts that vacancy can have. The program uses strategies such as growing food, greening of lots, and storm water management.

Local food systems development has been a goal of the city for the past several years. The 2009 Baltimore Sustainability Plan outlines twenty-nine goals for creating a "healthier, stronger Baltimore," which included (as its second goal) establishing Baltimore "as a leader in sustainable, local food systems." In pursuit of this goal, in 2013 the Baltimore City Planning Commission adopted *Homegrown Baltimore,* a new urban agriculture plan for the city. Homegrown Baltimore (HGB) simultaneously promotes the goals of the Baltimore Sustainability Plan, the mission of the Baltimore Food Policy Initiative, and the mission of Vacants to Value (Baltimore City Planning Commission 2013). Specifically, HGB addresses the goals of these various initiatives by developing an urban agriculture plan, putting more land into agricultural production, and clearing and maintaining vacant land for interim and future uses (figure 3.11).

Urban agriculture has a long history in the city. There is evidence of people gardening on vacant lots as a means for civic improvement and beautification in the city dating as far back as 1910 (Baltimore City Planning Commission 2013). In 1973, a Neighborhood Garden Committee was formed to clean vacant lots and provide soil so that city residents could garden. The Neighborhood Garden Committee was subsequently replaced by the Adopt-a-Lot program, which still exists today. Urban agriculture currently takes many forms in the city, including farms, community gardens, school gardens, home gardens, rooftop gardens, aquaculture projects, apiaries, and orchards (Baltimore City Planning Commission 2013).

The promotion of urban agriculture on vacant land has received renewed attention in the city in recent years. In 2010, the Planning Department conducted a GIS mapping land inventory to identify all city-owned land suitable for urban agriculture. Necessary site charac-

Figure 3.11. Homegrown Baltimore's Linkage to Baltimore City Initiatives. *Source:* Baltimore City Department of Planning (2013).

teristics were determined based on meetings with local farmers. Parcels were considered if they were city-owned and larger than one acre. They also needed to meet certain physical criteria, including tree coverage, slope, and location within a flood line. Parcels slated for development or parkland were excluded. The first assessment identified thirty-five acres and sixteen sites, and more parcels have been identified subsequently. If the city were to include nonadjacent, smaller plots in this inventory, 240 acres would meet the criteria, which is roughly 0.5 percent of the city's total land area.

As outlined in HGB, the City is now advocating for the development of more urban agriculture because of its potential to increase food security, provide access to fresh fruits and vegetables, create jobs, and bestow environmental benefits. To realize this goal, the City has decided to prioritize small-scale farms in weak-market areas with high unemployment. Another approach for using urban agriculture as part of vacant land management has been the Power in Dirt Program, begun in 2011. This program helps volunteers revitalize vacant lots, often through community gardening.

Comprehensive Strategies

The Housing Market Typology (HMT) originated with *PlanBaltimore!* in 1997 and was developed by the Planning Department and the Housing and Community Development Department (Kromer 2002). The HMT was updated in 2011 with the assistance of The Reinvestment Fund. Designed to aid in city efforts to strategically match limited resources to neighborhood housing market conditions, the HMT is a market classification scheme based on "cluster analysis," a method of statistical analysis applied to data that exhibit "natural" groupings or clusters. The cluster analysis in Baltimore was performed on the basis of nine housing market variables. Based on these variables, each section of the city was grouped into one of five cluster categories: Regional Choice, Middle Market Choice, Middle Market, Middle Market Stressed, and Distressed.

The HMT is used both by the Vacants to Value (V2V) program to address vacancy issues and by Code Enforcement for assistance in designing interventions and strategies for neighborhood conditions. The Housing Authority developed V2V in 2010 with the goal of strengthening neighborhoods, eliminating blight, and spurring development and revitalization efforts across the city. The V2V program is considered by the city to be a mechanism for encouraging change by reenvisioning Baltimore as a vibrant and growing city.

According to the Housing Authority, the majority of vacant properties in the city are in severely distressed areas (11,000, or 65% of the total) and cannot be rehabilitated because development demand is insufficient. The remaining 5,000 vacant properties (31%) are in "transitional neighborhoods." Last, a limited number of emerging markets have been identified in distressed areas which, with resource assistance from code enforcement, could support the rehabilitation of 700 properties (4%) (Baltimore Housing).

Using the HMT as a guiding framework for determining the ideal solution in a given area, V2V employs a comprehensive seven-point strategy (City of Baltimore):

1. Streamline the disposition of city-owned properties.
2. Streamline code enforcement in stronger markets (on transitional blocks).
3. Facilitate investment in emerging markets.

4. Target home-buying incentives.
5. Support large-scale redevelopment in distressed areas.
6. Demolish and maintain severely distressed blocks.
7. Provide concentrated green, healthy and sustainable home improvements.

V2V spawned several other city initiatives as well (see chapter 5).

Challenges and Critiques of Baltimore's Abandoned Housing Strategy

According to urban planning scholar James Cohen, an inherent tension exists between the neighborhood planning model in Baltimore's abandoned housing strategy and the need for a more comprehensive approach (2001). This causes a struggle between a more top-down policy and one that incorporates a deeper level of community input, as city interests are often in conflict with neighborhood interests. As outlined by Cohen, the primary challenges to Baltimore's abandoned housing strategy are: (1) the expense (both social and financial) of neighborhood revitalization planning when the need for consensus and a comprehensive approach are taken into account; (2) property acquisition; (3) prevention of abandoned housing; and (4) rehabilitation and marketing of new houses, particularly with regard to increasing the desirability of row house design and making rehabilitated properties affordable (2001).

In addition to the critique of Baltimore's vacant housing strategies as being piecemeal and counterproductive, researchers have noted weakness in data collection, environmental practices, and community response. Using Philadelphia's Neighborhood Transformation Initiative (a housing market typology-type model) and strategies from several other cities as a comparison, Culhane and Hillier (2001) observed the lack of data being used to guide operational decisions around housing vacancy in Baltimore and identified a need for increased modeling and evaluation in the City's process:

> Little is likely to change [in relation to abandoned housing] unless city governments assume leadership and make a persua-

sive case to both public and private sources for a well-targeted effort with a high probability of impact. To do so, cities need to create citywide planning strategies for land aggregation and neighborhood stabilization and to develop analyses of the risks and opportunities associated with redevelopment opportunities in specific markets. (449)

Vacants to Value constitutes Baltimore's primary response to the need for a more strategic, targeted approach, as is a demolition selection process from early 2013 (which we discuss in chapter 5). Even given these new efforts, Baltimore can learn from the successes and failures of other cities facing similar challenges with depopulation and abandonment.

City residents have also expressed dissatisfaction with the City's efforts to abate vacancy and abandonment. East Baltimore residents surveyed between 2000 and 2002 voiced numerous negative reactions to demolition and redevelopment in their neighborhoods (Bowie et al. 2005). In addition to feeling that the development projects were conducted without proper notification, residents expressed concerns about environmental and safety hazards (including rats, lead paint, and asbestos) and a particular fear that these environmental threats were due to social inequities. Interviewees also reported a range of psychological impacts from the demolitions, including relocation, disruption of ordinary life, and inattention to the needs of the community. Last, residents provided recommendations for how development projects could be improved, which included increasing notification and education about the projects, strengthening community involvement, and enhancing the safety and security of the demolitions sites. A more recent evaluation of Baltimore's antivacancy efforts is critical of the slow pace of putting properties into receivership, excessive sales to for-profit developers and uneven levels of development across neighborhoods. While a nonprofit developer, the Philadelphia-based Reinvestment Fund, has been quite successful in acquisition and redevelopment in distressed neighborhoods, the amount of credit for this that can be claimed by Vacants to Value is unclear (Perry Abello 2016).

The high level of distress in certain areas of the city poses a particular challenge for planners and other city officials. As one city employee stated, "you could eat up your whole budget just on East Baltimore." This highlights a theme that emerged in our conversations about how to design action plans in light of considerable budgetary constraints. City officials expressed a notable conflict between targeting money in one area versus spreading the funds more evenly across the city. Some expressed the opinion that targeting funds in a more strategic manner would have a larger impact, while others emphasized the importance and political necessity of equitable distribution of demolition dollars across the city.

In areas of the city with less blight, management strategies tend to center on where demolition is cheapest. As we will show in chapter 5, the vacancy is so extensive in certain areas such as East Baltimore, however, that the city has instead used a more targeted selection process for demolition clusters to bolster existing redevelopment efforts.

As an example, many of the city officials with whom we spoke pointed to the targeted demolition efforts in the Oliver neighborhood, geared at strengthening existing development interest and reinvestment initiatives. Oliver was highlighted as a special case because of the large number of nonprofits that have adopted the neighborhood in recent years. Thanks to these reinvestment efforts, vacancy in Oliver is down by a third. Demolition in this neighborhood revolved largely around a desire to support these initiatives.

Assessment

Baltimore's demolition management strategy today is iterative and seeks to incorporate many different stakeholder and agency priorities. City officials with whom we have spoken regarding vacancy and abandonment generally agree about the need for a city approach that is multipronged, prioritizes blight elimination, and employs strategic demolition in areas with high vacancy and concentrated rehabilitation where possible. Interim uses (such as greening) were also stressed as critical placeholders until the market unfolds or other uses are identified.

Funding constraints loom large in these conversations, and there is considerably less agreement about the most effective and equitable way to spread limited resources across a city struck by such a high prevalence of blight and abandonment. Within the Planning Department, a new discussion appears to be emerging about the importance of explicitly identifying goals and values that can be more transparently integrated into the decision-making process.

Recent evidence regarding strategies for blight reduction and elimination and economic development in distressed communities in Baltimore similar to ones we will discuss in detail later in the book is mixed, but on balance encouraging. Arising from Baltimore's complicated legacy as a city defined by structural racial discrimination and inequality of opportunity, and permanently changed by the weeks of unrest following the 2015 death of Freddie Gray in police custody, it appears that Baltimore represents an encouraging trend of African American–elected officials, responsible to a majority-black electorate and aware of progressive strategies for social policy, embracing an ethic of action on behalf of disenfranchised communities, rather than a traditional strategy of focusing on communities like the Inner Harbor that cater to tourists and whiter, more affluent residents. Unlike Flint and Fall River, Baltimore does not see itself as a shrinking city—but aside from cities like Detroit, it's hard to imagine many cities in Baltimore's position seeing themselves as such.

From evidence of positive change in distressed communities in areas of Baltimore near Johns Hopkins University resulting from community-anchor institution investments (Kaufman 2016; Dubb 2018) to acquisition and redevelopment of vacant houses through incentives like the Vacants to Value Booster grants (Perry Abello 2016), there is evidence that, in an era of limited funds for large-scale city-led investments, the city is nurturing creative partnerships with large nonprofit anchor institutions and community-oriented nonprofit developers to address the causes as well as the symptoms of disinvestment and decline. These encouraging signs are consistent with evidence of growth and diversification in population, residential neighborhoods, and economic activity across the greater Baltimore region (Greater Baltimore Committee and Baltimore Metropolitan Council 2018). We have also documented in this section impressive efforts by city planners to design responses to blight and abandonment. We note, however, that we found little evidence in our stakeholder interviews that city planners envision a large role for community-level engagement in strategy design. (We will address this issue in chapter 5.) It appears that community residents, empowered by the Freddie Gray protests, are increasingly advocating for themselves regarding city initiatives such as the "Complete Streets" transportation bill (Lipsitz Flippin 2018). In comparison to other large cities attempting to address systemic, structural, and historic racial bias and evidence of long-term distress and shrinkage, Baltimore has focused its attention, resources, and expertise on creative responses to these concerns that may produce a more equitable and opportunity-rich city in the future.

3.4 Fall River

Fall River is an example of another kind of postindustrial city, with its roots in an earlier era of economic growth that has long served as an entry point for immigrant ethnic whites. Unlike Baltimore and Flint, Fall River has not suffered the same level of long-term effects of sustained white flight and has really only in the past twenty years engaged the challenges and opportunities associated with a multiracial and multiethnic populace. However, like Baltimore and Flint, Fall River has a mayor who reflects that city's diversity and seeks new strategies to reverse a long decline in population and economic activity. Thus, Fall River offers us a new opportunity to explore the topics of this book: How does a city shrink? And what can be done to formulate a better plan for shrinkage?

A 2007 initiative in Massachusetts identified eleven cities that shared histories as gateways for new immigrants at the early stages of the Industrial Revolution, have lost their manufacturing base, and have lacked resources to compete in the technology-rich environment of Massachusetts. Mayors of these Gateway Cities signed a compact pledging cooperation on activities to take advantage of unrealized potential and to reduce the economic gap between them and the rest of the state (The Massachusetts Institute for a New Commonwealth 2007). Since 2007, fifteen more Massachusetts cities have been designated by the state legislature[6] as Gateway Cities, satisfying the following criteria: population between 35,000 and 250,000, with an average household income below the state average, and an average educational attainment rate (BA degree or above) below the state average. The challenges Gateway Cities face are significant: their poverty rate is 19.8 percent, double that of the state (MassINC undated); they have only 6.3 percent of the state's high-technology firms, compared to 60 percent in Greater Boston (The Massachusetts Institute for a New Commonwealth. 2007); relatively low property values make them unattractive places for new development, yet high rents make them increasingly unaffordable for many of their residents (Mohl 2016).

There are multiple opportunities for growth, in the Gateway Cities, however: these include leveraging the presence of immigrant communities to encourage immigrant entrepreneurship via place-making and local economic development (Foreman and Larson 2014), commuter rail service to the South Coast of Massachusetts that includes the Gateway Cities of Fall River and New Bedford (Metzger 2018), and an education vision that takes advantage of diversity, cultural institutions, and local providers (MassINC 2018).

Here we offer a closer look at Fall River, one of the original eleven Gateway Cities. To its residents, it is not a "shrinking city;" to them, it is home, though some industrial buildings are abandoned (see figures 3.12 and 3.13). We provide a glimpse into the city's history, how it came to

Figure 3.12. Typical Residential Neighborhood in Fall River.

Figure 3.13. Street View of Quequechan Mills District in Fall River.

be a global capital for cotton textiles by the end of the nineteenth century, and why it is has been in steady decline since the beginning of the twentieth century. Last, we describe the city's response to its economic and population decline, the kinds of policies the city has employed and what has worked and what has not.

A History of Fall River's Rise and Fall

From its humble beginnings in 1811, Fall River quickly attracted the attention of industrialists who recognized the city's waterfront location as ideal for the construction of textile mills: within thirty-five years, it was a city of 9,000 inhabitants, 2,000 of whom worked in the textile industry (Herald News 1978a). By the beginning of the twentieth century, Fall River had more spindleage than any other city in the United States and was widely recognized as one of the great textile cities of the world (*Herald News* 1978a; Noth 2008; Phillips 1946).

The city's impressive stature and its vast employment base, however, peaked by 1920 with a population of 120,485. In December 1920, workers saw a single-month wage cutback of 22.5 percent; shortly thereafter, mills began to close (Philips 1945). The city dominated the cotton market, but mills in the Southern United States began to put Fall River's mills out of business. This, combined with labor strikes, legislation that shut down the city's steamship line, and financial downturns, emptied the city of jobs and started a pattern of depopulation that would continue for nearly a hundred more years (Phillips 1945; *Herald News* 1978b). As one 1978 retrospective on the city's decline put it, "the most fatal of all setbacks was the Depression of 1929 when corporations folded like empty cardboard boxes" (*Herald News* 1978a). The flight of businesses left millions of square feet of mill space vacant, generating a hazard in the form of uncared-for buildings left behind (Ibid.).

The Pocasset Mill No. 2 was just one victim of the economic malaise of the late 1920s. A cotton mill of impressive size and output, it provided jobs for hundreds and was shuttered when the economics of cotton shifted away from this Massachusetts port city. Abandoned and vacant, the mill's floor was soaked with oil from bygone days of operation. On February 2, 1928, a demolition crew was working nearby on another vacant mill and a spark flew into Pocasset Mill No. 2. The resulting fire spread across the mill and within eight hours consumed thirty-six buildings, including most of the city's historic downtown (*Herald News* 1978c).

What the Numbers Tell Us

The city's population has been falling steadily since 1920. Today, the U.S. Census Bureau estimates the city's population to be 88,930—a loss of 26 percent since the 1920 peak (see table 3.2). Largely suburban Bristol County, which contains Fall River, has enjoyed a 25 percent rate of population growth between 1970 and 2016, as compared to an 8.2 percent loss in Fall River (U.S. Census Bureau 1970, 2016). Much of Fall River's population loss since 2000 has taken place in the downtown and areas bordering the interstate highway I-195 (figure 3.14).

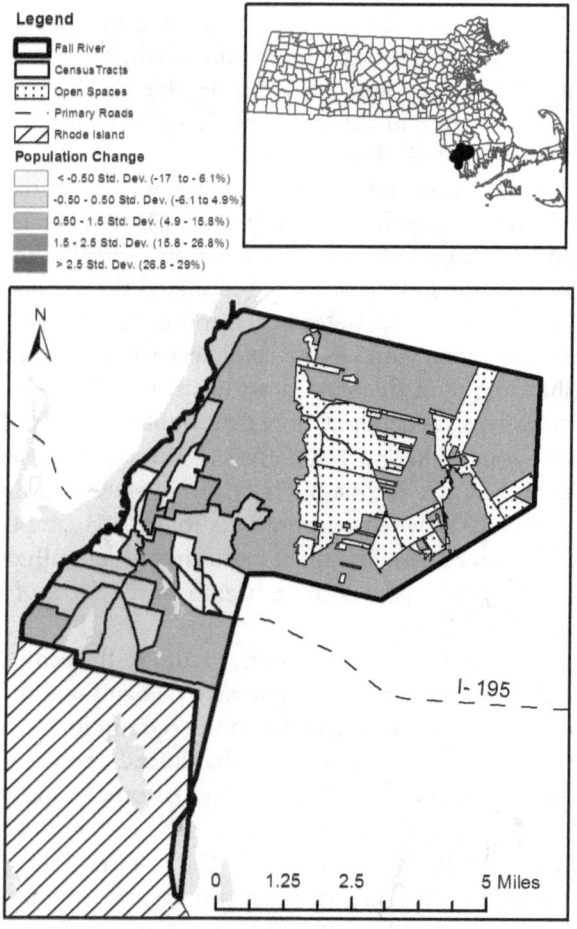

Figure 3.14. Population Change in Fall River, 2000–2016.

Fall River has a larger foreign-born population (19.8%) than Bristol County (11.7%) or Massachusetts as a whole (12.2%). Similar trends apply to residents who speak a language other than English, who are over twenty-five and have less than a ninth grade education, who are unemployed, and who have an income below the poverty line.

A close examination of demographic data across five decades, since 1970 (see tables 3.9 and 3.10), show three particularly compelling patterns: a diversification of the racial and ethnic characteristics of the population, an increase in the number of housing units, and a jump in the number of abandoned buildings. The confluence of these three patterns is worth more detailed review.

Let's begin with diversity: in 1970, the city was 99.1 percent white, with only 220 residents identifying as Hispanic or Latino. By 2016, the white population dropped to 82.5 percent, and all other racial groups grew—accounting for 13,126 residents (from a mere 855 persons in 1970). This increase in diversity is associated generally with reductions in discriminatory housing practices, redlining, and racial zoning, as well as increased immigration and the exodus of white populations to the suburbs (Sugrue 2005; Vicino 2008; Silver 1984); this population change is also associated specifically with the city's growing stock of poorly maintained

Table 3.9. Population & Race/Ethnicity in Fall River: 1970–2016

Year	Total Population	White Population	%	Black/African-American Population	%	Hispanic/Spanish Population	%
1970	96,898	95,779	99.1	278	0.3	220	0.2
1980	92,574	91,395	98.7	427	0.5	2,187	2.4
1990	92,472	90,076	97.2	952	1.0	1,577	1.7
2000	91,938	83,815	91.2	2,283	2.5	3,040	3.3
2010	88,857	77,349	87.1	3,466	3.9	6,562	7.4
2016	88,930	73,370	82.5	4,111	4.6	9,015	10.1

Data sources:
1970 Social Explorer, Census 1970 (T13: Race; T13: Spanish Origin or Descent Indicator [15%])
1980 Social Explorer, Census 1970 (T13: Race; T13: Race by Spanish Origin Status)
1990 Social Explorer, Census 1970 (T13: Race; T13: Hispanic or Origin by Race)
2000 Social Explorer, Census 1970 (T14: Race; T15: Hispanic or Latino by Race)
2000 Social Explorer, Census 1970 (T54: Race; T55: Hispanic or Latino Origin by Race)
2016 Social Explorer, ACS 2016 5-year estimates (T13: Race; T14: Hispanic or Latino by Race)

Table 3.10. Fall River Housing & Economic Characteristics: 1970–2016

Year	Total Housing Units	Other Vacant	Unemployment Rate	Total Employed	% Below Poverty Level
1970	34,129	406	5.2	40,278	10.9
1980	37,017	897	7.7	38,608	14.8
1990	40,375	916	10.0	40,226	14.3
2000	41,857	1,091	7.0	39,674	17.1
2010	42,750	1,057	13.2	38,613	20.2
2016	43,198	3,809	12.3	37,869	22.0

Data sources:
1970   Social Explorer, Census 1970 (T107: Housing Units; T111: Vacant Housing Units by Type of Vacancy for Year-Round Housing Units; T88: Poverty Status for Families; T56: Unemployment Rate)
1980   Social Explorer, Census 1980 (T80: Year-Round Housing Units; T83: Vacancy Status; T40: Unemployment Rate for Civilian Population; T100: Poverty Status In 1979 [short version])
1990   Social Explorer, Census 1990 (T72: Housing Units; T75: Vacancy Status by Type of Vacancy; T29: Unemployment Rate for Total Population 16 Years and Over; T99: Poverty Status in 1989 by Race)
2000   Social Explorer, Census 2000 (T155: Housing Units; T158: Vacancy Status; T73: Unemployment Rate for Civilian Population in Labor Force 16 Years and Over; T183. Poverty Status by Sex)
2010   Social Explorer, Census 2010 (T68: Housing Units; T71: Vacancy Status); ACS 2010 5-year estimates (T37: Unemployment Rate for Civilian Population in Labor Force 16 Years and Over; T114: Poverty Status in 2010 for Children Under 18; T115: Poverty Status in 2010 for Population Age 18 to 64; T116: Poverty Status in 2010 for Population Age 65 and Over)
2016   Social Explorer, ACS 2016 5-year estimates (T95: Occupancy Status; T96: Vacancy Status by Type of Vacancy; T33: Employment Status for Total Population 16 Years and Over; T37: Unemployment Rate for Civilian Population in Labor Force 16 Years and Over; T114: Poverty Status in 2010 for Children Under 18; T115: Poverty Status in 2010 for Population Age 18 to 64; T116: Poverty Status in 2010 for Population Age 65 and Over)

and lower-cost multifamily rental housing, which has become attractive to lower-income residents, who are disproportionately members of communities of color (The Public Policy Center at UMass Dartmouth 2016).

The second pattern that appears in Fall River's demographic trends is the growth in the number of housing units during a period of population decline. The city had 34,129 housing units in 1970 and 43,198 by 2016 (see table 3.10). If vacancy rates grew (from 1.2% in 1970 to 8.8% in 2016), why was there a net increase in occupied units? The growth of housing units (during a period of population shrinkage) can be most easily explained by a decrease in the average household size during this period. In 1970, Fall River had 32,949 households; by 2016, that number grew to 38,366. During that same period, the average household size in the city shrank from 2.87 persons per household to 2.3 (Census 1970, 2016). A city with fewer people was spreading out into more households in more housing units.

A final trend observed is the increase in abandoned buildings reported in the city. In 1970, the Census reported 406 "other vacant" properties, an indicator of the number of vacant and abandoned buildings. By 2016, that number had dramatically increased to 3,809, a trend similar to that of Flint and Baltimore. Figures 3.14, 3.15, and 3.16 show that areas within

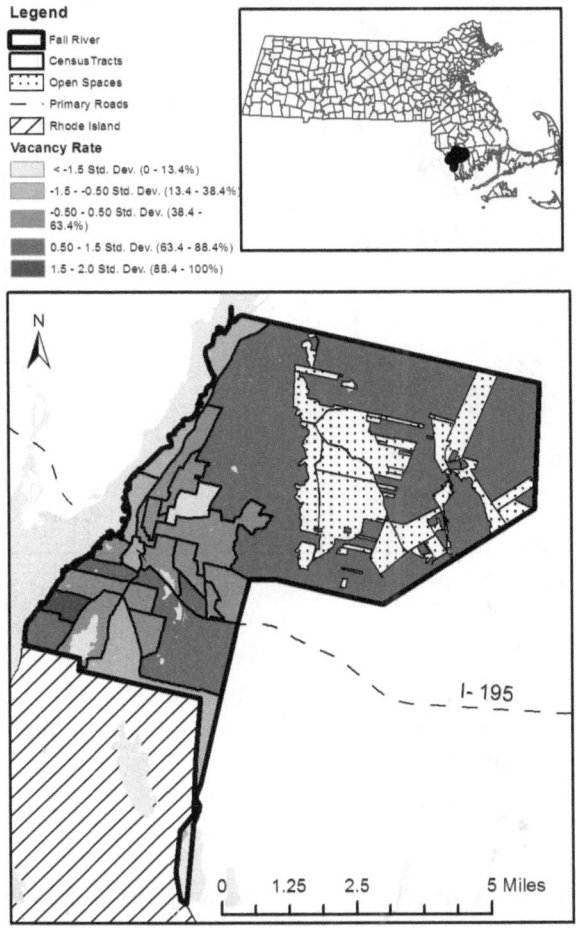

Figure 3.15. Housing Vacancy in Fall River, 2016: Percentage of Housing Units Classified as Other, Vacant.

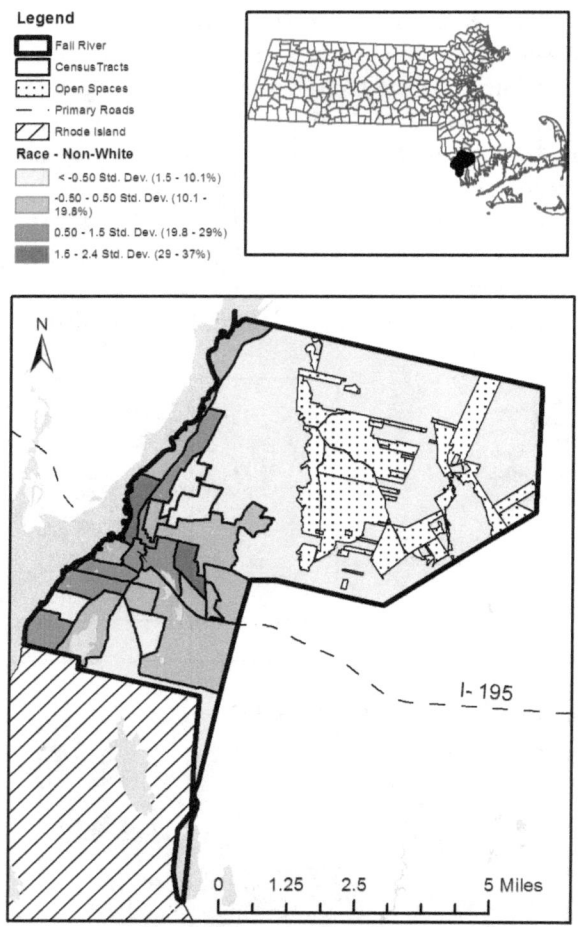

Figure 3.16. Nonwhite Population in Fall River: Nonwhites as Percentage of Population.

Fall River that have had the greatest population loss are also those that have the greatest number of housing vacancies and the highest concentrations of nonwhite populations.

Policy Responses

As Fall River shrank in population throughout the twentieth century, it became more diverse and its households expanded, but the numbers of vacant and abandoned buildings increased. Throughout this period, the city's response was primarily short-term oriented and lacked long-range planning. A hallmark of the city's plan was the re-use and demolition of abandoned mill buildings—something officials saw as a pressing issue, prodded along by real estate development interests. The combination of fewer cotton mills and a weakening demand for multistory industrial structures made these white elephants a major priority for city leaders.

A quick tour of Fall River today shows that the city has been relatively successful in making the necessary regulatory changes and policy inducements required to retrofit, re-use, and demolish the city's mills. According to our interviews, the city aggressively changed zoning from industrial to residential and commercial, and granted variances on a case-by-case basis to encourage real estate developers to take on these empty buildings. Industrial mills have been turned into senior housing, offices, and, during Halloween season, one building at 33 Pearl Street is turned into a "Factory of Terror" amusement center.

Surprisingly, during much of this period of population contraction (1920–2000), city officials felt that the problem of housing abandonment was not severe. But, for much of the twentieth century, the residential housing stock appeared to have stayed largely occupied, with just those several hundred abandoned buildings—that is, up until the foreclosure crisis, when the numbers more than doubled. As Fall River's housing foreclosure rate increased, so too did state and national rates, generating external interest in the city's problems. As a result, around 2007, policies started to explicitly try to address the growing numbers of vacant and abandoned homes in the city.

City officials have focused on their goal of identifying where abandoned buildings are located and then coordinating a response across agencies (Health Department, Code Enforcement Department, and Police Department) to deal directly with the worst offenders. They proactively work with the Registry of Deeds to forecast foreclosures sales: "[We] go out to inspect and start conversations with the bank to identify what they can do with these new properties. We put together a plan with new vacants whereas older ones are going to need to be knocked down . . . we are trying to be proactive rather than reactive." City officials try to rehab the buildings, but when repairs are too costly, the city will demolish the building and make efforts to build parks or open space on the land.

A Massachusetts Attorney General's program, Building Blocks, was also adopted by the city. The program tries to link the legal issues surrounding housing code violations, public safety concerns, and absentee landlords with foreclosed properties. By aligning state and local resources, the Building Blocks program has allowed Fall River officials to concentrate on the most challenging of its abandoned buildings and go after negligent owners.

We asked city officials how decisions about vacancy and abandonment are made. The response was that all parties—neighborhood associations, mayor, city council, and other agencies—work together in a collaborative, somewhat informal manner. "It is more of an organic process—squeaky wheel gets the grease. No specific metrics or criteria are identified. We listen to what the neighborhood associations ask for and try to make funds evenly distributed." One interviewee went on: "We don't want to put all funding in one area, but some areas need more help than others." What this long-time city official was saying was that a goal of the city's efforts is to achieve some level of equity amongst neighborhoods. But this official also said that the "squeaky wheel gets the grease"—that is, however much city leaders may want to achieve a goal such as equity in the distribution of city resources around vacancy, they often feel pressure to respond to the person who calls, who emails, who demands action.

Another clear goal of city leaders in Fall River is to be accommodating and welcoming to real estate developers. Beyond just being flexible with zoning, serving the needs of developers appears to be a longstanding aim of city leaders. "Fall River is a developer-friendly city, it goes out of its way to get development moving in the city. Developers know that coming in," explained a long-time city official. Garnering a reputation as "developer-friendly" was a driving factor in many policies and strategies created, with an eye toward attracting the interest of developers in reusing mills, rehabilitating older homes, or building new housing. This interest may be driven by an overall alignment between local government and developers, a phenomenon described by Logan and Molotch (2007) as the "growth machine." But more tangible, immediate concerns may also be behind the developer-friendly motif: "When a building is occupied, when [the] surrounding neighborhood is cleaned up, there is a spillover effect. I think the city was aggressive, if an apartment burned, developers knew they could quickly redevelop it. Quick turnover. If they needed approval from the Boards, they can get approvals in less than three months, as compared to a typical approval process that can stretch to a year," explained a city official.

A final aim of Fall River's City Hall in addressing population decline and vacant/abandoned properties is the broader goal of making their city a more attractive community, in general, for all kinds of investments and migrants. One city official explained this aim: "Try to attract folks to come to the community, try to attract businesses to come to the community. Try to do everything we can to improve the quality of life here in the city. With more people and more businesses, we will improve the quality of life here. Incentives for first time homebuyers to move into the city, emphasis on creating a more livable community." The city's challenge is that such a goal can be difficult to conceptualize and operationalize. If you want to make Fall River more attractive, how do you measure "attractiveness?" How can you get different stakeholders to agree on what that means? And, assuming you could, how would you measure it? How do you know if you are making progress? Are population and job growth the only indicators? Can Fall River "improve" and be more attractive while continuing to lose population?

Fall River's approach has been based largely on (1) studying the data to assess areas of highest need and (2) using a mixture of code enforcement and demolition to clean up the worst offenders. This may not be the most long-range approach, but the city has made great efforts in recent years to increase transparency in municipal decision making and encourage open dialogue with neighborhoods rather than imposing a top-down mandate around blight management. City officials noted a growing recognition within city government that a prerequisite for success in mitigating the vacancy problem is taking "a global approach and get[ting] at the crux of the problem."

The Building Blocks program has been the city's primary tool with which to take on the vacancy problem in Fall River. Through Building Blocks, staff from numerous city agencies work together to identify and inspect vacant residences, report code violations, and work with property owners to bring their buildings back into compliance (Attorney General of Massachusetts 2012). The city has also made a deliberate effort to get the community involved in these monitoring and enforcement efforts. This strategy is data-driven; a city team even developed an app with a heat map to help officials zero-in on the most distressed part of the city.

In 2013, Fall River received a grant from Bloomberg's Cities of Service program. The Cities of Service coalition supports innovative solutions revolving around civic engagement; Fall River used the money to build an urban tree farm on land where homes had recently been demolished. The project has been recognized by other Massachusetts cities as a model for the creative re-use of abandoned property. This endeavor is a notable example of a more proactive approach to vacancy management executed by the city.

Despite recent citywide and neighborhood inclusive efforts to attack blight in the City, Fall River's inductive approach to vacancy management—letting the data tell city officials where to focus—provides only a limited and imperfect way for values and goals to be defined or implemented. All this approach can do is observe where the problems are and attack them; this means that, ultimately, the city acts on a piecemeal basis without a clearly articulated plan for the future. Decisions about rehab versus demolition, about tree farms versus parks, are made in response to discreet conditions instead of a broader collective vision about concrete means and ends.

Since 2016, Mayor Jasiel Correira, reelected handily in 2018, has aggressively moved to consolidate economic development power in the mayor's office, stabilized municipal finances, and attracted an Amazon distribution center employing nearly 1,000 full-time, permanent workers (about one-third of which are from Fall River) (Jasinski 2019). These signs of progress, amplified by his profile as a hands-on mayor, pitching in to plow snow from city streets after a storm, are imperiled by an ongoing investigation by the FBI into misuse of funds of the U.S. Department of Housing and Urban Development (Siefer 2018). In an example of the political challenges associated with economic redevelopment and good governance in smaller cities, Mayor Correira won a recall election in 2019, was defeated for reelection in 2020, and is on trial on Federal corruption charges at the time of this writing (Fortin 2019; Borchers 2020).

Assessment

Five policy goals were most clearly articulated in the previous section: identify vacant or abandoned properties, respond to the most serious cases, be equitable among neighborhoods in the allocation of resources, be welcoming to real estate developers, and make Fall River more attractive. For those goals, it is possible to offer a rough assessment of success. The city has moved forward on the first four of these goals: officials have been effective in identifying vacant properties, they have a track record of addressing the most severe sites, they have spread their resources among several city neighborhoods, and they have generated a reputation for being developer-friendly. That final goal, making the city more attractive, is a greater challenge. One city official we interviewed offered a particularly dismal outlook on the direction Fall River is headed: "I see it heading in the wrong direction."

Something is wrong. With so much going on, with five fairly well-thought out goals and action behind them, why does there still exist such negativity within the city's own leadership? Despite the efforts made to date, Fall River has not confronted the core demographic transition that it has faced over the last century. The city has done little to effectively restructure or re-use its physical plant for a smaller population. Some zoning adjustments here or there have helped put mills into new uses and a dozen homes renovated through affordable housing programs helped affected families, but the city has yet to tackle the kind of big-picture, wholesale rethinking and rebuilding necessary to truly make the city more attractive.

3.5 Across Three Shrinking Cities: What Can We Learn?

Having profiled three cities wrestling with issues of decline and distress, we now return to the central theme of this book by asking: what evidence have we gathered that data, analytics, technology, and decision modeling might enable shrinking cities to make better decisions? Which of these tools and methods would be most appropriate for which type of city? In what ways could they be best used? The sample city studies shed light on these questions by explaining (1) the major goals that cities have when it comes to addressing depopulation, (2) the ways in which cities make decisions related to depopulation, and (3) the types of future uses they consider.

As we have discussed in chapters 1 and 2, data and technology tools inspired by the big data and smart cities movements enable shrinking cities such as the three we have studied to collect, share, and use data that enable a variety of stakeholders, at different levels of technical expertise, to design responses to shrinkage that balance efficiency, effectiveness, and equity, using best evidence and stakeholder values.

Across our three sample cities we discovered a wide range of policy approaches and decision-making frameworks. Flint chose to hone in on blight elimination and equity planning, Fall River sought transparency through a loosely coordinated interdepartmental strategy for managing vacancy, while Baltimore developed a clearly articulated vacant building and demolition action plan (see table 3.11). Some cities prioritized participatory planning, while others employed a more centralized approach and relied heavily on localized championing when determining where to invest time and resources.

There is no one-size-fits-all solution for decision making or policy outcomes (see table 3.12). Our examination of three cities illustrates the varied ways in which shrinking cities make decisions about depopulation, vacancy, and abandonment. These are difficult conversations to have; reaching consensus around management strategies is even harder. The extent to which political leaders feel comfortable opening up about their decision-making processes to key stakeholders or even to the general public varies. Consideration of a city's size (Baltimore's population is almost eight times that of Fall River), the diversity of its economic base, and its historic relationship with depopulation, among others, will all have a bearing on the ways it approaches decision making.

Table 3.11. Comparing Sample Cities: Primary City Goals

	Baltimore	Fall River	Flint
Equitable Distribution of Resources throughout Neighborhoods		X	X
Blight Elimination	X		X
Redevelopment	X		
Identify and Catalog Vacant Property	X	X	X
Address Worst Cases	X	X	
Be Welcoming to Investors	X	X	
Make City Physically Attractive		X	X

Table 3.12. Comparing Sample Cities: Primary Decision-Making Systems and Processes

	Baltimore	Fall River	Flint
Centralized	X		
Participatory			X
Squeaky Wheel		X	
Evidence-based	X		

In our conversations with city officials and employees, we consistently found that despite the intention to set a clear policy agenda, the necessary conversations for determining values and goals are not taking place in a systematic way. This leads, in most cases, to uncoordinated approaches that lack explicitly defined metrics and criteria by which to select policy options or evaluate the success of outcomes. In some cases, as we will show in a more thorough discussion of Baltimore's process later in the book, this can generate discrepancies between stated goals and policy actions.

Facing both uncertain population growth projections and more blight than can be managed with limited municipal and federal dollars for demolition, shrinking cities are under great pressure to find cost-effective and equitable solutions to the vacancy problem. Data, analytics, technology, and decision modeling, though far from offering a single optimal or most-preferred solution, can play a role in helping cities to select from a portfolio of options determined based on explicit articulation of values, goals, and constraints. For example, where the city officials in Flint and Baltimore discussed the pull between spreading funds equally across all neighborhoods and focusing investment in targeted areas, data analytics could offer a set of alternatives using clearly defined inputs. This primarily quantitative, model-driven approach is not intended to replace the planners' current toolbox but to offer the potential for a more transparent process and a set of equally desirable options from which planners can choose.

These tools can also play a role in the consideration of future uses for vacant buildings and lots. Each city profiled in this section has grappled, on some level, with the future uses of land left behind by demolished, abandoned homes. One of us (Hollander) recently traveled to Denmark and learned about the challenges that many Danish cities face with regard to depopulation. These places are beginning to act strategically by demolishing vacant and abandoned property, a necessity this nation of 5.6 million has never faced before. As birthrates and immigration fall, however, Denmark (like most Western European countries) is expected to decrease in population, and demolition appears to be the most practical answer. Unfortunately, the Danes have not yet developed plans for what will happen to the land left over when buildings are removed—an area where U.S. cities have generally been ahead of the curve.

For the three cities studied here, five uses were most frequently mentioned for land left behind after demolition: stormwater management, parks/green-space, urban agriculture/forestry, amusement center, and interim uses (see table 3.13). Parks, green-space, urban agriculture, and

Table 3.13. Comparing Sample Cities: Future Uses Considered

	Baltimore	Fall River	Flint
Stormwater Management	X		X
Parks/Greenspace	X	X	X
Urban Agriculture/Forestry	X	X	X
Commercial Uses	X	X	X
Interim Uses	X		X

forestry were future uses utilized by all four cities. The first two, parks and green spaces, are generally seen as amenities and as passive places where residents can congregate, play, or just appreciate nature. Urban agriculture and forestry are geared to put newly vacant land into a productive, income-generating use. In most cities, prior to the building of the city, most land was in some form of agricultural or forest use. These shrinking cities are simply reversing the process by returning abandoned land to its former, productive use. The key idea here is that because residential housing demand is low, these cities are considering nonresidential, income-generating uses. This also explains why commercial uses were popular in all four cities.

When developing income-generating uses is not possible, a use such as stormwater management makes sense because it offers a direct, quantifiable financial benefit to water districts (which are often allied with city governments). Last, interim uses such as land banks in Flint, and community-managed open spaces in Baltimore offer the opportunity for future development or investments, should the right developer come along. In the meantime, interim uses can weigh heavily on a city's maintenance budget.

Now that we know how a small group of U.S. cities responded to depopulation, we can more closely examine decision modeling as a smart shrinkage tool. In chapters 4 and 5 we examine Fall River and Baltimore in more detail to better understand the range of decision models and maps that can support individuals, community-based organizations, and government as they respond to shrinkage, distress, and blight. In chapter 6 we explore how information technology applications that employ the tools we have used can increase the ability of community residents to take charge of a redevelopment agenda.

Notes

1. For the purposes of this book and much other research on urban decline, the census category "other vacant" is used as a proxy for abandoned homes (Hollander 2010; Hollander 2009; HUD, 2008).

2. Following Yin (2018), we employed multiple research methodologies to achieve triangulation around key concepts and ideas: interviews with at least two officials in each city, review of the extant literature on each city, review of contemporary policy and planning issues, and initiatives in newspapers and policy reports.

3. According to the Imagine Flint Master Plan, the document "has a long-range perspective and is the one official policy document that provides a coordinated approach to community-wide decision making" (Imagine Flint 2013a, 3).

4. Any building in a block of row houses where the block as a whole contains 70 percent abandoned property (Clagett 2003).

5. A parcel of real property subject to a tax lien or liens with a lien or liens to value ratio equal to or greater than 15 percent, as determined by the Baltimore City Department of Housing and Community Development. The parcel must also contain a structure that poses a serious menace or public health/safety/welfare; have building code violations; or be subject to liens greater than $1,000 for work done by the City of Baltimore.

6. Section 3A of Chapter 23A of the General Laws of Massachusetts.

CHAPTER 4

Data and Modeling Preliminaries

An Application to Fall River, Massachusetts

4.1 Introduction

In chapter 2 we presented the case for, and against, the collection of models, methods, and applications inspired by innovations related to big data and smart cities that might be relevant to the problem of decision support for shrinking cities. In chapter 3 we presented case studies of three U.S. cities confronting challenges of shrinkage, decline, and distress, and the roles that urban planning, data, and technology could play—but *don't*, at least not yet—in supporting these efforts. In this chapter we summarize our knowledge of data-driven innovations to motivate one application, rooted in decision science, as applied to one of our case study cities. Our goal here is to demonstrate how a particular application, motivated by planning and policy concerns, might be the basis for innovations that could incorporate a broad range of research and practice insights and reflect the needs and concerns of communities most affected by shrinkage and decline.[1]

To introduce our analysis, we summarize what we have learned about data, models, and applications presented in previous chapters that are relevant to the problems of shrinking cities and blighted communities. Our focus is on data, models, and applications that support the design of interventions that may be especially useful to communities and the residents who live there and the constituent-focused nonprofits that represent and serve them. This collection of ideas, which we refer to as an "idea space," is presented in table 4.1. These concepts are summarized as broad

Table 4.1. "Idea Space" for Data and Tech-Inspired Interventions in Shrinking Cities and Distressed Communities

Theory/Concepts	Models, Tools and Technologies	Best Practices, Cases and Applications
Big data	Machine learning and data mining	Liveability indexes (Geers and Economou 2014)
		Neighborhood classification (Appel et al. 2014)
		Housing Market Typology (Kromer 2002)
	Dashboards	My City Forecast, to summarize urban quality of life (Hasegawa et al. 2015)
	Data visualization	"Terf" virtual world for urban planning and design (Jutraz and Zupancic (2015)
	User-generated data	"Landscapiness" mobile app for improved daily engagement with the environment (Tisma et al. 2015)
	Social media	Twitter use by planning opponents (Williamson and Ruming 2015)
Community-based research and technology design	Participatory action design research	Public education and community development through on-line and in-person communities (Mayorga 2014)
Operations research, decision science and analytics	Problem-structuring methods	Values design for local anti-foreclosure interventions (Keisler et al. 2014)
	Community data analytics	YouthHub initiative for labor market readiness (Gardner et al. 2019)
		Youth community mapping of blight (Teixeira 2016)
	Community-based operations research	Multiobjective parks design to balance coverage, connectivity, and accessibility (Sefair et al. 2012)
	Predictive analytics	Development of constructs to predict the probability of housing abandonment (Morckel 2013)

Theory/Concepts	Models, Tools and Technologies	Best Practices, Cases and Applications
	Math optimization	PAIRS metric to quantify partnership potentials between cities (McLarty et al. 2014)
	Community operational research	Models for increasing accessibility to affordable fresh food in underserved communities (Wang et al. 2018)
	Decision support systems, planning support systems, public participatory GIS	Decision support for low-income family housing search (Johnson 2005)
		SeaSketch for marine planning (Goldberg et al. 2018)
		CommunityViz for urban community planning (Aggett and McColl 2006)
Game design and data-driven civic engagement	Participatory game play for community change	@Stake for cellphone roleplay; Community PlanIt for group in-person planning simulations (Gordon and Walter 2015)
	Gaming simulations of community-based planning problems	Gaming design for pedestrian planning and crowd control (Raghothama and Meijer 2015)
	Technology-enabled citizen participation in planning	ChangeExplorer for real-time citizen feedback on planning initiatives (Wilson et al. 2019)
Community-engaged planning and interventions	Local engagement and user-driven data collection	311 services (O'Brien 2018)
	Relationship-building for applied research, collaborations and advocacy	Urban Research-Based Action Network
		Boston Area Research Initiative
Collaborative planning spaces	Participatory visualization and democratic participation	Carticipe, Better Reykjavik, Mayor, I Have an Idea, UrbanData2Decide

categories—specific examples of models, tools, and technologies, as well as best practices or cases. We propose the following categories: big data; community-based technology design; operations research, decision science, and analytics; game design and data-driven civic engagement; community-engaged planning and interventions; and collaborative planning spaces.

Our idea space represents a wide range of models, tools, and technologies. Examples of big data include machine learning and data mining, dashboards, data visualization, user-generated data, and social media. Operations research, decision science, and analytics encompass problem-structuring methods, community data analytics, community-based operations research, math optimization, community operations research, and decision support systems. Game design and data-driven civic engagement is a rubric that allows for mostly analog and in-person game play as well as digital and remote simulations. Community-engaged planning and interventions supports creative data gathering, as well as collaborations between practitioners, researchers, and community members. Collaborative planning spaces encompass many web-based applications for community participation in discussions of changes to local infrastructure and services.

We discuss some examples of best practices, cases, and applications especially salient to shrinking cities and distressed communities. While the Housing Market Typology has actually been used in Baltimore and other cities (Kromer 2002), many others could certainly be applied to places such as the case study cities we examined in the previous chapter. My City Forecast, a big data-based dashboard (Hasegawa et al. 2015), could support large-scale master planning efforts such as those done in Flint and Baltimore. User-generated data, through novel applications (Tisma et al.'s [2015] mobile app for daily engagement; Wilson et al.'s [2019] mobile app for citizen input on local planning projects) or use of existing social media (Williamson and Ruming 2015) can provide insights distinct from administrative datasets. Problem-structuring methods (Keisler et al. 2014), community data analytics (Gardner, Snyder, and Zuguy 2018; Teixeira 2016), and community operational research (Wang, Touboulic, and O'Neill 2018) could provide special value to smaller cities where community engagement and control of institutions is a current subject of debate. Advanced decision-modeling methods are useful for generating detailed policy and planning prescriptions, whether developed to support community-level interventions, such as park design (Sefair et al. 2012), or city-level proposals, such as partnerships (McLarty et al. 2014), or as "engines" for decision aids such as decision support systems and public participatory GIS (Johnson 2005; Goldberg, D'Iorio, and McClintock 2018; Aggett and McColl 2006). Game play and game design is especially useful to engage community members with no special training or expertise in models, methods, or technology (Gordon and Walter 2015; Raghothama and Meijer 2015). Finally, interventions in communities, whether based on extensive data collection and analysis or model development, or done interactively and inductively with qualitative methods, require active development and management of collaborative relationships across stakeholder groups, as exemplified by the Urban Research-Based Action Network (https://urbanresearchnetwork.org) and the Boston Area Research Initiative (https://www.northeastern.edu/csshresearch/bostonarearesearchinitiative).

In the remainder of this chapter, we focus on applications of operations research, decision science, and analytics to provide planning support across communities within a city facing shrinkage and distress. By doing so, we illustrate the challenges of developing planning recommendations for professionals who may have deep local understanding of the communities they serve, but who may not have the means to assess potential impacts of alternative development strategies that may have different impacts on communities at different levels of social and economic vitality. We provide an application of community-based operations research and math optimization to Fall River, Massachusetts, in the last section of this chapter.

4.2 Data Analytics and Decision Modeling for Smart Shrinkage

In the previous chapter we learned how planners and community members in Flint, Baltimore, and Fall River have devised responses to problems of abandoned buildings, vacant land, food deserts, and systems of disinvestment and structural barriers to opportunity. Many of these responses rely on targeted investments and creative uses for vacant and abandoned buildings in communities where traditional residential and commercial development is unlikely to be economically viable in the short term. While planners, policy analysts, advocates, and other stakeholders play essential roles in community development responses to shrinking cities and distressed communities, the responses they devise tend to rely on traditional methods drawn from disciplines such as urban planning, real estate, and economics. It is less common that practitioners seeking to develop community-level interventions are conversant with the variety of methods described in the previous section's Idea Space, which represent the cutting edge of research motivated by real-world problems. In this section we focus on that portion of the Idea Space devoted to operations research, decision science, and analytics. We do this because we believe that the science of data and decision analytics can provide unique insights into identifying, formulating, and solving problems that take advantage of people's values and experiences while generating policy and planning recommendations designed to represent improvements over the status quo—and, in some cases, optimal, or best-possible solutions.

As we argued in chapter 2, the availability of data, in and of itself, need not be transformative. Instead, the value of data comes from the uses to which it is put. "Data analytics," or simply "analytics," represents a variety of methods of extracting value from data. Analytics is commonly understood to comprise three related activities (Liberatore and Luo 2010). The first of these, *descriptive analytics*, represents tabulations, statistical analyses, and visualizations that provide improved insight into current and past organizational processes and outcomes. The second activity, *predictive analytics*, encompasses models and methods to estimate the future state of an organization's activities or the environment within which it works. The last activity, *prescriptive analytics*, describes models and methods intended to generate policies, rules, and insights regarding individual and organizational decisions that reflect the values of stakeholders, that are optimal, or most preferred according to commonly accepted metrics. In the remainder of this section we use the terms *prescriptive decision modeling*, *prescriptive analytics*, and *decision analytics* interchangeably.

To understand the significance of these methods, we define important concepts related to performance management, or the ways in which analytics can be used to improve the way organizations achieve their missions through products, services, programs, and initiatives. Building blocks of performance management consist of inputs, which are resources an organization uses to achieve goals; outputs, indicators that show how an organization uses its resources; and outcomes, indicators that show the impact of a program or initiative on participants, or the amount of progress made toward an organizational goal. Impact measures for performance management include efficiency, or relative use of outputs per unit of input; effectiveness, or level of achievement of organization or social goals; and equity, or perceived fairness of distribution of goods, services, outputs, or outcomes across geographies or population groups.

Private-sector firms typically use output measures such as production levels, throughput and inventory, and outcome measures such as revenue, profit, or market share. Efficiency impact measures are often money-based metrics such as return on investment. Effectiveness impact measures depend on the sector a firm operates in; for example, health care effectiveness measures are population health measures; military effectiveness measures are levels of security. Social equity is not usually a primary consideration for private-sector firms; however, many firms have increasingly embraced a broader range of impact categories represented by the "triple bottom line": people (contributors inside and outside the firm related to products), planet (sustainability), and profit (Hammer and Pivo 2016).

In contrast, government and nonprofit organizations rey on nonmonetary output measures such as number of program participants, cases closed, and meetings held, and outcome measures such as labor market participation, food insecurity, and recidivism. Examples of efficiency impact measures are donor retention, client satisfaction, and program expenses versus total expenses. Examples of effectiveness impact measures are ecosystem health, for an environmental nonprofit, or housing cost burden, for a housing nonprofit. Social equity is typically a central concern, and can be measured by health disparities, discrimination in housing, or political inclusion (Gaynor 2017). Efficiency, effectiveness, and equity impact measures can be classified using a theory of change (DuBow and Litzler 2018) or a "toolbox" approach (Penna 2011).

Private-sector firms commonly use data analytics to make critical decisions. Much of the literature on big data and data analytics reflects the perspective of the corporate private sector, since it not only understands the potential of big data but has the capital to pursue the latest data analytics tools (McAfee and Brynjolfsson 2012).

However, the big data and analytics movements have had significant impacts on not-for-profit organizations as well. Cities such as New York, Boston, Chicago, and Baltimore have embraced the "CitiStat" model by which multiple datasets related to maintenance, health, crime, and human services are linked, summarized, and made public so that government officials can be held accountable for meeting performance goals (Perez and Rushing, 2007). Initiatives such as the Boston Indicators Project (www.bostonindicators.org), the Metropolitan Philadelphia Indicators Project (recently discontinued), and Atlanta's Neighborhood Nexus (www.neighborhoodnexus.org) represent efforts by nonprofit organizations to develop large datasets describing measures of neighborhood and regional health in order to support and coordinate planning, organizing, and interventions at the local and regional level. The London Datastore, a data portal created by the Greater London Authority (https://data.london.gov.uk/) provides open access to over 700 datasets related to jobs and the economy, transport, housing, and other categories, in raw form and distilled into indicators. The National Neighborhood Indicators Project (neighborhoodindicators.org) is a collaboration of partners such as these to democratize access to information and to support the strategic use of data by local organizations, rather than the preparation of independent reports. The Reinvestment Fund's PolicyMap (www.policymap.com) is a web-based mapping application that enables practitioners and researchers at all skill levels to create maps at a variety of levels, from neighborhoods to the entire United States, using over 15,000 datasets in demographics, housing, lending, consumer spending, education, and many other categories.

Despite these efforts, the level of awareness and productive use of data sources such as these by local organizations, who are often the intended beneficiaries, is not as high as one might expect or hope. Many nonprofit organizations are constrained by the demands set forth by their funders (Stoecker 2007). Funders are often reluctant to grant organizations the right to use funds for increasing technological capacities (Al-Kodmany 2012). Limited technical and organizational resources may make it difficult for a CBO to develop IT applications that may allow the analysis and sharing of data they desire (Wallace 2014; Boyd and Crawford 2011; Stone and Cutcher-Gershenfeld 2002). According to Patrick Ball, head of the Human Rights Data Analysis Group,

> If you're looking at poverty or trafficking or homicide, we don't have all the data, and we're not going to . . . That's why these amazing techniques that the industry people have are great in industry, but they don't actually generalize to our space very well. (Wallace 2014)

We note that most of the leading examples of cities making most advanced use of data and analytics are larger, more affluent cities rather than smaller, shrinking, or distressed cities that are the focus of this book.

Prescriptive decision modeling uses qualitative and quantitative analysis to generate recommendations that optimize one or more objectives. This approach enables stakeholders to articulate values that support neighborhood-level interventions; to identify specific decision alternatives associated with desirable social outcomes; to develop strategies that are improvements over current practice as well as consistent with their own values; and to perform sensitivity analyses to learn how changes in the model affect important outcome measures. We emphasize prescriptive decision modeling in the remainder of this chapter. We do so because of our belief that planning and policy analysis, as typically taught and practiced, often lacks empirical support for assertions that a given course of action is more-preferred, or most-preferred, or optimal, as compared to the status quo and thus provides stakeholders with empirical methods to guide real-life interventions that draw explicit connections between values, data, outputs, outcomes, and social impact. However, we acknowledge that applying prescriptive decision modeling in real-life contexts is challenging: it requires evidence about the efficacy of an intervention whose associated impacts are to be quantified and objectives to be optimized; available data to formulate a decision problem; judgment about the most-appropriate solution method; and patience to engage community stakeholders in a meaningful way, even if a consultancy approach might be quicker.

Prescriptive decision modeling is widely used for many private-sector applications such as logistics, finance, marketing, and human resources. It is of great use in those fields where an organization's goals and values are well defined, the range of decision alternatives is reasonably easy to explain to those without specialized training, and a model's recommendations can be implemented in practice in straightforward ways, especially with information technology (consider how UPS improves the routes it uses to deliver packages as quickly and cheaply as possible). Decision modeling is more difficult to apply in public-sector domains, where values conflict, there are multiple objectives, and technical resources are limited. It may even be the case that those who wish to solve a problem cannot agree on what the "real" problem is, or that solutions to a widely understood problem turn out to be unacceptable to key stakeholders due to disagreements about priorities to be put on objectives, or on conflicting objectives themselves. A current example is the controversy in Boston regarding the results of planning models intended to make school start times more beneficial to older students, to enable impacts of start-time changes to be distributed more equitably among communities, and to redesign bus schedules to support these start-time changes (Scharfenberg 2018).

The use of data and decision analytics for housing and community development has been a focus of study in operations research and related disciplines for over thirty years. Surveys of work in this area (Johnson 2012a, 2011) demonstrate a wide range of descriptive, predictive, and prescriptive models, as well as decision support systems to automate the process of policy analysis and recommendations. We start, however by distinguishing between a traditional, quantitative, top-down, and technocratic perspective, on data and decision analytics, and a more mixed-methods, multidiscipline and collaborative and community-focused perspective.

Data and decision modeling is usually presented (e.g., see Albright and Winston 2016), as a process led by technical experts who consult with clients who bring a problem statement. An example of this from housing and community development is the following. A community development corporation may want to know how it can develop and implement a housing strategy to optimize social outcomes for community members. In consultation with clients, technical experts will transform the problem statement into a specific decision problem, that is, how many and what kinds of housing units should the organization develop, and where should they be located, to optimize multiple objectives such as expected social value (an effectiveness measure) and distribution of housing units across communities to reflect relative housing needs (an equity measure). This optimization is performed subject to constraints such as minimum production levels and maximum resource availability per planning period (efficiency measures). Technical experts may solve the problem using appropriate analytic methods and present a range of decision alternatives, of which the client will choose a most-preferred solution for implementation using planning and policy tools for community engagement, financing, construction management, marketing, and property management.

An alternative approach to data and decision modeling assumes that "clients" are not just a source for problem statements and do not only approve technical solutions, but instead are partners who formulate and solve decision problems in full collaboration with technical experts. This relationship, and the analytic methods that support it, are known as "community-engaged operations research" (Johnson 2018a). "Partners" represent not only nonprofit organization analysts, but community stakeholders who may not have special expertise in data and decision analytics or even technical aspects of planning and policy applications such as housing and community development. Community partners work with technical experts to formulate decision opportunities that may or may not use traditional data and decision models and reflect a critical approach to power and social identity. Next, they identify appropriate data sources (both qualitative and quantitative data), acquire, store, and process these data, and collaboratively solve decision problems using qualitative as well as quantitative methods in an iterative manner. "Solving" could have multiple meanings here: generating insight about the problem statement, generating new or unexpected decision alternatives, as well as the conventional understanding of choosing a most-preferred or optimal course of action. Alternative approaches to performing community engaged operations research are community-based operations research (CBOR; Johnson 2012) and community operational research (COR; Johnson and Midgley 2018). CBOR allows for nonprofit organizations to speak on behalf of local stakeholders, and relies more often on quantitative data and decision analytic methods. In COR, technical experts work directly with community members, emphasize qualitative and mixed-methods problem-solving approaches, and put as much weight on generating collective knowledge about the decision opportunity as in generating specific policy and planning alternatives.

Quantitative decision-modeling approaches compatible with community-engaged operations research include multiobjective decision making (MODM) and multiattribute decision making (MADM). MODM considers the problem to be solved to be composed of many individual decisions whose outcomes, in the aggregate, comprise a strategy that can be applied across multiple neighborhoods or multiple property parcels. As an example from decision modeling for foreclosure response (see Johnson et al., 2016), a MODM approach would determine how a budget for property acquisitions might be allocated across multiple target neighborhoods, which particular foreclosed properties of different types (e.g., owner-occupied versus multi-family rental) to attempt to acquire, and the time period in the future in which a particular acquisition would be performed. On the other hand, a MADM approach might treat decision alternatives, or strategies, as defined in terms of a relatively short list of potential actions characterized by multiple attributes (e.g., neighborhood interventions, such as residential property acquisition, commercial development, or developing green spaces); the goal of this analysis would be to choose the single most-preferred course of action according to stakeholder perspectives on the levels of attributes and the value placed on the various attribute types.

Qualitative decision-modeling approaches compatible with community-engaged operations research include problem structuring methods such as value-focused thinking (VFT; Keeney 1992, 1996; Keisler et al. 2014). In VFT, the goal is to conduct conversations with community stakeholders that generate fundamental values that motivate a community intervention, and from those, decision alternatives associated with means, or intermediate values that are causally associated with fundamental values, and attributes that allow measurement of the extent to which certain decision alternatives achieve fundamental objectives. Other problem-structuring methods, including soft systems methodology, cognitive mapping, and strategic choice approach, sometimes referred to as "Soft OR" (Mingers 2011; Rosenhead and Mingers 2001), are associated with community OR, while facilitated modeling (Franco and Montibeller 2010) is often applied in corporate as well as community contexts.

We now describe data and decision analytics applications to housing and community development generally, and then focus on applications most salient to issues of municipal shrinkage and distressed communities. Descriptive research in housing and community development includes cost-benefit analyses of housing mobility programs (Johnson, Ladd and Ludwig 2002) and evaluation of alternative national policies for renovation public housing stock using statistical models of housing duration (Gleeson 1992). Prescriptive research includes long-term policy modeling for housing mobility (Caulkins et al. 2005), land acquisition for residential and commercial development (Wright, ReVelle, and Cohon 1983; Gilbert, Holmes, and Rosenthal 1985), and multiobjective optimization for affordable and subsidized housing location (Johnson 2006; 2007). Gabriel, Faria, and Moglen (2006) use multiobjective optimization to generate alternative collections of land parcels in suburban Maryland for residential development that reflects the perspectives of a government planner, an environmentalist, a conservationist, and a land developer. Nigar Neema, Maniruzzaman, and Ohgai (2013) use genetic algorithms with geographic information systems to generate Pareto optimal solutions to the problem of designing parks and open space using land parcels for urban areas in developing countries. Demetriou, Stillwell, and See (2012) developed a math programming–based decision support system to address the consolidation of scattered land parcels in a rural area of Europe to support economic development.

Examples of decision support systems for housing include an application to assist in the search for affordable and assisted housing by low- and moderate-income families (Johnson 2005) and applications to forecast demand and allocating resources for military housing (Forgionne 1991; Forgionne and Frager 1998). A lack of consideration for issues of equity, inclusion, class, and race has led to applications of OR/MS to housing and community development that have resulted in negative impacts on low-income and African-American neighborhoods (Wallace 1989; Schmidt 2011).

Data and decision analytics for shrinking cities and distressed communities is distinguished from more general applications for housing and community development in a number of ways. First, the planning context is that of declining population and economic activity; aging, neglected, and abandoned physical infrastructure such as housing, public spaces, and public services; overrepresentation of low-income persons and communities of color as compared to the larger metropolitan area; and limited fiscal resources to develop high-impact, but often costly, interventions. Second, planning interventions more often reflect the values, priorities, and expertise of nonprofit professionals, public-service officials, and for-profit organizations than those of residents of distressed communities, who are more likely to be politically underrepresented (sometimes ineligible to vote due to criminal justice system involvement), less visible in community discussions, and lacking in awareness and use of technology and analytic tools. Thus, issues of political power, social standing and influence, equity, evidence of beneficial social impact of proposed interventions (not just financial outcome and various output measures), and authentic community engagement are likely to play a prominent role in data and decision analytic responses to shrinking cities and blighted communities.

In this context, descriptive analytics may answer a variety of questions about neighborhood and property characteristics and recent trends, using data at varying levels of specificity. Pettit and Kingsley (2011) show that questions such as: "Which zip codes in my metropolitan area have the highest foreclosure inventory?" can be answered using neighborhood-level data from national sources, such as the Local Initiative Support Corporation's Foreclosure Risk Scores; questions such as: "What are the properties with repeated code violations?" can be answered using local administrative data that may not have yet been joined with other datasets such as code violation data; and more complex questions such as: "How long has a property been in real-estate-owned status?" can be answered only with multiple linked datasets, perhaps visualized using geographic information systems, such as assessor's data with ownership identifiers. The Reinvestment Fund's Market Value Analysis (Goldstein 2011; The Reinvestment Fund 2014) uses cluster analysis to produce fine-grained classifications of neighborhoods according to their potential for residential and commercial development consistent with neighborhood stabilization and revitalization. This analysis uses multiple data sources on housing vacancy, land uses, sales prices, mortgage foreclosures, and others to create a typology of Census block groups.

Predictive analytics enables organizations to make educated guesses regarding the future trends of certain indicators of neighborhood health. Appel and colleagues (2013), in their study of neighborhoods in the city of Syracuse, sought to identify neighborhoods likely to face increased levels of vacant properties in the near future, as well as specific properties at high risk of future vacancy. This analysis was performed at the neighborhood level using linear regression to create prediction functions, and at the individual property level using machine learning algorithms. Both analyses integrate large volumes of property- and neighborhood-level data from multiple sources, and are integrated into a city-level vacancy analysis system. Morckel (2013) has developed constructs such as market conditions, gentrification, and physical neglect from administrative data to predict the probability of housing abandonment. These analyses could be adapted to determine which neighborhoods, and which parcels within them, are likely to remain in a blighted state suitable for smart shrinkage responses, or to transition to such states, absent significant community development interventions now or in the future.

Prescriptive analytics addresses generation of specific responses to symptoms and causes of shrinking cities and distressed communities that accommodate concerns of neglect, disenfranchisement, and low participation by residents identified above. Jacobs and associates (2013) develop and apply a structured decision-making approach for vacant property re-use to a neighborhood in Cleveland, Ohio. This process integrates stakeholder values elicitation and analysis, extensive data on distressed properties and the neighborhoods in which they are located, and multiattribute decision-making methods using stakeholder values and local data fused into a web-based application. Examples of re-use alternatives under consideration include: take no action; use parcel for bioretention via stormwater management; or convert parcels into community gardens. This application currently is intended to facilitate learning about the characteristics of decision alternatives for property parcels and the impacts of pursuing one of these alternatives as opposed to generating actionable recommendations across large numbers of parcels. Morckel (2017) has applied suitability analysis from geographic information systems to rank vacant parcels in distressed communities for transformation to a naturalized state (not redeveloped for housing or business). Johnson and colleagues (2014) have applied spatial analysis and multiobjective optimization to the problem of setting investment types and levels for neighborhoods at various levels of decline in Fall River; we explore this model in the next section. Johnson and associates (2016) have developed mixed-methods decision-modeling approaches for identification, acquisition, and redevelopment of housing at various stages of foreclosure in low-income communities in the Boston area. No decision support information technology applications known to us have been specifically designed for the needs of shrinking cities and distressed communities and implemented in the field.

This recent work is encouraging evidence that the data analytics and decision-modeling research for housing and community development is increasingly connected across disciplines, shows evidence of real-world implementation, and uses theories and principles that support generalization of research approaches across diverse regions and housing types.

The remainder of this chapter is devoted to an exploratory study of smart shrinkage responses at the neighborhood level using multiobjective decision making in Fall River. In the next chapter, we present a MODM application to the smart shrinkage problem at the level of individual parcels that arose from extensive engagement and participation by planning analysts and decision makers in Baltimore.

4.3 Neighborhood-Level Decision Making for Vacant Land Management

The smart shrinkage decision problem we explore here can be described as follows: what types of neighborhood-level infrastructure investments, and at what funding level, can preserve and enhance quality of life for current and potential residents of multiple communities in a shrinking city? The primary beneficiaries of these investments are communities facing sustained decline in population and economic activity, as well as nonresidents who may visit or work in targeted communities. Understanding that planning interventions may derive political legitimacy by addressing needs of diverse communities, however, infrastructure investments suggested by a decision model can occur in less-impacted neighborhoods as well as those bearing the primary burden of shrinkage and distress. The example we explore in this section comprises the fifth and sixth steps of the geodesign study process, referred to as "impact models" and "decision models," respectively (Steinitz 2012).

Traditionally, large-scale planning investments that could be improved with the use of decision models are designed and implemented by city- or regional-level organizations, with limited input by community stakeholders.

However, political legitimacy also relies on collaboration with community stakeholders to formulate and solve problems of primary importance to them, as opposed to solely agencies or government. When this collaboration is done primarily with community-based organizations, the smart shrinkage decision problem is solved using a community-based operations research approach (Johnson 2012b); when this collaboration is done directly with community members, as well as the local organizations that serve them, the smart shrinkage decision problem is solved using community operational research (Johnson and Midgley 2018).

Our focus on residents as distinct from nonresidents arises because of our understanding that neighborhoods that may be the target of investments in human and physical infrastructure can be divided into two broad types. The first category is comprised of those likely to respond well to neighborhood stabilization and revitalization initiatives that support traditional residential and commercial activities, consistent with the community development framework of Mallach (2008). The primary beneficiaries of these investments are *current and future residents*, who typically seek affordable, high-quality housing located in neighborhoods that provide access to opportunities for education, employment, and recreation; *nonresidents* who may travel to these neighborhoods to work, shop, and engage in recreational activities would also benefit. These might be classified according to Market Value Analysis as applied to the City of Baltimore as "Middle Market Choice," "Middle Market," and "Middle Market Stressed" (City of Baltimore 2010) and be targets primarily of smart growth initiatives.

The second type of neighborhood we consider is that which is not likely to respond well to traditional stabilization and revitalization efforts because high levels of vacancy and blight make it unlikely that investments in housing and commercial development will substantially improve the quality of life of current and future residents, or make the neighborhood substantially more attractive to nonresidents who would shop, work, and recreate there. Instead, different types of investments are necessary to support the transformation of portions of these distressed communities into areas more suitable for nonresidential land uses similar to those defined by the application of structured decision modeling to Cleveland (Jacobs et al. 2013), for example, community gardens or environmental remediation, as well as other passive uses such as recreation and artistic expression. These neighborhoods might be classified by Market Value Analysis as "distressed" and be the target primarily of smart decline initiatives.

The approach we present uses multiobjective decision modeling to choose levels of residential- and nonresidential-focused investment to jointly optimize several social objectives, subject to constraints on investment levels within and across neighborhoods. Examples of residential-focused investments include roads, housing, stores, libraries, and the like. Examples of nonresidential-focused investments are parks, bioretention areas, locations for artistic expression, and land-banked parcels with the minimum maintenance to remain feasible for future land uses for specific social goals.

We assume that different neighborhoods will respond differently to residential-focused versus nonresidential-focused investments—that is, that they exhibit distinct changes in social and economic outcome measures. Here, we assume that the primary outcome measure of interest is perceived quality of life, and that these responses, as a function of investment levels, may show varying measures of economies of scale. Finally, we assume that there is a single variable or index that is strongly associated with a neighborhood's propensity for growth or decline, as well as that neighborhood's quality of life (as perceived by residents, or nonresidents who may derive direct benefit from proximity to or visiting neighborhoods in question). Here, we use the measure of housing vacancy, which Hollander (2010) has identified as a promising metric of shrinking cities and Mallach (2012) has used as a basis for making recommendations for neighborhood development initiatives.

For *high-impact neighborhoods*, quality of life increases at an increasing rate according to increasing levels of investments. For *low-impact neighborhoods*, quality of life increases at a decreasing rate according to increasing levels of investment. For *moderate-impact neighborhoods*, quality of life increases at a rate that corresponds to the increase in investment levels. In economic terms, high-impact neighborhoods enjoy increasing economies of scale for local investments; moderate-impact neighborhoods enjoy constant economies of scale, and low-impact neighborhoods see decreasing economies of scale.

With these assumptions, we develop a decision model to choose levels of residential- and nonresidential investments to optimize four objectives: neighborhood satisfaction; proximity of neighborhoods chosen for investments; and the fairness with which residential as well as nonresidential focused investments are allocated across neighborhoods, subject to constraints on investment levels—over the whole city, and by neighborhood. The decision variables, or quantities whose values determine the objective functions, include the level of residential- and nonresidential-focused investments in each neighborhood. The impacts of residential and nonresidential investments in specific neighborhoods depends on scale economies observed for these neighborhoods, that is, whether a given neighborhood is known to be high-impact, moderate-impact or low-impact. Constraints, or functional expressions that determine permissible values for decision variables, include the following: residential-focused and nonresidential-focused investments in each neighborhood should not exceed defined maximum levels; total residential-focused and nonresidential-focused investments across all neighborhoods should not exceed defined maximum values. A complete presentation of this decision model may be found in Johnson, Hollander, and Hallulli (2014).

This model, which is an example of the nonlinear multiobjective optimization problem, can be solved using a variety of analytic methods (Cohon 1978; Collette and Siarry 2002; Ehrgott 2005; Ehrgott and Gandibleux 2002; Miettinen 1998). The outputs of this optimization process are a series of neighborhood-level investment strategies, each of which can be assumed to be equally preferred by a decision maker (nondominated, or noninferior) in the absence of detailed information about decision-maker preferences. These results can be visualized in two ways: according to objective function values (*objective space*) and according to the actual levels of investment types by neighborhood (*decision space*).

We apply our decision model to a variety of data for Fall River. In collaboration with a planner from Fall River's government, we use Fall River's 2010 Consolidated Plan to characterize Census tracts according to low-income population, the presence of at least one Community Development Block Grant Investment type (street improvements, walking beat police, a new East End branch library, and parks and playgrounds), and population growth between 2000 and 2010 ("growing" if greater than 2%, "declining" if less than 2%, and "stable" otherwise). If a tract has a growing population, we assume it would respond strongly to residential-focused investments and weakly to nonresidential-focused investments. If a tract has a stable population and at least one CDBG investment, we assume it will respond in a linear way to both types of investments. We assume that all other tracts, which are declining in population and may have a low-income population, no CDBG investments, or both, would respond strongly to nonresidential-focused investments and weakly to residential-focused investments.

We define levels of investment based on the amount budgeted for the HOME program (designed to increase the supply of affordable rental and owner-occupied housing) and the Community Development Block Grant (CDBG) program (which supports tasks including street improvements, home rehabilitation, economic development, and senior centers). Given political and popular opposition to the notion that a city is "shrinking" (see the example of Baltimore), we also assume that in the short term, Fall River could not be expected to spend large amounts on nonresidential growth. Therefore, we set the total residential-focused growth budget to 80 percent of the total development budget. Nonresidential-focused growth is assigned the remainder of the budget. The total amount budgeted for neighborhood-level residential- and nonresidential focused investments greatly exceeds the total funds available as estimated from the Year One Annual Action Plan from the Fall River Consolidated Plan. This reflects an assumption that neighborhood stakeholders would have much longer lists of potential projects than the city can accommodate in a single year. As a speculative exercise, we acknowledge that CDBG funds are tied to qualifying geographies; thus it is possible that our model might recommend neighborhood-level expenditures over and above the amount for which a neighborhood qualifies.

We have used these data to solve the smart shrinkage decision problem for Fall River. For certain values of model structural parameters, our problem is a linear multiobjective optimization problem that can be solved quickly using the simplex algorithm. Other values of structural parameters yield a nonlinear decision problem that must be solved using specialized methods. Figure 4.1 (on page 140) shows how different alternative strategies, represented as lines with different shades and data point shapes, perform according to the four objectives that our model optimized.

This display, known as a value path (ReVelle 1987), shows that each alternative investment strategy represents a particular level of achievement, scaled from 0 to 100 percent, on each of the four objectives. Since the lines all cross, there is no single investment strategy clearly preferred to all others—they are all nondominated, by design. This is consistent with the theory of multiobjective optimization (Cohon 1978).

To give a sense of the range of objective function values associated with various combinations of objective function weights, we start with "corner solutions" that arise when we optimize one objective and ignore the others. To solve this problem, we apply a weight of one on one objective and zero on all others. The results correspond to solutions 1 through 4 in figure 4.1. We see that solution 3, the "corner solution" corresponding to maximizing equity associated with residential-focused investments,

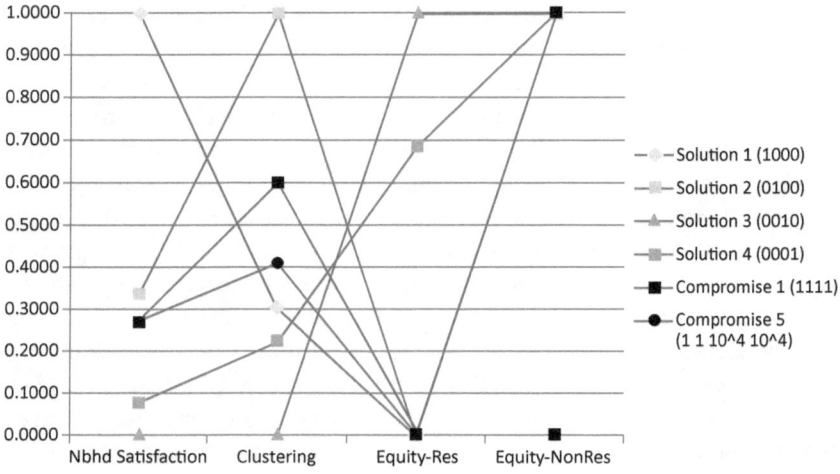

Figure 4.1. Neighborhood-Level Planning Model Objective Space Results: Corner Solutions and Two Compromise Solutions.

maximizes equity associated with nonresidential investments as well. Next, we examine "compromise solutions" in which nonzero weights are applied two or more objectives to determine if there might be one or more solutions that do at least reasonably well on two or more objectives. Compromise 5, a solution associated with large weights on the two equity objectives and weights of one on the neighborhood satisfaction objective and the clustering objective, respectively, performs moderately well on the neighborhood satisfaction and clustering objectives, achieves maximum value for the residential equity objective, and achieves minimum value for the nonresidential equity objective.

Another objective-space view of our model outputs is shown in figure 4.2, which displays investment levels by neighborhood for two nondominated solutions: one that maximizes neighborhood satisfaction, in the top panel, and the compromise solution, in the bottom panel.

The bars representing levels of residential investment are much higher than the bars representing levels of nonresidential investment because we assumed that most investment in the short term, to be politically feasible, would continue to be devoted to traditional residential investment. In another city, such as Flint or Baltimore, where there is a broader acceptance of a range of investment strategies associated with neighborhoods that

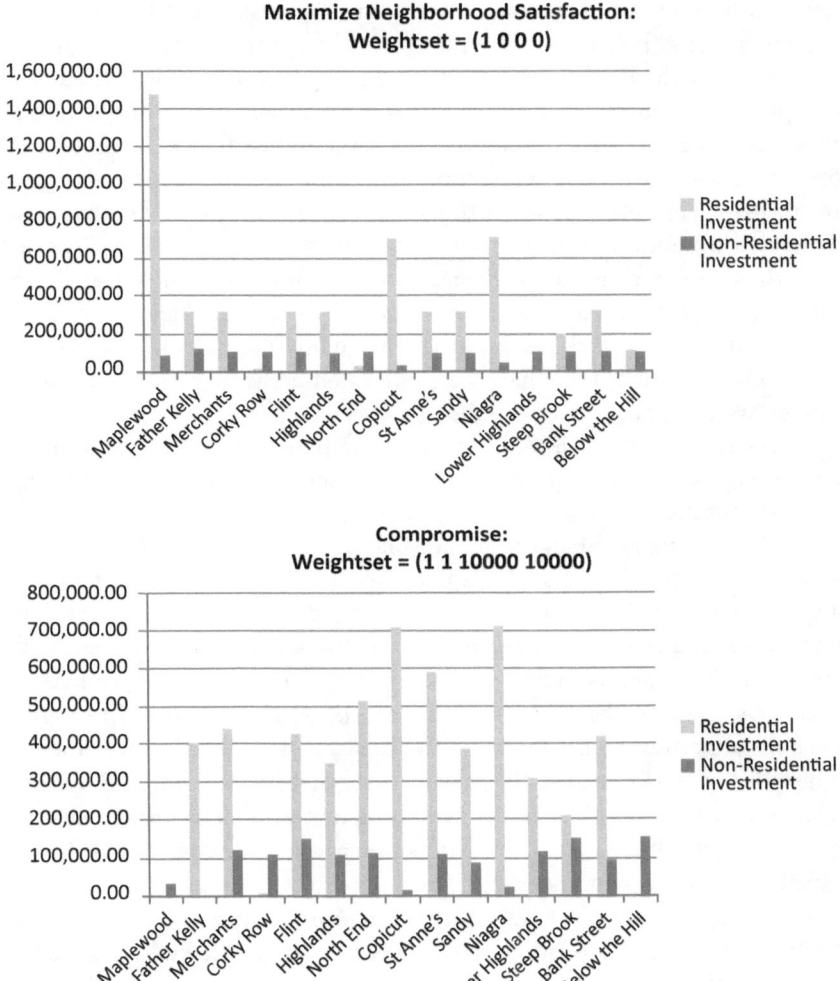

Figure 4.2. Neighborhood-Level Planning Model Decision Space Results: Two Non-Dominated Solutions.

might be more accepting of residential versus nonresidential investments, the heights of the bars might be more equal.

We see that the solution that maximizes neighborhood satisfaction greatly prizes the Maplewood neighborhood of Fall River over all other neighborhoods, and allocates relatively little nonresidential funds to any particular neighborhood. By emphasizing the equity objectives while incorporating the neighborhood satisfaction and clustering objectives, the compromise solution, in contrast, does a much better job in allocating funds across many neighborhoods, and targeting certain neighborhoods for nonresidential investments consistent with the satisfaction received from them. We note that while this prospective analysis yields solutions, generated by optimization methods, that are preferred to the status quo according to our constructed dataset, we cannot assert that our analyses represent actual improvements over the status quo in Fall River. That would require a research design in which we observe outcomes in neighborhoods for which funds have been allocated according to our decision model prescriptions, which we did not use.

A decision-space view of our model outputs is shown in the form of a map. Figure 4.3 displays investment levels across neighborhoods in Fall River for the compromise solution shown in the bottom panel of figure 4.2.

The left panel of figure 4.3 displays levels of residential-focused investments; the right panel displays levels of nonresidential-focused investments. Consistent with the underlying data on vacancy rates and population changes over time, residential investments are concentrated outside of the region containing the central business district, while neighborhoods closer to the CBD (with the exception of Steep Brook) receive the bulk of nonresidential investments. The lack of residential investments targeted specifically at the CBD may indicate that Fall River would benefit from supporting appropriate residential or nonresidential growth strategies in neighborhoods outside the downtown, and may consider avoiding expensive programs to encourage relocation to the city center.

The meaning of these outputs of neighborhood-level analysis depends on the nature of the relationship between various stakeholder groups. Model outputs should probably be viewed as providing opportunities for stakeholders to craft their own strategies, using recommendations from models such as this as another factor in their decision-making process. City agencies or departments who have viewed themselves primarily as "decision makers"—the "traditional rationalists" and "Corbusian modernists" discussed in chapter 2—would probably see their goal as persuading community members and groups to adopt their recommendations. This is consistent with a traditional conception of public-sector OR.

A more contemporary view of planning, which accepts that full information for making "optimal" decisions is probably unavailable ("incrementalists"), or which advocates for pedestrian-focused and mixed-

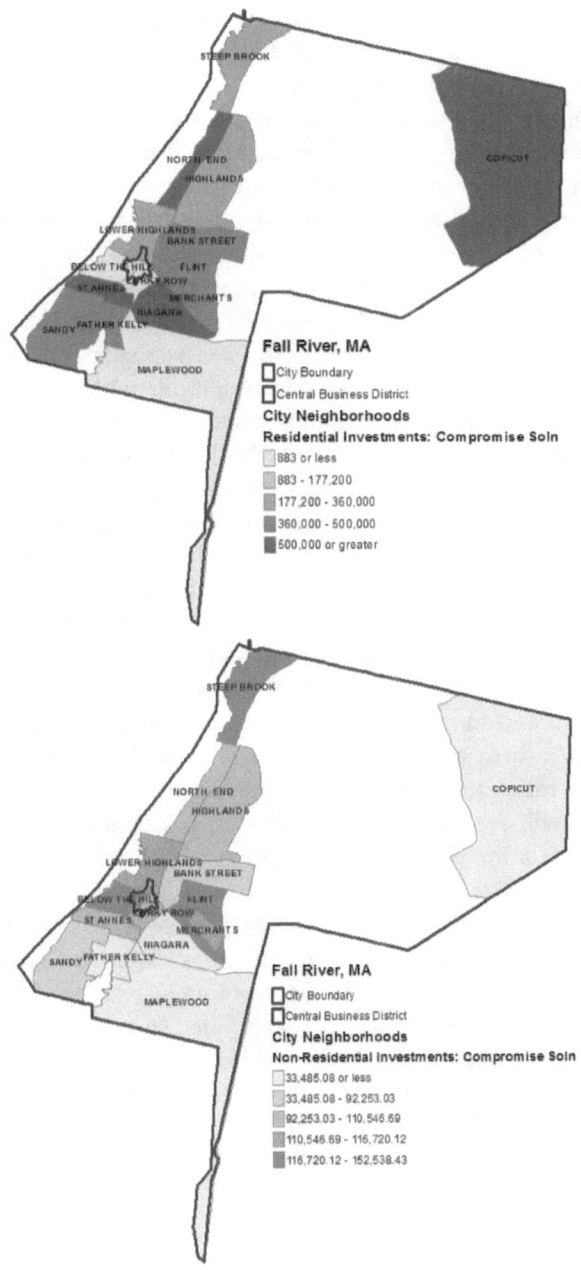

Figure 4.3. Neighborhood-Level Planning Model Decision Space Results: Compromise Solution—Residential and Non-Residential Investments.

income development ("neotraditionalists" or "new urbanists"), would be more likely to see community-based organizations, speaking on behalf of community members, as key partners for problem identification, model development, problem solution, and implementation of results is consistent with the conception of community-based OR. The most progressive views of planning, in which notions of social justice, equity, and inclusion are central to strategy design ("just city proponents") or where stakeholders are seen as coequal partners in developing solutions inductively and iteratively ("communicative/collaborative paradigm"), are consistent with the principles of community OR. The example we explore here, while inspired by principles of community-based OR, was validated by a city planner but did not benefit from extensive consultations with community-based organizations. Therefore, we cannot assert that this is an example of citizen-engaged decision modeling. Examples of citizen-engaged decision modeling, drawn from homelessness services and development strategies for slums, are described in Johnson and Chichirau (2020).

Since the graphical representations we have shown here—line charts in figure 4.1, bar charts in figure 4.2, maps in figure 4.3—provide complementary perspectives on solutions to the smart shrinkage problem, it is natural to imagine that an information technology application that combines the three views of the problem results, along with ways for users to build and modify the problem to be solved, could provide even more useful information to stakeholders. We will discuss this potential extension in much more detail in chapter 6.

As we will see in the next chapter, it is not easy to design useful decision models for planning interventions in shrinking cities and distressed communities at a more granular level—parcels, rather than only neighborhoods—that reflect the needs and concerns of traditionally disenfranchised groups as well as traditionally dominant groups such as professional planners. Nevertheless, this effort is essential to meeting the promise of interventions drawn from our "idea space" in which the social benefits of data-, model-, and technology-driven interventions exceed the costs, as described in chapter 2.

Note

1. Sections 4.2 and 4.3 are based on the work of Johnson, Hollander, and Hallulli (2014).

CHAPTER 5

Shrinking City Data and Decision Modeling

Baltimore, Maryland

5.1 Introduction

United States cities facing shrinkage and distress employ a wide array of approaches and policies to address problems of abandoned buildings, vacant land, and community disinvestment, as illustrated in the case studies of chapter 3. In chapter 4 we introduced a decision-modeling response to shrinkage at the neighborhood level, using the city of Fall River as an example. In this chapter we focus on the specific problem of building demolition and vacant land re-use at the parcel level. Many questions remain about the precise processes used by cities to implement aggressive demolition and repurposing programs, including: Which properties do they target and why? How do they choose new uses for selected properties? A central aim of this book is to explore whether data analytics and decision modeling can help shrinking cities do a better job of developing planning responses to urban vacancy and abandonment. In this chapter we examine actual decisions regarding vacant and abandoned property acquisition and repurposing, and use these observations to identify elements of a more purposive approach to this problem using qualitative and quantitative decision modeling methods. We apply this approach to the city of Baltimore.[1]

As the United States emerged from the Great Recession, Maryland received $950 million in 2013 from the General Mortgage Servicing settlement of a lawsuit against the nation's five largest mortgage servicers for abuses associated with foreclosure abuses, fraud, and unethical mortgage servicing practices (Maryland Attorney General n.d.). The city of Baltimore used $10 million of these funds to support efforts toward acquisition and demolition of 4,000 blighted properties, resident relocation, and homeowner down payment assistance under the Vacants to Value (V2V) program (Sharrow 2013), as described in chapter 3. In the remainder of this chapter we will examine the internal decision-making process Baltimore used in 2013, present a decision model for vacant land acquisition, consolidation and redevelopment, and use the findings from our decision model to develop a more general values-based modeling approach that can be applied to many neighborhoods, cities, and regions.

5.2 Demolition, Vacant Land Re-use, and Growing Greener in Baltimore

To begin our study of actual practices in vacant land redevelopment, we present results of semi-structured interviews[2] with seven Baltimore city employees in the Department of Planning, Office of Sustainability, and the Land Resources and Permits and Code Enforcement Divisions of the Housing Department. Interview questions were designed to generate insights about the decision-making process used by the City in the winter of 2013 when evaluating which vacant properties to target for demolition and future re-use. The interviews were guided by several questions about the planning process, but were open in nature to allow for the discussion of topics and concepts not highlighted by the specific interview questions. A snowball technique was used for recruiting interview subjects. Below we describe the planning process as outlined for us by our Baltimore city interview subjects.

The first steps in the 2013 decision-making process involved rough calculations to determine the scale of blight in the city and the cost of necessary demolition. As V2V Strategy 6 states:

> Blighted blocks in distressed areas are characterized by high concentrations of vacant properties, many city-owned through default, truly abandoned, or in tax arrears. Generally, the housing market will not support the rehabilitation of these vacant properties and many of these blocks will ultimately need to be

demolished. Much of the land needs to be banked and open-space and non-housing uses promoted at least temporarily. (Housing Authority 2013)

The city had roughly 16,000 vacant structures at this time, the majority of which were located in "distressed" neighborhoods, according to the Housing Market Typology. These structures were considered high priority for demolition and re-use under the Growing Green Initiative (Baltimore City Department of Planning 2012). Dealing with just the first one-third of these properties would cost the city in excess of $165 million, much more than the $10 million the city received through the General Mortgage Servicing settlement.

To start the selection process for the first round of demolitions, GIS technicians from the Planning Department located potential vacant clusters throughout the city. A total of 620 clusters were identified based on blocks with the highest concentration of vacancy.

City officials from the Housing Authority, Office of Sustainability, Department of Planning (including community and historic preservation planners), as well as GIS technicians, then gathered for a series of meetings to select clusters of parcels that were highest priority for demolition, clearing, and eventual re-use (referred to henceforth as "demolition clusters"). With the Housing Department as the lead agency, members of the selection team examined maps of the 620 identified vacant clusters alongside the Housing Market Typology to prioritize clusters for demolition. The team closely studied the entire city, parcel by parcel, with the applied collective knowledge of the various agencies involved. Areas suitable for large-scale demolition (high vacancy with low occupancy rates) received special emphasis. Each city agency or representative was able to share parcel-level knowledge such as excessive code violations, pockets of high crime, areas of concern for community residents, and neighborhoods with existing redevelopment efforts underway. This information, along with agency-specific goals such as sustainability and crime reduction, was applied to help identify priority clusters for demolition. Individual re-uses were not identified or assigned at this stage.

The configuration of these demolition clusters was complex: as shown in figure 5.1, owners might retain title to some parcels, while others might have ownership reverted to the city. Some might be owned by the Housing Authority of Baltimore City, and still others might be public parks. Some

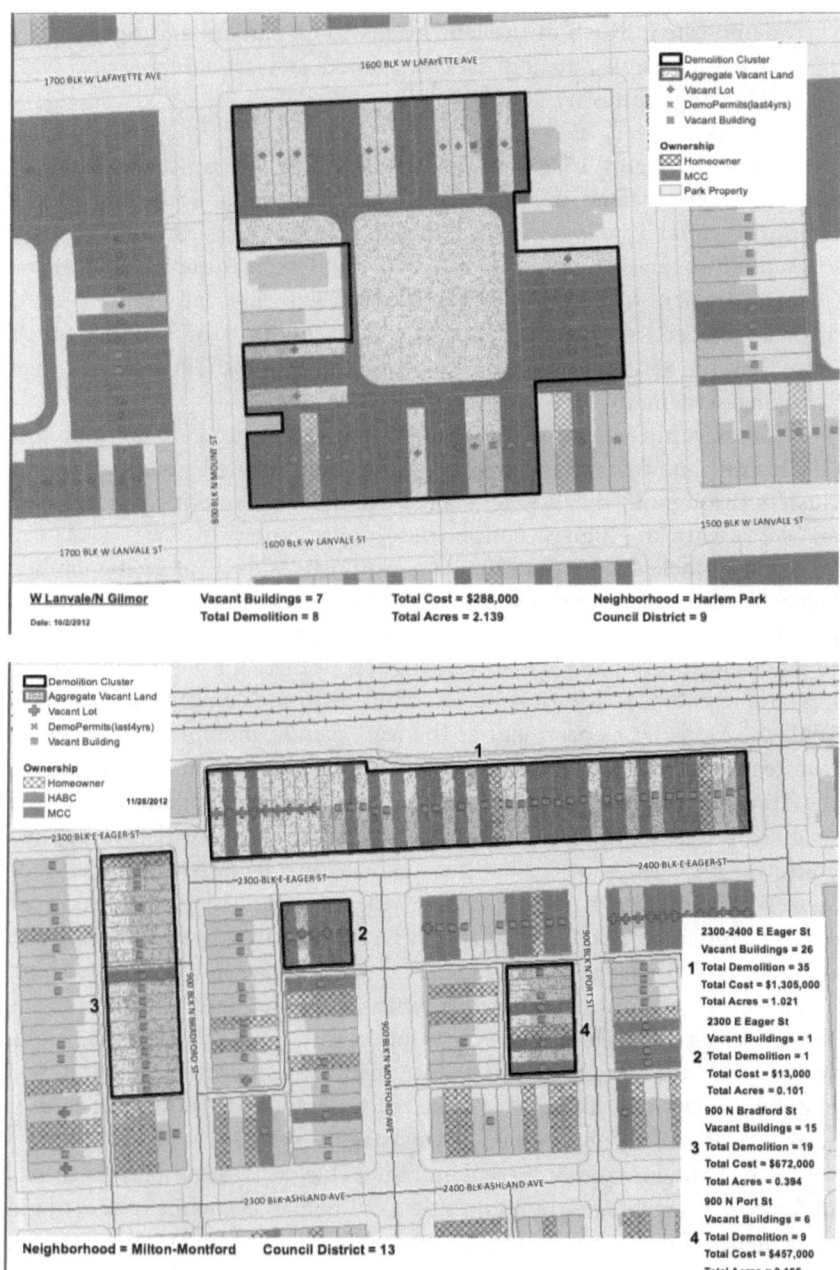

Figure 5.1. Examples of "Demolition Clusters" in the City of Baltimore. *Source:* Baltimore City Department of Planning (2013).

properties might have had demolition permits issued sometime in the past four years, while others might be currently legally occupied by residents who wished to remain where they were.

Moreover, these clusters had nonuniform shapes: some were directly adjacent to occupied units for which the city had no plans for acquisition and demolition, and others consisted of noncontiguous collections of parcels.

Clusters such as those shown in figure 5.1 could be characterized by many different metrics: number of vacant lots, number of renters and/or homeowners who would be required to relocate if the houses they lived in were demolished, the cost of acquisition and demolition, the preferred postdemolition land use, and so on. One sample of twenty-four demolition clusters identified by the Department of Planning, for example, contained 474 vacant lots, requiring 588 demolitions, comprising over forty-three acres, and requiring over $14 million for property acquisition, resident relocation, demolition, and securing properties—before including the cost of the eventual re-use.

The primary criterion used by decision makers in the selection of clusters was cost. While no dollar cutoff per block or cluster was specified, the City aimed to achieve cost-effective outcomes that involved minimal acquisition, relocation, or building of structural support walls. In this case, "effective" was defined as generating the largest impact for the lowest cost. Relocation has high social and economic costs, and retaining walls are expensive, so blocks with significant occupancy were generally ruled out. According to one city official, "[the] goal was to have whole block outcomes as much as possible." Again, no specified cutoffs were applied for the number of relocations allowable per block or cluster, but given that relocation costs exceed demolition costs, cost served as an acceptable proxy for the occupancy criteria.

Beyond cost and relocation, the criteria metrics used primarily reflected a desire to support more stable neighborhoods through blight removal and targeted demolition. The city transformed this goal into practice by investing in areas identified by the Housing Market Typology (Kromer 2002) as having significant market demand or being near to preexisting redevelopment efforts. According to officials we interviewed, demolition of clusters adjacent to areas with high owner-occupancy and existing redevelopment efforts had the twofold advantage of (1) supporting more stable neighborhoods by removing pockets of crime and physical disorder; and (2) clearing the land for interim use or redevelopment in the future. There was also a focus on the elimination of crime hotspots.

When asked how each of these priorities was weighted in the selection process, city officials expressed that, rather than using an explicit weighting system, each of the priorities was considered on a parcel-by-parcel level. Agency representatives evaluated individual clusters based on how well they met various agency and cost criteria. Clusters that could meet multiple criteria were given higher priority than those that were only able to meet one or two. Overall, conversations with Baltimore city officials revealed a large number of stated priorities and very little evidence that tradeoffs or relative preferences for certain objectives over others were considered. Instead, a case-by-case decision process was employed, meaning tradeoffs were not measured and objectives were not weighted accordingly.

5.3 Examining Vacant Land Management Practice: A Pilot Study

We now examine specific vacant land data in Baltimore to gain a deeper understanding of how planners and other professionals made decisions about property acquisition and repurposing. Our focus is on five neighborhoods in East Baltimore that our Baltimore city partners agreed would serve as a useful test bed for our analysis: Better Waverly, Coldstream Homestead Montebello, East Baltimore Midway, Oliver, and Broadway East. These neighborhoods are adjacent to each other, located fairly close to downtown Baltimore, and are classified as "distressed" according to the Housing Market Typology. However, some of them, according to city planners, have high levels of distress throughout, while others have pockets of blight mixed with more stable areas.

To gain insight into the process through which planners decided which clusters to choose for demolition, we assembled a set of twenty-six clusters, chosen at random from the 138 available in the five target neighborhoods, for use in a small, "toy" instance of the vacant parcel decision model that we will discuss in more detail in section 5.5. Of these twenty-six clusters, we selected two of the clusters chosen by the city for demolition for closer examination of the city's reasons for choosing them, augmented by two other clusters selected by the city for demolition that were not part of the toy model. We also selected for closer examination six other clusters from the twenty-six used in the toy model for closer examination that the city did not choose for demolition.

Figure 5.2 shows the five target neighborhoods, the 138 vacant clusters within these neighborhoods under consideration by the city for redevelopment in 2013, when this study was performed, and the four

Figure 5.2. Interview Map.

clusters of those available that were selected by the city for demolition and possible redevelopment. The ten clusters that are the basis of our qualitative analysis to follow are listed in the lower left of figure 5.2 and identified with numbers on the neighborhood map.

The first question we posed to interview subjects from the city was whether there was anything special or unusual about the City's cluster selection process in the five East Baltimore neighborhoods. We learned that the overriding concern was the level of distress across the neighborhoods, and the primary decision-making conflict between targeting money toward revitalizing one area versus spreading the funds more equitably across the city emerged as a theme within the development of action plans while working with a limited budget. Some City officials expressed the opinion that targeting funds in a more strategic manner would have a larger impact, while others emphasized the importance and political necessity of the equitable distribution of demolition dollars across the city.

In other parts of the city, the focus is often on areas where demolition is cheapest. As described in chapter 3, vacancy in East Baltimore is so extensive that the City is primarily interested in being strategic in the selection of clusters so as to bolster existing redevelopment efforts. As an example of this, many of the City officials with whom we spoke pointed to the targeted demolition efforts in the Oliver neighborhood, which were geared at bolstering existing development interest and reinvestment initiatives. Oliver was highlighted as a special case due to the large number of nonprofits that have adopted the neighborhood in recent years. Thanks to these reinvestment efforts, vacancy in Oliver had been reduced by a third. Selection of clusters in this neighborhood largely centered on a desire to support these initiatives. Similarly, there had been strong community advocacy for redevelopment in Coldstream Homestead Montebello.

We now discuss specific clusters in the East Baltimore sample that were selected by the city, and those that were not, and the rationales provided by city planners for each decision they made.

East Baltimore Clusters Selected by the City

Cluster 1: 2700 Block Tivoli Avenue. The 2700 block of Tivoli Avenue is located in Coldstream Homestead Montebello (CHM), a relatively stable neighborhood with a high percentage of owner-occupancy in the northern sections. According to a 2008 community master plan for the neighborhood, this block of Tivoli was cited as being the number one priority of the community for demolition because of high crime and drug rates. The City hoped to strengthen the more stable areas of the neighborhood by removing the blighting in this triangle.

Cluster 2: 1100 Block East Linval Street, 1400 Block Ensor Street, 1400 Block Holbrook Street, 1700 Block Ensor Street. Cluster 2, located in the Oliver neighborhood, was cited as being a priority of both the City and the community for blight elimination in order to help stabilize the surrounding areas.

Cluster 3: 1400 Block North Dallas Street, 1600 Block Lansing Avenue, 1600 Block North Bethel Street. The majority of the parcels in Cluster 3, also located in Oliver, are on inner blocks, which means that they have smaller, less marketable homes.[3] Clearing out inner blocks is a strategy that cleans up blight and helps to showcase the considerable redevelopment work already underway in a given area.

Cluster 4: 1500 Block North Regester Street, 1700 Block Crystal Avenue. By demolishing Cluster 4, the City hoped to eliminate blight in order to bolster the surrounding area for redevelopment. The demolition of these blocks is a short-term boon to other redevelopment efforts, but in the long term it also clears the blocks for future redevelopment possibilities.

The primary reasons for selecting these four clusters were (1) requests from the community or community organizers, city councilpersons, and others; (2) preexisting City priorities; (3) drugs, crime, and blight elimination; (4) the bolstering of more stable areas and nearby development efforts; and (5) the cleaning out of inner blocks to showcase existing redevelopment. The theme of a cluster-by-cluster evaluation was also quite evident, suggesting that, despite some generally agreed-on objectives, the City did not appear to have a clear or consistent decision-making rationale that translated across all of the selected clusters.

In general, City officials were much more knowledgeable about the details of these four clusters than they were for the remaining clusters in the sample that were not selected. Several officials were able to provide parcel-level information about specific buildings and development projects, and could also demonstrate strong familiarity with community groups and neighborhood concerns. This indicated a solid working knowledge among City officials of neighborhood-level issues within the City. It also reflected the significance of community advocates and other stakeholders working on behalf of specific neighborhood concerns. The sheer volume of vacant clusters in the city makes intimate knowledge of each cluster nearly impossible, but certain clusters will inevitably rise to the top (with assistance from advocates). It is likely, then, that these clusters would not only be the ones with which City officials were most familiar, but also that they would eventually be chosen for targeted demolition and redevelopment efforts.

It should also be noted that, despite a stated objective of cost-effective outcomes, a number of the clusters selected by the City for this first round of demolition had very high aggregated costs. The aggregated costs for each cluster include demolition plus the cost of any necessary relocations or building of structural supports. Cluster 1, for example, had a total cost of well over one million dollars, potentially eating up a big percentage of any demolition budget. The total cost of all twenty-four clusters selected by the city, across all neighborhoods (including the five target neighborhoods discussed here) was slightly more than $14 million, exceeding the $10 million budget allocated for this first round of demolitions. None of the City officials interviewed spoke to this discrepancy.

East Baltimore Clusters Not Selected by the City

Cluster 5: 2700 Block Fenwick Avenue. The 2700 block of Fenwick is the eastern-most section of the CHM triangle discussed above for cluster 1. This cluster was a priority for the City but, given the amount of relocation necessary and the community's concerns about neighboring blocks, it was not selected for the first round of demolitions.

Cluster 6: 1700 Block North Bethel Street. No information about the reason for not selecting this cluster was provided in the interviews. It was noted that Bethel is an inner block (in the Oliver neighborhood) and that eventually cleaning it out would be good for the mostly intact blocks adjacent to it.

Cluster 7: 2000 Block East Hoffman Street. The Housing Department identified this cluster as being a second-tier priority. According to City officials, this cluster was expected to be selected for the second round of demolitions.

Cluster 8: 1400 Block North Gay Street. The 1400 block of North Gay, also in the Broadway East neighborhood, had already largely been demolished. The few remaining structures in the cluster (roughly six) were mostly occupied. While this explains why this cluster was not selected for demolition, there was little consensus among interviewees as to the status of this cluster going forward.

Cluster 9: 1300 Block North Broadway. In addition to rehabilitation potential and historic architecture, this block had a relatively high level of occupancy, making it an expensive choice for demolition at that time.

Cluster 10: 2600 Block Greenmount Avenue. This cluster in the Better Waverly neighborhood was not selected for this round of demolition due to its high level of occupancy. Most of the vacant buildings on the block have already been demolished and the remaining buildings are predominantly occupied.

The overall themes for reasons that these clusters were not selected by the City for the first round of demolitions were (1) second-tier priority (including clusters that were already mostly demolished or on the list for the next round of demolitions); (2) excessive relocation or acquisition required; (3) pressure to spread funds equitably across the city; and (4) rehabilitation potential or historic value. Minimizing cost was the most consistent objective expressed as justification for these clusters not being selected. The weighing of tradeoffs (i.e., whole block outcomes vs. cost or concentrated efforts vs. spreading funds) was not explicitly cited as part of the selection process concerning these or other clusters.

Cluster Selection and Redevelopment: The Big Picture

The Planning Department estimated that the city had funding over the next ten years to demolish only 20 percent of the 620 identified demolition clusters. For this small fraction of clusters where the city could (eventually) take action, the city wanted to answer the following questions: Which clusters should be chosen for acquisition, demolition, and repurposing in such a way as to offer the greatest value for money? Which postdemolition greening options, either temporary and permanent, would be most appropriate given city strategies for neighborhood stabilization and revitalization, and resident needs as understood by local development organizations and the city? We have discussed how the city justified its decisions to select, or not select, specific clusters in our sample set of neighborhoods. We are interested in a slightly different, and more difficult question: How could the City solve this "smart shrinkage" problem in a holistic way for all 620 demolition clusters?

The first primary challenge in solving the smart shrinkage problem is identifying candidate properties for acquisition, demolition, and repurposing. Previously we showed that the officials from multiple agencies selected clusters of properties primarily on the basis of occupancy rates, vacancy levels, crime levels, code violations, and other criteria. While city officials described this process as performed on a parcel-by-parcel basis, this could be automated through spatial-analytic methods such as suitability analysis (Morckel 2017b).

A second primary challenge in solving the smart shrinkage problem is identifying appropriate new uses for vacant properties. While new uses in economically robust areas typically include housing, commercial establishments and offices, vacant lots in distressed communities may be transformed to support a range of less-traditional uses as well (Detroit Future City 2015; Morckel 2015; U.S. Department of Housing and Urban Development 2014). Active uses include parks, community farming, and "pop-up" stores and sites for cultural activities. Passive uses include stormwater retention, community gardens, "naturalized" sites using trees, grasses, and native plants, and sites for public art. City officials also specified a small set of alternative uses without explicit reference to available research. In section 5.5 we describe how we operationalized the process of determining which clusters might qualify for particular city-defined uses.

After identifying a range of potential re-uses, the planning organization must decide which specific vacant clusters to acquire, how, if at all, to combine certain clusters into larger units, as well as the specific re-uses to which they should be assigned. This step requires detailed knowledge of social costs and benefits of various uses, and local preferences for different uses. While research is available on cost-benefit analysis for vacant parcel re-use (Kim 2016; Heckert and Minnis 2012) and elicitation of local preferences for parcel re-use (Jacobs et al. 2012), our work with the city generated only limited, direct measures of social costs and benefits and did not address preferences of local residents or other stakeholders.

To complete the process of choosing candidate clusters and assigning appropriate uses, one could, in principle, list all of the candidate clusters in a spreadsheet and simply select those clusters that might meet certain requirements, such as percentage vacant lots or numbers of families to be relocated, and represent certain re-use types, such as "Clean + Green," "Neighborhood Park," or "Urban Agriculture," and stop when the total cost of acquisition and repurposing is just less than, or equals, the defined budget limit. (In management science, this solution strategy is referred to as a "greedy algorithm.") This procedure has a number of complications, though. If certain clusters qualify for multiple re-use strategies, how would we know which particular re-use strategy is most desirable, given the re-use strategies assigned to other clusters? The city might want, for political purposes, to distribute the chosen clusters about multiple neighborhoods, and not leave some neighborhoods unaddressed. The city might, on the other hand, want to take advantage of economies of scale in demolition by choosing clusters that are close together. Planners might have local knowledge that would enable them to decide whether, for neighborhood development purposes, some clusters should or should not be acquired together.

Accounting for all of these considerations, the planners realized that a simple solution approach to the smart shrinkage problem would "paint themselves in a corner," yielding multiple alternative strategies with no clear way to distinguish between them. There were additional considerations not present in the problem that the planners were wrestling with as well. On what basis had they chosen certain re-use options for particular parcels? How had they accounted for the needs of various stakeholders? How would they know that the re-uses they had identified would best meet the social and economic needs of the neighborhoods in which the clusters were located? Was it clear that the clusters that they had developed were, indeed, the most desirable aggregation of underlying parcels?

These concerns have significant real-world consequences. If planners could not develop a clear and consistent rationale for a plan encompassing acquisition, demolition, and re-use, would the plan gain the support of the mayor or of community groups comprised of citizens who would be affected by it? Could disagreements within the group of planners regarding a most-desirable strategy make it impossible to recommend any particular plan to the mayor? How could planners respond to appeals by residents and community groups to include this cluster, or spare that cluster from demolition? It was to develop an evidence-based procedure to address these concerns that we assisted the Department of Planning in solving their smart shrinkage decision problem.

5.4 A Values-Oriented Approach: What Really Matters?

In order to develop a more systematic approach to the smart shrinkage decision problem, we consider how to formulate the problem, with a focus on core concerns. Using observations from the city's demolition selection process in winter 2013, we build a decision-modeling structure based on objectives that we think were important to the city's decision making, though the planners may not have stated them explicitly. We perform this problem-structuring process using principles of Keeney's value-focused thinking (1992), the method we introduced in chapter 4. Value-focused thinking provides an opportunity to address the conceptual limitations practitioners often face: they may think they understand problems better than they really do; they are under pressure to produce tangible results but may not have time to clearly articulate objectives; and they lack a structured framework by which to identify quantifiable metrics closely associated with their values and to recognize necessary tradeoffs between desirable but conflicting objectives.

The qualitative decision model we examine in detail here is called a "means-ends network." It represents the relationship between certain objectives, or values fundamentally important to solving the smart shrinkage problem (fundamental objectives) but which may be difficult to achieve using commonly available policy and planning tools, and other objectives or values also associated with the smart shrinkage problem, which can be more easily achieved in practice and that serve as means to achieve certain fundamental ends (means objectives). A means-ends network can be quite valuable in articulating rationales for planning and policy interventions and identifying potential courses of action that may differ from those understood to decision makers at the start of a planning process. Keeney refers to this as the distinction between "alternative-focused thinking" and "value-focused thinking."

The causal connection between fundamental objectives and means objectives represents the answer to the question, "In what ways might this fundamental (means) objective be better, or more directly, achieved?" This chain of relationships ends with constructs that can be understood best as alternative courses of action (decision alternatives) or alternative policy or planning strategies, comprising multiple specific decisions. The causal relationship between means and fundamental objectives can be understood in the opposite direction as well: for a given decision alternative (alternative strategy) or means objective, another more general or more fundamental objective represents the answer to the question, "Achieving this objective will help us better achieve what more fundamental objective?" We present a means-ends network below.

Another decision-modeling construct associated with value-focused thinking is a fundamental values hierarchy. Here, we seek to decompose fundamental objectives on the basis of logical (not causal) relationships, going from most general to most specific, ending in expressions that are best understood as attributes, or ways to measure progress of certain decision alternatives or alternative strategies toward achieving other more fundamental goals. We will not pursue this modeling exercise here.

The City's method for choosing objectives for the selection of this round of demolition clusters was an iterative one that sought to incorporate many different stakeholder and agency priorities. While using a collaborative model, most officials agreed in their identification of the City's goal for managing vacancy and abandonment as a multipronged approach that prioritizes blight elimination and employs strategic demolition in areas with high vacancy and concentrated rehabilitation where possible. Interim uses (such as greening) were also highlighted as strong alternatives until the market unfolds or other uses are identified.

City officials described the planning process as being an application of collective knowledge (from various agencies) to the vacancy problem. After the initial geospatial analysis, which provided a scope of the problem and a database from which to work, the team attempted to meet the priorities of all of the represented agencies. These priorities ranged from urban greening to crime reduction, code enforcement, and support of the housing market. Some City officials stated that the process used a number of metrics by which to determine objectives and outcomes, while others felt that the selection process was made using a more case-by-case evaluation, rather than a metrics-based one.

Based on the interviews, the City's criteria for this selection process seemed to center on the themes of blight elimination, neighborhood stability, support of existing redevelopment efforts, large-scale demolition, targeted investment, and equal distribution of funds across the city. Objectives based on functions of criteria, or values statements that result as functions of the criteria, are, then, the maximization of areas devoted to blight elimination, supporting existing redevelopment and targeted investment, and the maximization of whole-block outcomes, neighborhood stability, and equitable distribution of funds.

These building blocks are insufficient, on their own, to constitute a decision model. First, we must distinguish between objectives that have causal relationships (lie on different levels of a means-ends network), and those that do not (that is, they lie on the same level of a means-ends network). For example, it seems reasonable that neighborhood stability can be better achieved via more specific means objectives such as targeted investments and whole outcomes, while blight elimination and whole-block outcomes can be understood as similarly situated means objectives.

Second, we must infer from conversations with city planners which of their concerns are of fundamental importance, even if they cannot be achieved quickly or directly on the basis of specific interventions, as distinct from others that have a more direct relationship with planning actions such as acquisition, demolition, and repurposing. For example, maximizing equity of interventions is an expression of a general, fundamental value similar in spirit to other fundamental values not stated explicitly by planners, of maximizing economic efficiency of interventions, and maximizing the strategic impact, or effectiveness, of various planning actions.

Third, we must identify objectives that are at odds. For example, it is difficult to design an intervention that maximizes equitable distribution of funds across neighborhoods and also maximizes targeted investments. Similarly, it is difficult to design an intervention that maximizes blight elimination and also maximizes support for existing redevelopment. During the interviews, several City officials mentioned the political challenge of conducting projects within a city on a limited budget. Some officials recognized that a more targeted approach could have a greater impact, but that this approach may not be politically tenable due to its higher cost and a directive to spread the funds equally. Multiobjective decision making inherently involves conflicting objectives; it is precisely because of this issue that the discussion surrounding tradeoffs is so important.

Last, we must identify elements of the smart shrinkage decision problem that are expressed by decision makers as constraints, and determine if they can also be expressed as elements of a means-ends network (or, if we are pursuing this direction, a fundamental values hierarchy). For example, officials we interviewed expressed two important constraints as cost and relocation. The City was working within a defined budget of $10 million and wanted to maximize outcomes with this funding. Relocations were characterized by most of the officials as financially and socially costly. An important goal of this project, as articulated by one official, was to improve the quality of life of Baltimore residents. As such, officials made clear that, if people did not wish to be relocated, the City would work with them to make it possible for them to stay. Given all of these associated financial and ethical challenges, relocation is not just a proxy for cost—it is also a constraint in its own right. We can express this in a means-ends network by asserting that minimizing intervention costs is a means objective, which could be met by alternative (competing) strategies of minimizing resident relocation costs and minimizing acquisition and redevelopment costs. Meeting certain physical criteria for specific end-uses was mentioned peripherally, but did not seem to be a significant constraint in the City process.

The result of this analysis is a means-ends network for the generalization of the city demolition cluster selection process that we understand as the smart shrinkage decision problem, shown in figure 5.3. (For addi-

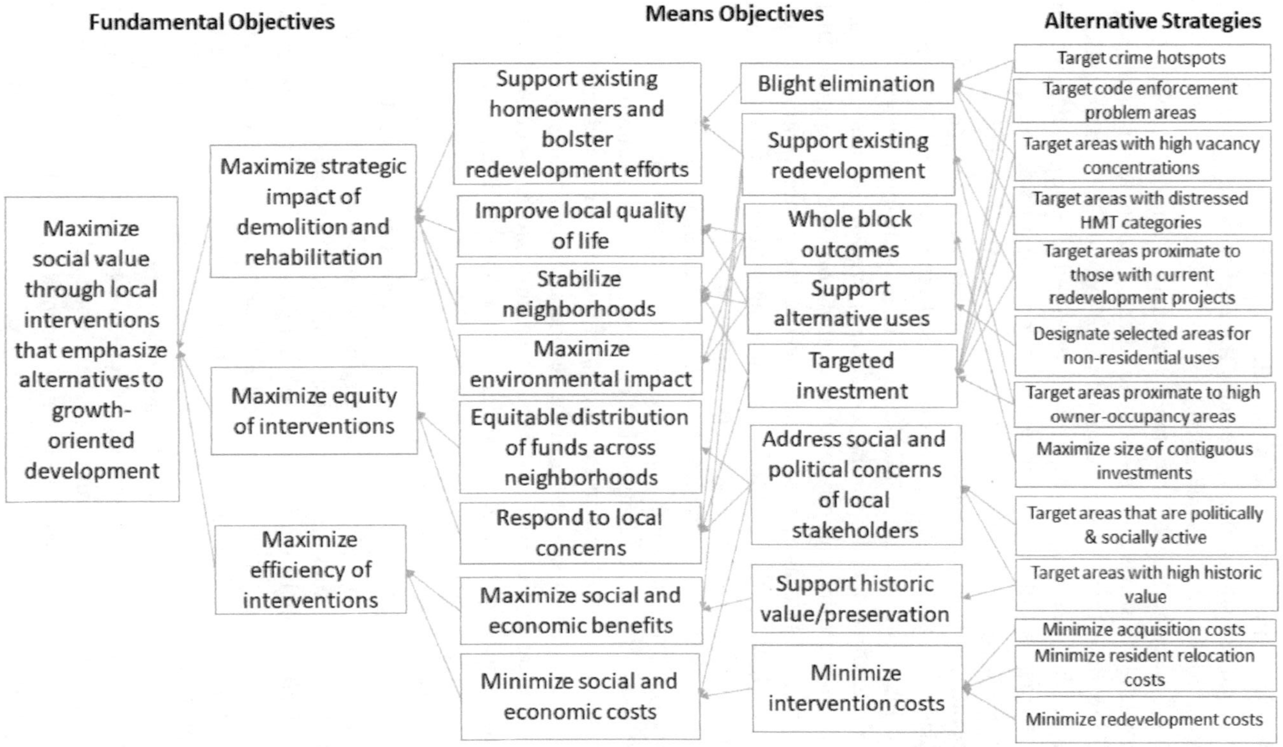

Fundamental Objectives

- Maximize social value through local interventions that emphasize alternatives to growth-oriented development
  - Maximize strategic impact of demolition and rehabilitation
  - Maximize equity of interventions
  - Maximize efficiency of interventions

Means Objectives

- Support existing homeowners and bolster redevelopment efforts
- Improve local quality of life
- Stabilize neighborhoods
- Maximize environmental impact
- Equitable distribution of funds across neighborhoods
- Respond to local concerns
- Maximize social and economic benefits
- Minimize social and economic costs

- Blight elimination
- Support existing redevelopment
- Whole block outcomes
- Support alternative uses
- Targeted investment
- Address social and political concerns of local stakeholders
- Support historic value/preservation
- Minimize intervention costs

Alternative Strategies

- Target crime hotspots
- Target code enforcement problem areas
- Target areas with high vacancy concentrations
- Target areas with distressed HMT categories
- Target areas proximate to those with current redevelopment projects
- Designate selected areas for non-residential uses
- Target areas proximate to high owner-occupancy areas
- Maximize size of contiguous investments
- Target areas that are politically & socially active
- Target areas with high historic value
- Minimize acquisition costs
- Minimize resident relocation costs
- Minimize redevelopment costs

Figure 5.3. Means-Ends Network for Smart Shrinkage Decision Problem.

tional details on the theory and application of value-focused thinking in another urban housing context, we refer the reader to Keisler et al. 2014 and chapter 5 of Johnson et al. 2016.)

Our understanding of the smart shrinkage decision problem that the City wishes to solve can be understood as being rooted in a primary fundamental objective "Maximize social value through local interventions that emphasize alternatives to growth-oriented development," which appears at the root of the means-ends network. To answer the question, "In what ways could this objective be better achieved," we identify three more specific fundamental objectives from conversations with city officials: "Maximize strategic impact of demolition and rehabilitation," "Maximize equity of interventions," and "Maximize efficiency of interventions." For each of these three specific fundamental objectives, we identify multiple objectives in the third column, each of which corresponds to goals that planners might state as the basis for specific local interventions, such as "Improve local quality of life," "Equitable distribution of funds across neighborhoods," and "Respond to local concerns."

At this point, we recognize that the themes that city officials had identified as motivating their planning efforts, such as blight elimination, neighborhood stability, and support of existing redevelopment efforts, correspond to means objectives in the third and fourth columns of objectives that serve more general objectives in the second and third columns. In turn, each of the means objectives in the fourth column can be associated with one or more specific strategies that can be implemented using common administrative and analytic methods. We note that, while both historic preservation and community requests were offered as justifications for selection or nonselection of given clusters in section 5.2, neither was mentioned by City officials as a specific strategy that might be considered alongside others in the last column, such as "target crime hotspots" (associated with the means objective "blight elimination") or "target areas proximate to those with high owner-occupancy" (associated with the means objective "targeted investment") This suggests a discrepancy between the perception and the actual operation of the City's "human-based decision model."

How might the means-ends network of figure 5.3 be used as a basis for solving the smart shrinkage decision problem in the five target neighborhoods of East Baltimore we have focused on? Our interviews and analysis of the human-based decision making in Baltimore offers both hope and concerns about the ability of a group of individuals to come together around clearly identified goals and objectives and maximize them effectively. The process described did result in decisions about which areas the city ought to prioritize, and there was some level of consensus reached. However, due to the very large number of parcels and clusters of parcels, the complex nature of the problem, and the conflicting missions of each agency within the city, the quality of the outcomes of this human-based process is less clear. In the following section we present a parcel-level vacant land planning model fueled by a desire to address shortcomings in the existing decision-making process for vacant property management in Baltimore. This model will provide specific guidance to planners regarding which clusters of parcels the city may consider targeting for acquisition and repurposing to balance multiple objectives, considering practical constraints such as budget availability. Our means-ends network, as shown in Figure 5.1, allows us to understand the scope and scale of decisions that, yielding a conceptually simple and tractable prescriptive analytical model, will serve to fulfill some means objectives in service of certain fundamental objectives, but not others.

5.5 Prescriptive Decision Modeling for Vacant Land Management

The smart shrinkage problem faced by the city of Baltimore is challenging. The 2,951 acres of vacant land are distributed quite widely across the city's 299 neighborhoods. However, the land defined by the Department of Planning as "clusters" eligible for acquisition and re-use is concentrated more narrowly in the central East, central West, Southwest, and Northwest portions of the city—those areas, as we showed in chapter 3, with the highest concentrations of African American residents and those that have faced the largest population declines. In order to "test-drive" our solution method in a small portion of the impacted neighborhoods of Baltimore, we agreed to perform intensive data analysis in five "focus" neighborhoods in the Baltimore East section first mentioned in section 5.3: Better Waverly, Coldstream Homestead Montibello, East Baltimore Midway, Oliver, and Broadway East. The Department of Planning selected 138 clusters in these five neighborhoods, through close examination of each parcel's characteristics, but not using an automated method such as suitability analysis as demonstrated by Morckel (2017b) for Flint, Michigan. These clusters may overlap, but are not identical to, vacant properties; some clusters are immediately adjacent to other clusters, while others are more isolated.

How might we decide which clusters to acquire, and the new uses to which those selected clusters would be put? We will refer to the decision model whose solution can provide an answer to this question as the *vacant land planning model*. As for our analysis in chapter 4, we refer to this study in the language of geodesign (Steinitz 2012), as comprising the fifth and sixth steps of the study process, referred to as "impact models" and "decision models," respectively.

The Department of Planning agreed on three new potential uses for any given cluster, based on the Growing Greener initiative. "Urban agriculture" refers to land leased to urban farmers to grow food commercially; "stormwater management" is defined as land used for reducing pollution in stormwater runoff and reducing risks of floods; and "future development" means holding, stabilization, and minor landscaping for a future time at which traditional residential or commercial development might be feasible. The planners also designated another potential classification for a cluster: "blight elimination." This term denotes a cluster whose present state is likely to generate undesirable social outcomes such as criminal offending, fires, or dumping, and for which some immediate re-use action, currently undefined, may be considered. Based on research and practice on alternative uses for vacant land available (U.S. Department of Housing and Urban Development 2014), our partners may not have examined the full set of alternative uses from which to choose their most-preferred uses. The planners worked with us to define characteristics of any cluster that would qualify it for each of the three re-use types or the blight elimination category; the results are shown in table 5.1.

We used suitability analysis (Morckel 2015) to apply these multiple criteria to all clusters in our sample and thus determine which clusters might qualify for which alternative uses. The city chose to combine certain clusters to ensure that there would be a nontrivial number of clusters qualifying for urban agriculture, resulting in a total of 118 clusters for the analysis that follows.

We found that ten of the 138 clusters qualified for urban agriculture, thirty-eight qualified for stormwater mitigation, thirty-five qualified for potential development, and seventy-six qualified for blight elimination. Moreover, while nine clusters did not qualify for any use or classification, and nine more qualified for only one use or classification, the remaining 100 clusters qualified for two (71), three (27), or even four (9) uses or classifications. Since the number of combinations of seventy-one clusters with two uses is 2,485, the number of combinations of twenty-seven clusters

Table 5.1. Vacant Land Planning Model: Criteria for Clusters

Urban Agriculture
- Cluster area size of half an acre or greater
- Slope of less than 5%
- Minimum tree cover of 25%

Stormwater
- Cluster area size of 1/8 acre or greater
- Slope of less than 5%
- Clusters within 20 feet of a storm drain

Potential Development Opportunity
- Cluster area size of a quarter-acre or greater
- Cluster's proximity within a maximum of 800 feet to any single known development ("Vacant to Value" cluster or "major initiative") OR to any single amenity (parks, existing or proposed transit stops, educational and hospital campus zones)

Blight Elimination
- Clusters are greater than 50% vacant
- Classified as a distressed HMT *or* be within 150 feet of a public safety hot spot (fire department priorities or police priorities list) *or* 150 feet of a high-visibility blighted area (major street, park or school) *or* have fewer than three owner occupied houses on the cluster.

Data: City of Baltimore, Department of Planning, with authors.

with three uses is 2,925, and the number of combinations of nine clusters with four uses is 126, the total number of combinations of clusters with at least two uses (along with nine clusters with only one possible use) is 5,545. It is cognitively challenging to evaluate this many combinations of clusters to optimize multiple objectives. This indicates that our smart shrinkage decision problem is likely to require computational skills not commonly found in planning practice.

The next step in solving the smart shrinkage problem in Baltimore is formulating an appropriate decision model. In prescriptive analytics, a key task is to identify one or more objectives to optimize (maximize or minimize), each objective being a function of actions assumed to be under the control of a decision maker, all functions subject to constraints, cr limitations, on the scope of actions that can be chosen. According to the principles of value-focused thinking, a decision modeler will engage in a collaborative, iterative process with stakeholder groups to determine what values are fundamental to the problem at hand, and then draw connections between core values and metrics that allow one to measure progress toward achieving those goals, and between core values and decisions that can help achieve those goals.

In the previous section we have performed a comprehensive application of these principles to identify important elements of the vacant land planning model. However, during our actual engagement with Baltimore planners, we understood that they were not focused on this sort of fundamentals-driven policy analysis involving multiple stakeholder groups. Instead, they appeared to be concerned primarily in demonstrating that they would make good, prompt use of limited municipal funds; hence, they seemed to prefer dollar-valued measures of decisions that corresponded to actual expenditures. Examples include the costs associated with land acquisition, demolition, and property repair and resident relocation (if necessary). The planners also expected that the city would transfer ownership or control of clusters used for urban agriculture and stormwater management to other entities, and therefore felt that any impacts that might accrue after the city relinquished control of these properties, temporarily or permanently, would not be relevant to the city's accounting. This sort of perspective, while common in practice, is contrary to basic principles of standing and bureaucratic and political "lenses" used in social cost-benefit analysis (Boardman et al. 2006). However, we felt that it was not appropriate for us, as applied researchers addressing a real-world, high-stakes problem, to introduce entirely new methodologies and perspectives to experienced practitioners.

As a result, our decision model reflected two concerns. The first is that the success of any particular acquisition strategy be measured in terms of the number of acres of clusters devoted to each of the four uses/classifications of urban agriculture, stormwater management, future development, and blight elimination. These constitute our model's objectives. The second concern is that the primary limitation on acquisition and repurposing be measured in terms of direct dollar outlays. This represents our primary constraint.

Even this narrowing of the conceptual scope of the decision problem yields a rich decision context. The 118 clusters under consideration for our problem show wide variation in area (0.05 acres to 2.3 acres) and cost (between zero and $3,677), though the relationship between the two is strong (correlation coefficient 0.8) and approximately linear. Most clusters are fairly small (0.28 acres on average) and moderately expensive ($327,652 on average). Within each of the four uses and categories, we found widely differing distributions of clusters according to area and total cost. For example, clusters eligible for urban agriculture varied widely across area and total cost, with a correlation between area and cost of 0.7. In contrast, clusters eligible for future development had generally small values for area and total cost, with a small number of outliers, and had a correlation coefficient of 0.84.

This is a hint that our objectives, maximizing the amount of land devoted to each of our four uses/classifications, are likely to conflict. That is, a cluster acquisition strategy that does well on one objective is not likely to do equally well on the other objectives. Thus, a naïve solution strategy initially identified by the Baltimore planners, which was to select clusters one by one to maximize an aggregate objective—total area—in order to use all funds available for acquisition and repurposing, would not reflect the varying impacts on the individual objectives of cluster area devoted to individual uses/categories. In addition, this "greedy algorithm" is likely to result in solutions that exclude certain clusters that might make better use of available funds.

The vacant land planning model we formulated in conjunction with the City of Baltimore Department of Planning consists of the following components: *Decision variables* represent the choice of clusters to acquire and the new use/category to which each cluster is assigned. *Objective functions* represent total acres of clusters devoted to each of four uses/categories, each a function of the decision variables.

The primary *constraint* on any cluster acquisition strategy is that the total amount spent on acquisition and repurposing, also a function of decision variables, not exceed a predetermined amount. We also require that a cluster can be assigned to only one use (urban agriculture, stormwater management, future development), and that if a cluster is assigned to blight elimination (not a formal land use, as explained above), it must also be assigned to a specific land use. Our model is assumed to generate recommendations for a single time period—say, a year—over which all relevant data are known fully and with certainty.

This representation of the vacant land planning problem is defined in operations research as a deterministic single-period multiobjective knapsack problem. Though there are specialized algorithms available to solve this problem (Collette and Siarry 2003; Kumar et al. 2008), we applied the well-known weighting method, popularized by Cohon (1978) and implemented using Frontline Solver's Premium Solver software (Frontline Systems 2011, 2015) with Microsoft Excel.

To solve the vacant land planning model, we set the budget for cluster acquisition and repurposing at $3.5 million, as recommended by the City of Baltimore. By applying the weighting method (Cohon 1978) as we did for the neighborhood-level smart shrinkage decision problem in chapter 4, we generated a set of nondominated solutions that, without additional information about decision-maker preferences, are assumed to be equally well preferred by the decision maker. (For additional theoretical and computational details of the general multi-objective math programming problem, we refer the reader to Cohon 1978 and appendices A and B in Johnson et al., 2016.)

Because the objective function values are measured in acres and the range of objective function values varies across objectives, it can be difficult to understand how the different nondominated solutions compare to each other. We adapt the concept of *value paths*, introduced in chapter 4, to display the relative performance of the different objectives, using a grouped (or 'multi-series') bar chart (figure 5.4). Here, the vertical axis represents the percentage of the maximum possible value achieved by each model instance (solution according to a given weight-set) for each of the four objectives. For example, a bar with a value of 1.0 (100%) means that, for that model instance, the corresponding objective achieved 100 percent of its maximum possible value across all nondominated solutions.

We first generated a set of "corner solutions," that is, solutions to the vacant planning decision model in which weights were set to one for one objective and zero for all others. As an example, the solution labeled "Maximize W" in figure 5.4 corresponds to the weight-set (0, 1, 0, 0), as stormwater mitigation is defined to be the second of four uses/classifications. By identifying corner solutions, we were able to verify the internal consistency of our decision model and to get a sense of the range of possible values for the various objectives.

Of greater interest to the City of Baltimore, however, were model results associated with weighting schemes more reflective of actual practice, in which two or more objective function weights were nonzero. We defined a range of objective function weights, starting with equal values for all objectives, corresponding to equal preferences for each objective ("Compromise 1" in figure 5.4). We then applied two weight-sets defined by the City of Baltimore. In the first, greater emphasis was put on stormwater mitigation and less on urban agriculture ("Compromise 3" in figure 5.4). In the second, greater emphasis was put on future development and less on urban agriculture ("Compromise 4" in figure 5.4). We see in figure

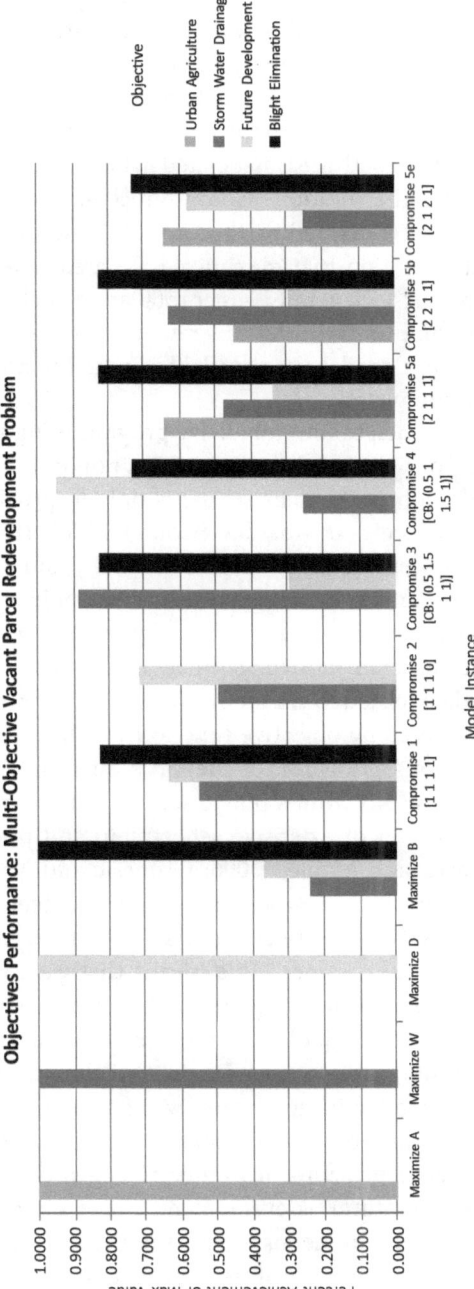

Figure 5.4. Vacant Land Planning Model Objective Space Results: Value Chart.

5.4 that no clusters were acquired for use as urban agriculture in the first four compromise solutions. Therefore, we defined additional compromise solutions based on weight-sets chosen to ensure that any solution would include at least one cluster assigned to urban agriculture ("Compromise 5a," "Compromise 5b," and "Compromise 5e" in figure 5.4).

We found that the total area associated with these nondominated solutions is greatest for the solution "Compromise 4," the second of two solutions using weight-sets defined by the City of Baltimore; the smallest area occurred for the solution that maximized the area devoted to urban agriculture ("Maximize A"). Generally, larger total areas of clusters acquired tended to occur for compromise solutions rather than "corner" solutions. In all cases, the decision model uses available funds for acquisition and repurposing almost completely.

A traditional approach to multiobjective programming states that the decision maker (City of Baltimore) decides which nondominated solution is most preferred; the job of the analyst (us) is only to provide as wide a range of alternative strategies as possible (Cohon 1978). If our planning partners decided that certain solutions produced by our model, using assumptions about weights to be assigned to various objectives that they have specified are inconsistent with their expectations, then they would need to rethink the decision-modeling process. They could modify the decision model and data related to clusters, or decide if their policy/planning preferences, as represented by objective function weights, do not actually reflect their organization's priorities, or the city's mission. Deciding how to understand and use results from a public sector–focused multiobjective decision model is a subject of extensive scholarship and practice insight (e.g., see Gabriel, Faria, and Moglen 2006; Grubesic and Murray 2009).

As we showed in chapter 4, solutions to multiobjective decision models can be visualized in the space associated with decision variables as well as objective function values. This means that each of the eleven nondominated solutions shown in figure 5.4 has a corresponding map illustrating uses to which particular clusters (if selected) are assigned. Figure 5.5 shows "decision space" values for the two compromise solutions associated with Baltimore Planning–defined weights.

Uses for various clusters receive different shadings: in Figure 5.5, the dark shaded-clusters represent stormwater management and the light-shaded clusters represent future development. Since blight elimination is defined to occur contemporaneously with the three uses, clusters that qualify for blight elimination as well as a particular use are shown in heavy black outline. The identity of selected clusters, and especially the

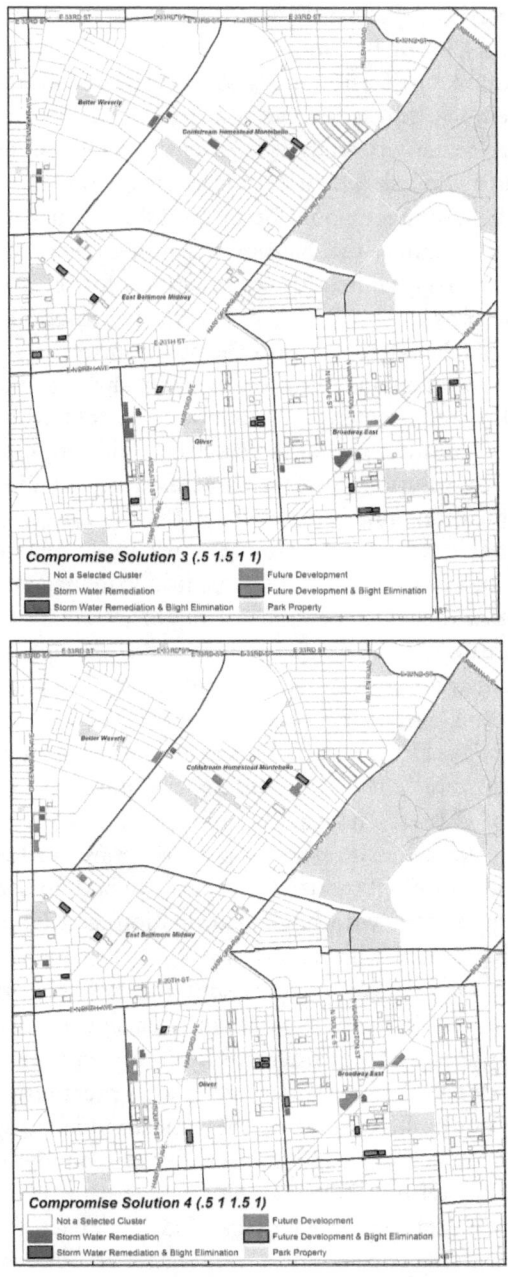

Figure 5.5. Vacant Land Planning Model Decision Space Results: Compromise Solutions Associated with Objective Function Weights Suggested by City of Baltimore.

assigned uses, varies significantly across these two compromise solutions suggested by the City of Baltimore.

It is common in decision analytics to explore variants of the basic decision problem to address specific concerns of the decision maker. This is referred to as "sensitivity analysis." For example, it is often the case that a decision maker will ask why a certain decision was not chosen by the model, or what the impact would be of modifying a particular modeling assumption. For example, the Baltimore planners were surprised that a particular cluster that qualified for consideration for re-use in urban agriculture did not appear in any of the "base case" solutions in figure 5.4. To "force" this particular re-use into the solution to the smart shrinkage problem, we imposed a constraint to the smart shrinkage decision model that enforced this requirement. We found, consistent with the theory of mathematical programming, that the resulting solution was less "efficient" than the base case solution: fewer total acres were recommended by our model for acquisition and repurposing. The Baltimore planners were also uncomfortable with the distinction we made between the "land use" categories of urban agriculture, stormwater management and future development, and the "classification" of blight elimination. What would happen if we treated blight elimination as a formal land use? We found that by dropping the constraint that a cluster receive the "blight elimination" designation only if it has been acquired for one of three defined land uses, we "relaxed" the original decision model. As a result, we were able to generate more "efficient" solutions as compared to the base case: the total area of clusters chosen was greater, and the amount of funds expended for cluster acquisition and repurposing greater for the modified model than for the original model. (However, we had no data on the costs that would be associated with blight elimination as a land use, so these results should be treated with caution.)

The "base case" model results, and the two sensitivity analyses discussed above, are indications that our decision-modeling approach can provide planners with considerable flexibility to represent and solve problems associated with smart shrinkage in ways previously unavailable to them. However, our multiobjective mathematical modeling approach is not a panacea. First, we acknowledge that our decision model is preliminary, limited, and quite stylized. For example, it makes no effort to associate specific acquisition decisions with a range of social impacts that city officials consider important: improvements in resident health outcomes, reductions in criminal offending, and improved environmental quality. We have not considered the cost of regulatory change in the optimization problem, for example changing uses of parcels in residentially zoned districts to nonresidential uses. We have considered only one portion of Baltimore for our analysis. We consider only a single period within which acquisition decisions would be made, whereas the City recognizes that acquisition decisions should address choices that must be made years into the future, when certain clusters not available for analysis now may become available at some later point when social and economic conditions may change. Although our model was developed in close cooperation with city of Baltimore planners, the lack of participation by community members or community-based organizations in this process limits our ability to claim that this represents an example of community-engaged decision modeling. Similar to our reflections on the outcomes of decision modeling in chapter 4, we cannot claim that the portion of Baltimore we studied for this decision model is actually better off for our efforts. That judgment would require an experimental design, in which actual outcomes are observed for some neighborhoods that had development proceed according to the recommendations of our model, and others proceed according to normal planning methods. Such an exercise, though quite valuable in principle, went well beyond the scope of our project.

Importantly, the unit of analysis on which our decision model is constructed is the cluster—a collection of parcels defined by the Department of Planning—rather than parcels themselves. While a decision model based on parcels would require many more decision variables than the one we have solved, such a model would provide significantly more flexibility in assembling clusters from parcels based on many assessments that may be beyond the cognitive capacity and professional expertise of planners (e.g., see the literature on consolidation of land parcels for farming, parks, and residential "smart growth" development of Gabriel et al. 2006; Nigar Neema, Maniruzzaman, and Ohgai 2013; Sefair et al. 2012; and Demetriou, Stillwell, and See 2010). Finally, our model is linear, whereas social concerns such as equity, political feasibility, or social impacts might be better modeled as nonlinear in order to capture scale economies and diseconomies.

To address these concerns, planners and policy-makers may have to think differently about model-based problem solving. First, they may have to address more complex measures of social impacts. Second, they may have to become more comfortable with fundamental decision-scientific notions of feasibility, optimality, and tradeoff that give decision models their power in practice. To do this, it will be necessary to routinely use

174 | Supporting Shrinkage

models like the one we have presented. Such use can be done through decision support systems that integrate data management, data display through mapping, model creation and solution, and sensitivity analysis (e.g., see Timmermans 1998; Malczewski 1999). In the next chapter we will discuss public participatory GIS (first introduced in chapter 2) that engage stakeholders in a more direct way, and that can be adapted to the smart shrinkage context.

5.6 Man versus Machine

What can we learn from the "human" approach to vacant parcel selection and re-use in sections 5.3 and 5.4 with the "machine" approach of section 5.5? To answer this task, we will compare similarities and differences in stakeholders; methods; identification of variables, objectives, constraints, and metrics; community input; discussion of goals; and the weighting applied to achieve most-preferred outcomes. This will help us learn how similar the City's objectives were to the model's objectives and how closely our decision model was able to capture the values embedded in the City's process.

Process Comparison

The key stakeholders were relatively consistent across the two problem-solving approaches. All officials interviewed identified the Housing Department as being the lead in the selection of demolition clusters. The researchers from UMass Boston and Tufts were the lead in the technical aspects of the decision model process, however, while the Office of Sustainability headed up the Baltimore side.

The steps involved in each process had a number of differences, due largely to the fact that the City's demolition selection methodology, while more metrics-based than in past iterations, was ultimately a human-led, organic process with a high degree of subjectivity at play. The model, on the other hand, while subject to the biases and assumptions of the researchers and the Baltimore team, was more explicitly and inherently metrics-based in its approach.

During the interviews, City officials identified the strengths and weaknesses of the current City process, particularly as compared to approaches used in the past (table 5.2). Identified strengths included a

Table 5.2. Strengths and Weaknesses Identified in City Demolition Cluster Selection Process

Strengths	Weaknesses
Interagency approach	Not talking about post-demolition cluster uses enough
More funding for strategic/active demolition	Conversation about goals and balancing objectives not explicit enough
More strategic approach than before	Very little community input*
Using HMT and other information to identify areas for demo/rehab/reuse	Case-by-case decision making*
Targeting areas with existing redevelopment	
Metrics to evaluate success	
Prioritization system	
Less piecemeal/emergency-focused	

*Not expressly stated as weaknesses

Source: Interviews with City of Baltimore officials.

more strategic, less piecemeal approach than prior attempts to manage vacancy in the city; a new interagency approach; and the use of metrics for evaluating success. Weaknesses observed included the lack of discussion about post-demolition cluster uses and the lack of explicit conversations about goals and objectives.

The City's case-by-case approach was not explicitly presented by them as a weakness of their solution strategy. Given the City's interest in more thoroughly incorporating decision analytics into their current process, we have extrapolated from the interview themes the assumption that the City wishes to pursue innovations to the decision-making process that include more clearly defined objectives and metrics. Also, City officials expressed mixed opinions regarding the amount and quality of community input in the process. Officials acknowledged that the community had very little input in the cluster selection process. While no officials explicitly identified the lack of community input as a weakness, engagement with the community is essential if a more transparent and equitable approach is desired.

The selection of inputs for each process also varied considerably. The primary difference in the decision variables used by the City versus the model relates to the focus. While the model used decision variables built around specific end-uses (e.g. urban agriculture, future development, storm water), the City variables were oriented more toward overarching strategic goals for addressing vacancy (e.g., stabilizing neighborhoods and targeted demolition to support existing redevelopment). End-uses, especially alternative re-use options, were not as explicit in the City process as in the model.

This lack of backend use discussion, observed by one City official as a weakness in the process, seems inconsistent with the Growing Green Initiative and other City programs intended specifically for alternative re-use options. It also suggests that the City's process is focused primarily on demolition and blight removal without explicit consideration in the selection of clusters of what comes next. This means that process outcomes (e.g., cost of demolition) are prioritized over the optimization of social outcomes. One official found this approach problematic, noting that "blight elimination is only a mid-point." According to this official, talking about backend uses is critical, especially considering the City's goal of getting more families to live in Baltimore. As she put it, "[We] need to balance the directive to redevelop with the need to clear blight." Since the date of our study, Baltimore has received $700 million for increased vacant land management (Thomas 2016), and anchor institutions in the city have partnered with community-based organizations to address vacancy and blight (Kaufman 2016). However, we have no evidence the city or its partners have used decision models or decision support systems to rigorously formulate, solve, and evaluate models for vacant land management.

The objective functions were quite different between the City's case-by-case approach and our model-based approach. The City's objectives (e.g., maximize whole-block outcomes, maximize area devoted to targeted investment) were less straightforward than those of the model (e.g., maximize area devoted to urban agriculture). The constraints for each were largely linked to cost, although the size of the budget was dramatically different in the model ($3.5 million for the 138 clusters in five neighborhoods) versus the City's demolition cluster selection ($10 million citywide). Additionally, adherence to physical criteria, such as slope and size of lot, were more clearly outlined as constraints in the model, due to the specifically defined end-use inputs.

Despite several City officials' assertions that metrics were a part of the selection process, no one with whom we spoke was able to identify defined and measurable criterion by which cluster eligibility was assessed. In our solution to the smart shrinkage decision problem, for example, clusters eligible for urban agriculture had to meet certain physical metrics, defined as clusters a half-acre or greater with slope less than 5 percent and tree cover less than 25 percent. According to interviewees, the input variable in the City process of "area devoted to targeted investment" had several metrics associated with it, including areas with high owner-occupancy, high concentration of vacancy, existing redevelopment efforts, and association with the Housing Market Typology. However, no specific cutoffs or thresholds were identified with regard to any of these metrics. We probed on the level of specification on some, but not all, of these metrics; thus, it is possible that more detailed metrics existed, but were not revealed in the interview process.

Requests from the community or advocacy on behalf of a given neighborhood by stakeholders such as community organizers and city councilpersons, were mentioned by most City officials as being strong determinants in the selection of particular clusters. It was clear from the frequency with which community advocacy was brought up in the interviews that supporting these requests is a strong value underlying the City's decision making, suggesting that these requests or forms of championing are serving as an implicit metric in the City's process.

It was not clear to us from interviews that the City used weights or priorities in any explicit way to prioritize some objectives ahead of others. An official we talked to reflected that our decision-modeling process had encouraged the City team to have a more explicit conversation regarding goals and objectives. She observed that, without the model, these conversations happened within the group, but in a much more organic and less purposeful way. She noted that this conversation about how to prioritize objectives is a difficult but important one for the City to be having and that doing this in a deliberate way is most desirable. In contrast, our decision model used the weighting method of multiobjective mathematical programming to generate a range of alternative strategies for acquisition and redevelopment. The "weight-sets" used in this process are used to quantify decision-maker preferences about the problem to be solved.

Of course, for the model-building process, encompassing input variables, objectives, constraints, metrics, and weights for goals and objectives, to reflect stakeholder values, there must be extensive conversations among different groups, about values and priorities. In the spirit of community-based operations research, these conversations must include community-based organizations and advocates; in the spirit of community operational research, these conversations must include local residents as well. If such comprehensive conversations about values and objectives occur, then the set of solutions created by the model are more likely to capture what is most important to stakeholders. In neither case, for the city-led cluster selection process, or the researcher-led modeling process, can such wide-ranging conversations be said to have occurred.

Comparison Summary

The city-defined selection process (section 5.3) and the model-defined selection process (section 5.5) both focus on five East Baltimore pilot neighborhoods. We have previously described significant distinctions between the two solution processes with respect to decision variables, objectives, constraints and goals, and objectives preferences. In addition, the city-defined solution process, as we understood it, did not include or imply specific criteria by which some demolition clusters would qualify for acquisition and repurposing, while the model-defined process used an explicit site-suitability process to determine which clusters met criteria for any of three defined land uses. Moreover, we found that four clusters in the target neighborhoods did not qualify for consideration by our decision model because they did not meet the eligibility criteria for any of the three alternative uses. Therefore, they were not included in any optimization weighting or compromise solutions produced by the decision model. These clusters were, however, considered by the city planners we interviewed (and two of these were actually chosen by the planners). This indicates that the city planners may not have had explicit land-use eligibility criteria in mind when deciding which clusters to acquire for demolition, contrary to our findings when we engaged in a deliberate planning exercise as described in section 5.5.

In the case, described in section 5.3, of the two collections of parcels that the city reported selecting in our interviews but which our model did not select, our informants cited community advocates and organizations as being strong motivations for selection. Thus, a selection metric that was important to the city was not expressed to us as a relevant metric when designing our decision model. This is an indication that the city's decision process may not have reflected a rigorous focus on value-based model building—a point we highlighted in our value-focused decision modeling in section 5.4. We also acknowledge that neither the city's decision process nor our own incorporated direct participation by community members or the organizations that represent them. We compare the city's cluster selection process and our decision analytics–based cluster selection process in table 5.3.

Table 5.3. Cross-Case Comparison of Process and Outcomes

Comparison Category	City†	Model††
Stakeholders	Housing (lead) Planning Office of Sustainability	Housing Planning Office of Sustainability (lead) Researchers
Process	620 possible clusters in choice-set GIS analysis for cluster identification Case-by-case analysis for cluster selection	138 possible clusters in choice-set GIS analysis for cluster identification Criteria metrics for cluster eligibility Weighting of mathematical model for cluster selection
Objectives	Maximize whole block outcomes* Maximize support of existing redevelopment* Maximize blight elimination*	Maximize urban agriculture Maximize storm water Maximize potential redevelopment Maximize blight elimination
Constraints	Cost (max budget of $10 million for 620 clusters)	Cost (max budget of $3.5 million for 138 clusters) Considerations of feasible designation of clusters to specific end-uses
Metrics	Not clearly defined	Defined eligibility metrics (see table 10.1)
Weighting of goals and objectives	Not explicit	Explicit
Clusters not eligible for selection**	None	Four

†Set of ten clusters discussed in Section 5.3
††Set of 118 clusters used in model runs reported in Section 5.5.
*Objectives not clearly defined
**By the city, or by optimization model, within any use category (Urban Agriculture, Stormwater Management, Future Development), according to criteria discussed in Section 5.5

There was little overlap in the set of clusters selected by the city versus our decision model. As discussed in section 5.3, the reasons given by the City for not selecting certain clusters were related mostly to the clusters being second-tier priorities, being too costly (requiring too much relocation), or having historic or rehabilitation value. This is an indication that there are other objectives and metrics at play in the City process not included in our decision model.

This point is made clear by the fact that the objectives used in the vacant land planning model reflect the values that the City articulated to us for the making of the model, but do not match the values that were articulated by City officials during the qualitative interviews. This discrepancy in both the stated objectives and the resulting solutions points to a conflict between the two processes. What is the source of this conflict? Did we misunderstand the values of the City or not probe carefully enough about those values when designing the model? Did we not engage a wide enough spectrum of stakeholders in the process? Were the criteria misapplied in selecting eligible clusters? Or is there a divergence between the actual criteria applied and the mental version of the objectives used by the City?

5.7 Conclusion

The study of the city-led selection process in section 5.3 and our decision-modeling process in section 5.5 did not yield identical choice sets (the collection of candidate clusters). This makes it impossible to perform an ideal "apples-to-apples" comparison that might demonstrate that our optimization model-based results here are necessarily better than ad-hoc decisions made by city officials. Doing so would require a formal experiment with common outcome measures and trained, objective evaluators—surely a challenging and promising exercise. Such an experiment could yield even stronger findings regarding distinctions between the way that practitioners conceive of and solve a decision problem associated with priorities that come from political decision makers (the Vacants to Value initiative, for example), and the way that a formal modeling process would generate and solve a decision problem intended to meet the same goals.

Our comparison of the two solution approaches in section 5.6 did uncover some important results: the values that motivate the judgments and decisions of decision makers are complex, subtle, and sometimes hidden.

The importance of this for analytics approaches to smart shrinkage is that decision modeling, which relies on explicit understandings of data, values, decision variables, objectives, constraints, and solution methods, requires a commitment to uncovering hidden criteria and making visible a "mental" or idealized model familiar to practitioners but which may yield results inconsistent or incompatible with a more structured, transparent, and evidence-based modeling process that practitioners may say they prefer. In order to implement a decision-modeling process that accurately represents the values of the decision makers, the entire decision process (and not just the model) needs to make clear the assumptions and values of the decision makers. In addition, a modeling process that explicitly reflects concerns for concerns of community members and the organizations that represent them would require a different notion of "decision makers" and a willingness to work with, and not just on behalf of, the community. In turn, this would require that the city consider modifying their strategic goals to include meaningful community participation in an evidence-based, decision model–driven planning process.

Such a decision process, which would address issues of community engagement, mixed-methods for analysis, a critical approach to problem identification, and construction and solution processes that may be iterative and as interested in process and learning as specific recommendations, has been a part of the operations research literature for over twenty years (Rosenhead and Mingers 2001; Midgley and Ochoa-Arias 2004; Eden and Ackerman 2004; Johnson 2012; Johnson and Midgley 2018). We believe that the application of these methods, in an amalgam of processes described in chapter 4 as "community-engaged operations research" (Johnson 2018a), has the potential to leverage the knowledge and commitment of planning practitioners as well other important stakeholders, including residents, advocates, and activists, in designing responses to vacant properties and blight that combine theoretical rigor, clarity, and consistency of modeling assumptions to produce results that reflect efficiency, effectiveness, and equity. We also believe that use of research designs that allow comparison of planning outcomes for neighborhoods in which decision modeling has been applied to those for otherwise similar neighborhoods in which decision modeling has not been applied could generate persuasive evidence as to the efficacy of decision modeling for neighborhood redevelopment.

In the next chapter we use these principles for critical, community-focused, and evidence-based solution approaches to the smart shrinkage decision problem—both for the neighborhood-level planning model of chapter 4 and the vacant land planning model of this chapter—to identify requirements for a computer-based decision aid that combines spatial data, decision modeling, and stakeholder engagement in a way that meets the special needs of shrinking cities and distressed communities.

Notes

1. This chapter is based on the work of Davenport Whiteman (2013) and Johnson, Hollander, and Davenport Whiteman (2015).
2. We received an exemption from the Tufts Institutional Review Board and the anonymity of the interviewees has been preserved.
3. Baltimore has a street grid structure of primary streets with much narrower streets running between. These smaller streets are referred to as "inner" or "interior" blocks.

CHAPTER 6

Technology, Data, and Community-Building Where People Matter

In chapters 4 and 5 we presented applications of data analytics and decision modeling for smart shrinkage to the cities of Fall River and Baltimore. These studies came about because we wanted to build expertise in helping public organizations make better decisions about land acquisition and land uses in shrinking cities and distressed communities. Our results show that, with appropriate methods and technical support, cities can develop diverse and appropriate strategies for community development that can represent an improvement over the status quo. We noted the positive role that community engagement and values-based modeling can play in contested and complicated enterprises such as smart shrinkage.

However, our case studies did not achieve all of the goals we had set for them. They did not represent deep engagement with community members, and they did not result in professional-quality, public-facing planning support applications that might address the potential for smart decline responses inspired by the three case study cities. We have argued in chapter 2 that there is an unmet opportunity for new systems of people, data, technology, and models to take advantage of the promise of big data and smart cities. We will address this opportunity here.

In this chapter we identify the functional, social, and planning requirements of a planning support system specially designed to meet the needs of multiple stakeholders, especially community members, in areas that have traditionally not had the resources to lead in the design of strategies for neighborhood and regional development. These requirements reflect current knowledge of community data analytics, community-engaged operations research, and public participation geographic information systems. This knowledge, in the context of geodesign, big data, and smart cities applications has the potential to transform citizen engagement with urban planning and community development. We will conclude by summarizing the benefits and costs of big data and smart cities innovations that might address needs of shrinking cities and distressed communities, and evaluate the potential of one of these, public participatory geographic information systems, to enable users to make best use of multiple problem-solving tools and methods.

6.1 Community Engagement and Problem Solving in a Spatial Context

An information system and process that enables community residents to actively participate in the process of gathering and analyzing spatial and nonspatial data in order to set priorities and solve problems related to local development would seem to be a promising application for shrinking cities and distressed communities. For over twenty years, the terms "public participatory geographic information system" (PPGIS), "participatory GIS" (PGIS), and "volunteered geographic information" (VGI) have been used by researchers to denote different versions of this system and process (McCall 2017). In recent years, "geodesign" and "community geography" have served to provide a high-level description of a comprehensive planning methodology for which PPGIS, PGIS, and VGI represent special cases (Steinitz 2012). They also provide a way to ensure that resource-limited communities like the ones that are the focus of this book can take best advantage of expertise and technology represented by PPGIS, PGIS, and VGI to build local technical capacity and ensure that community voices and values are central to interventions based on spatial analytics and technology and decision science (Robinson, Block, and Rees 2017). We focus on PPGIS, PGIS, and VGI because our primary interest is on community-level interventions rooted in decision analytics in which local stakeholders play a primary role in collecting, organizing, and analyzing data for formulation and solution of qualitative and quantitative decision models. Geodesign, in contrast, is most often practiced in a middle geographic range from "larger geographic areas to watersheds and regions"

(Steinitz 2012, 21), while community geography supports local decision making but is not centrally focused on decision modeling.

The distinctions between the PPGIS, PGIS, and VGI can be understood in terms of process emphasis, institutional sponsors, data collection, and sociogeographic focus, among others. Generally, PPGIS represents systems sponsored by government planning agencies, for use by marginalized and disadvantaged communities in urban and regional contexts within developed countries. PPGIS use data derived from individual residents that are considered the property of the sponsors of the mapping project, with primarily digital (quantitative) mapping technologies, with the goal of enhancing public involvement to inform land use planning. In contrast, PGIS is more commonly understood to have the goal of community empowerment through collective data gathering that is primarily sponsored by nongovernmental organizations. PGIS users assert ownership of their data, using qualitative (nondigital) as well as quantitative mapping technologies. While PGIS has its roots in rural communities and in developing countries, it is currently more often applied in urban contexts. VGI focuses on aggregating spatial data gathered from many residents, sometimes without their knowledge, other times intentionally in the spirit of citizen science, using Web 2.0 technologies. These collected and processed data are intended to be shared widely (Brown and Kyttä 2014; Ghose 2017; Verplanke et al. 2016; Goldberg, D'Iorio, and McClintock 2016).

Of these systems, we believe that public participatory GIS is the most appropriate system for use by residents of underserved or marginalized communities, including those in shrinking cities or regions of the United States, in conjunction with nonprofit organizations collaborating with city planning agencies, to assert ownership over the process of setting development priorities. A contemporary description of PPGIS by Ghose (2017) emphasizes the political-economy context, neoliberalism, within which urban development often occurs, and the need for PPGIS to support different kinds of knowledge acquisition and use. Ghose identifies the following necessary characteristics for successful PPGIS development:

> (i) equitable access to both spatial data and GIS technologies among socially marginalized citizens; (ii) incorporation of grounded, indigenous, experimental and local knowledge with public datasets for marginalized citizens to contest or reshape policies; (iii) discouragement of top-down, rational planning

approaches in policymaking; (iv) inclusion of both qualitative and quantitative data in GIS; (v) alternate forms of mapping, representation to capture complex social processes and cultures; and (vi) alternate forms of geospatial technology designed to suit the needs of indigenous and socially marginalized groups. (504)

However, successful design and implementation of PPGIS faces a number of practical challenges. Developing a productive PPGIS process, system, and outputs requires active participation by residents, access to appropriate technologies, and good governance. In their study of marine spatial planning, Goldberg and McClintock (2015) emphasize the need for stakeholder participation throughout all steps of the planning process. Radil and Jiao (2016) argue that community-based planning for urban development requires a planning process that reflects autonomy and control, rather than "simple consultation or informing," to use the language of Arnstein's (1969) ladder of participation.

Moreover, these studies demonstrate that engaging a community may entail not just working with a relatively small number of individuals whose opinions and judgments may be used to generate consensus on planning priorities, but instead working with large groups of people—crowds—who need not have specialized knowledge or training. If this community engagement reflects a diversity of opinion, independence and decentralization, and aggregation, then PPGIS processes can support the sorts of land use decisions that are a central focus of this book (Brown 2015). Pánek (2016) describes a number of technology platforms that support democratization of spatial decision making in ways that go well beyond use of ubiquitous corporate-owned technologies such as Google Maps. There is a need for PPGIS project managers to have and apply mediation and conflict resolution skills. Where PPGIS are used in conflict situations and display contested data, managers should understand that showing differences of opinion or value can lead to political polarization (Sieber 2006).

Finally, the notion of participation itself can be contested. Conrad and colleagues (2011) describe large and striking discrepancies between conceptions of public participation in a planning process in Malta by public respondents as compared with planners and policy-makers. The authors found that public respondents put greater weight on "good communication skills" and "provision of appropriate and adequate information" than planners and policy-makers, while the latter group emphasized "technical competence" and "scientifically rigorous collection and analysis of data" more than the former group. Balancing the priorities of diverse groups is integral to the long-term success of participatory action. This activity reflects the need for skilled facilitation and stronger monitoring and evaluation methods that adequately define individual and group preferences.

In addition, Ghose (2011) calls attention to the current neoliberal environment, describing a system that has defunded social services while reducing support for nonprofit organizations that have traditionally filled the gap between public need and available government resources, requiring community-based organizations to cooperate with government on its own terms. Thus, while PPGIS can lead to more effective decision making by some disadvantaged communities, an organizational capacity gap, along with a technology gap and power imbalance limit the effectiveness of CBO-led PPGIS initiatives (Ghose 2011; Ellwood and Ghose 2001). As a result of these limitations, city entities such as planning agencies or offices of community development can dominate the agenda and control resources needed for community-based organizations to work on behalf of their constituents.

Geodesign and community geography can enable users of PPGIS to obtain community data that are technologically advanced and support community change. An example of a geodesign tool helping to promote community change is HarassMap (https://harassmap.org/en/). Developed in 2010 with the support from the University of Cairo, HarassMap is used to engage Egyptian society in mapping and monitoring sexual harassment. This initiative is intended to enable citizens to take action when sexual harassment happens in their presence (HarassMap 2019). The HarassMap uses Web and mobile technologies to crowdsource incidents of sexual harassment from all over the country and is used in public reports and targeted educational programs across Egypt (HarassMap 2014).

Systemic barriers to access appropriate data and technology is a recurring theme in studies of PPGIS and community-based data analytics generally. Elwood and Ghose (2004) discussed a general lack of financial resources, technical capacity, and organizational flexibility on the part of community-based organizations in Milwaukee that participate in PPGIS activities, especially those organizations whose goals and missions do not closely match those of local government revitalization programs. Johnson's (2015) study of smaller, mission-driven, community-focused nonprofit organizations in Boston revealed a disjunction between the understanding of "big data" by smaller nonprofits versus larger public and for-profit organizations, and a gap between available resources and actual usage of data analytics and IT applications. O'Brien (2018) documents significant progress in improving access to detailed data by CBOs in lower-income and marginalized communities through data intermediaries such as the Boston Data Portal, but acknowledges that ordinary citizens and the community-based organizations that serve them have demonstrated limited interest in data services provided through a centralized process that emphasizes quantitative data and data literacy. Robinson and associates (2017) emphasize opportunities to work closely with community residents, often nonexperts, to reduce barriers to spatial data for increased knowledge of local conditions and phenomena and community co-ownership of knowledge derived from spatial data. The increased interest in and use of tech-driven solutions requires greater training in the use of PPGIS and other spatial technologies and their potential community and social impacts.

The process of bringing a PPGIS to life in a community can be quite challenging. PPGIS system design starts with a participatory "deliberative-analytic" process to generate ideas from the public that include statement of a goal, brainstorming ideas, negotiating items, voting on ideas, and evaluating outcomes (Jankowski 2011). These steps are formalized in the Enhanced Adaptation Structuration Theory (EAST2). EAST2 draws connections between values, concerns, expectations, and information needs of stakeholders, the nature of the convening organization, the rules that govern participation by stakeholder groups, group size, complexity level of the technology, the process setting for application use (synchronous versus asynchronous), and alternative systems architectures (Jankowski and Nyerges 2001). Choosing between alternative PPGIS applications requires addressing three key issues (Aggett and McColl 2006): decision support system effectiveness in supporting participatory decision making, supporting communities to make their own decision support technology solutions, and using an appropriate user needs assessment to select a DSS.

The role of formal decision models to identify most-preferred alternative courses of action, or to generate a range of strategies based on multiple objectives and decision variables that represent individual policy "levers," is ambiguous in PPGIS. Recent surveys of PPGIS (e.g., Brown and Kyttä 2014) emphasize contemporary issues such as participatory mapping, identification of spatial attributes, resident participation, and data quality rather than specific ways to generate recommendations for land uses using structured decision making, and acknowledge that there is little evidence that PPGIS has influenced specific land use decisions (see specifically Brown 2012). Moreover, many research priorities identified by Brown and Kyttä do not include topics related to decision modeling. Earlier reviews of PPGIS (Sieber 2006) discuss decision-modeling applications of PPGIS but acknowledge that integration of PPGIS into decision-making processes is difficult. A collection of studies of community participation and GIS from the late 1990s (Craig, Harris, and Weiner 2002) included a wide range of PPGIS case studies across city planning, environmental management, and development across the global South, but very little focus on specific ways to support decision making using a structured, model-based approach. An even earlier review of decision support systems in urban planning (Timmermans 1997) is robust on decision-modeling approaches, but has little to say about the nature of public participation in design of solution approaches or user applications.

To be sure, researchers such as Jankowski and Nyerges (2001) describe three different sophisticated applications of decision modeling in PPGIS, but only one of these represents an empirical study of an actual decision context for which decision modeling was used to identify a most-preferred planning strategy. PPGIS such as SeaSketch (Goldberg and McClintock 2015; Goldberg et al. 2016), a marine planning software, use a decision science technology called Marxan to design optimal placement of protection management zones (Marine Planning Partnership Initiative 2015). Despite a larger role for decision modeling in geodesign (Steinitz 2012), there is a disconnect between the rigorous modeling conducted in the field of operations research and decision support systems and the real application of PPGIS.

Evidence indicates that PPGIS could have a positive impact on communities seeking evidence-based local interventions based on spatial data and decision science. Recent work on decision support for interventions in distressed urban communities to address housing foreclosures has established a wide range of potentially useful decision-modeling strategies that could be integrated into a PPGIS, ranging from problem structuring to quantifying impact measures to designing response strategies (Johnson et al. 2016). However, that type of decision modeling response is highly dependent on local organization capacity and the nature of the problem to be addressed (Geertman et al. 2014). Principles of community-engaged operations research (Johnson 2018a; Midgley, Johnson, and Chichirau 2018; Johnson, Midgley, and Chichirau 2018) emphasize that learning about the problem may be as important as actually solving it. Another approach to empirical problem solving that is distinct from formal decision modeling is game design and game play. Here, participants solve specific instances of real-world problems using the norms and language of games, that is, quests to achieve a goal that may be more intuitive than decision modeling (Gordon and Walter 2016, Gordon, Schirra, and Hollander 2011). This represents an alternative approach to embedding decision support into PPGIS.

A final challenge associated with use of PPGIS in shrinking cities and distressed communities is evaluating the utility and impact of a chosen system. Aggett and McColl (2006) identify four elements of decision support system utility: transparency (the ability of users to understand and access data and decision-making rationales), flexibility (the ability to use separate components of a DSS separately or together), user-friendliness, and ability to communicate stakeholder interests within a participatory planning process. Aggett and McColl apply these principles to create a DSS evaluation framework, adapted from Jankowski and Nyerges (2001), in which systems can be assessed on three ascending levels of decision support capabilities: basic information handling support; decision analysis support, and group reasoning support.

Given these challenges and barriers to developing a PPGIS that is technically robust, well aligned with community needs, flexible and supportive of community engagement, capacity building, and decision making, and well positioned to influence real-world decision making in tangible ways, prompts the question of whether developing such a system is worthwhile. We believe the answer is a firm *yes*. We come to this conclusion based on documented beneficial impacts of PPGIS (notwithstanding more skeptical assessments of Brown 2012); a survey of the pros and cons of information technology applications inspired by the big data and smart cities movements in chapter 2; a description of unmet opportunities for community-participatory spatial decision support for community development in our three case study cities of Fall River, Flint, and Baltimore in chapter 3, and documentation of valuable insights from decision-modeling applications for shrinking cities and distressed communities in chapters 4 and 5.

On balance, we believe that the potential social benefits of a PPGIS specifically designed to meet the needs of shrinking cities and distressed communities could outweigh the financial and technological costs of developing such a system. In the remainder of this chapter we provide evidence for this assertion. We describe what such a PPGIS could look like, how it might be designed, and how we might know that it will make a difference to residents of cities like our three case study cities.

6.2 What Should a Planning Support Application for Shrinking Cities and Distressed Communities Do?

A public participatory planning support application for shrinking cities and distressed communities should be designed specifically to meet the needs of residents without any special GIS or analytics training, and the mission-driven and technology resource–constrained grassroots organizations that usually represent and serve them (Ghose 2017; Johnson 2015). While use of such an application can benefit from the guidance of a facilitator or "concierge" who can provide expert assistance in accessing and using datasets (Goldberg and McClintock 2015; Burnett 2020a), the goal of such an application should be to support independent individual and group data exploration and analysis for design of neighborhood-level planning interventions.

A PPGIS with robust decision-modeling capability will enable users to perform data exploration, problem structuring, decision model formulation and solution, sensitivity analysis, and guidance for implementation of recommended local development strategies. We define these terms below.

Data exploration means examination of spatial data that has been preloaded into the application, along with data acquired by users in real time, using standard GIS functions of pan and zoom, addition and modification of data layers, and creation of thematic (choropleth) maps based on area-level data. This means creating conventional descriptive maps that describe physical features and sociodemographic characteristics of communities; see Gorr and Kurland (2013) for examples of tutorials related to these tasks. More sophisticated data analysis such as clipping and joining of shapefiles, spatial analytic tasks of hot-spot analysis, and geodatabase design and interface modification (e.g., see Allen 2009; Allen and Coffey 2011) are probably beyond the scope of introductory data exploration.

Spatial data exploration for our PPGIS—what Jankowski and Nyerges (2001) refer to as "basic information handling support"—can be done using quantitative analysis of administrative data and 3-D exploration of local areas, and qualitative analysis of primary data. Examples of quantitative analysis of neighborhood characteristics include general datasets for transportation, housing, environment, and other domains, in applications such as PolicyMap (https://www.policymap.com/), Maptionnaire (https://maptionnaire.com/), Map Your World (http://mapyourworld.org/), Ushahidi (https://www.ushahidi.com/), and CommunityViz' Scenario360 (http://communityviz.city-explained.com/communityviz/scenario360.html). Specialized datasets such as the Child Opportunity Index display metrics specifically designed to highlight local variation in risk and opportunity measures for child development (http://www.diversitydatakids.org/research-library/data-visualization/what-does-child-opportunity-look-your-metro). Virtual representations of local areas are possible through applications such as CommunityViz' Scenario 3D (http://communityviz.city-explained.com/communityviz/scenario3d.html) and the ways2gether augmented reality app (Reinwald et al. 2014).

Examples of qualitative analysis of neighborhood characteristics are mental maps, that is, hand-drawn representations of localized features representing strengths and barriers to opportunity, and superpositions of quantitative and qualitative spatial data as described by Cope and Ellwood (2009). An approach for quantifying local data for representation on maps include crowdsourcing suggestions for local improvements via applications such as *Better Reykjavik* (https://betrireykjavik.is) and *Madame Mayor, I Have an Idea* (https://idee.paris.fr) and dynamically crowdsourced mobile map applications (see descriptions of these in chapter 2).

Data-informed *problem structuring* can be done using the principles of objectives and attributes identification via value-focused thinking (Keeney 2007, 1992). The outputs of this task should approximate values structures that trace out relationships between core values and objectives and decision alternatives, on the one hand, and attributes (metrics) by which progress toward achievement of important objectives can be measured, on the other. In chapter 5 we provided an example of problem structuring through value-focused thinking for vacant parcel use strategies.

Priority setting, values elicitation, and problem-structuring methods—part of Jankowski and Nyerges's (2001) second level of decision aiding methods referred to as "decision analysis support"—are well explored in the research literature (Jankowski and Nyerges 2001, chapters 3, 6, and 7; Jankowski 2011; Johnson et al. 2016, chapter 5; Keeney 2007; Rosenhead and Mingers 2001), but there is limited evidence that computerized representations of these methods currently exist within PPGIS. Maptionnaire (https://maptionnaire.com/) allows users to define and structure how the respondents can see and interact with questionnaires. Users may set branching rules and define the visibility of other respondents' map responses. In contrast, stand-alone applications such as ExpertChoice (https://www.expertchoice.com/2020) support problem structuring specifically for use with the Analytic Hierarchy Process multicriteria decision model (Saaty 1980). Explicit application of values elicitation and problem structuring largely remains a task for in-person deliberation.

Formulation and solution of decision models requires determining the kind of problem to solve, identification of objectives, constraints, and decision variables, assembling datasets to solve the problem, and application of appropriate analytic methods to solve the problem. In chapter 4 we described the mathematical programming problem of selecting types and levels of neighborhood-level investments to design growth strategies that can enhance aggregate social value for a city or region. In chapter 5 we described the mathematical programming problem of vacant parcel acquisition, aggregation, and use assignments. Of prime interest to residents, planners, and agencies in shrinking cities and distressed communities is the problem of identifying candidates for building demolition in a resource-constrained environment, which we discussed in chapter 3's presentation of Baltimore's blight response strategies.

Problem solving within a PPGIS, also part of Jankowski and Nyerges's (2001) second and third levels of decision-aiding methods, can allow for different conceptions of solutions. Game play and community operational research, both mentioned previously, allow for qualitative problem solving. The focus of this book, however, is on quantitative decision modeling for use in PPGIS. Generally, there are three approaches for doing so: multicriteria decision models for ranking a list of alternatives on the basis of attribute values and user-defined priorities for categories of attributes (Malczewski 1999; Jankowski and Nyerges 2001, chapter 5); mathematical programming for assembling optimal solutions from values of component decision variables according to objective functions and constraints (see chapters 4 and 5, this volume); and computerized simulation of real-world systems to generate most-preferred solutions (Grinberger, Lichter, and Felsenstein 2015; Ragothama and Meijer 2015).

It is crucial that problem formulation and solution be performed with community residents playing a leading role, as opposed to the usual practice whereby planners, academic experts or government administrators set the agenda and community residents critique the result. While citizen-engaged decision modeling is not a primary focus of most literature on PPGIS, ideas on how this could be done are provided through principles of community operational research and community-based operations research. Examples of applications that support community participation include SeaSketch's use of the Marxan decision-modeling technology for solving natural resource problems such as reserve design (Ardron, Possingham, and Klein 2013) and Jankowski and Nyerges's (2001, chapter 5) use of multicriteria decision models for health care resource allocation in a PPGIS. However, neither of these applications are particularly focused on urban decision making or shrinking cities. Another potential decision-modeling application relevant to shrinking cities and distressed communities could be the choice of new uses for specific parcels, vacant or not, corresponding to expressed neighborhood needs. This would be an example of a multicriteria decision problem. We explore this problem later in the chapter.

Sensitivity analysis refers to the process of systematically exploring the impacts of changes in a variety of model assumptions on model outputs. Examples of such changes include model parameters (e.g., coefficients of objective function terms, objective function weights, values of constraints) and model components (addition, deletion, or changes to objectives or constraints, in the case of mathematical programs, or changes to the set of decision alternatives, in the case of multicriteria decision models). Johnson and colleagues (2016) provide examples of sensitivity analysis for foreclosed housing acquisition and development regarding estimation of strategic value of acquisition opportunities (chapter 6; Johnson et al. 2012) and strategy design for property acquisition over multiple periods (chapter 10; Bayram, Solak, and Johnson 2014). Our presentation of multiple nondominated solutions to problems in chapters 4 and 5 are one example of sensitivity analysis; we also applied sensitivity analysis in chapter 5 through modifying the formulation of the decision problem itself.

Implementation of model recommendations denotes the process of translating results from a decision model into steps that can be performed by a variety of stakeholders, from residents to staff of community-based organizations to city agencies. Examples of implementation of recommendations from GIS and PPGIS include Penang Island, Malaysia (Meng and Tan 2002), and Wilhelmsburg, Germany (Poplin 2012). In the case of our analysis in chapter 4, that would mean negotiations between community residents and CBOs and the city regarding specific neighborhood investment priorities reflecting desired outputs from the decision model. In the case of our analysis in chapter 5, that would mean developing consensus between community-level stakeholders and city-level organizations on exactly which vacant parcels to acquire, to aggregate, and to assign to which use, according to specific decision model outputs.

We provide examples of real-world problems that might support development of PPGIS-based solutions. Johnson and colleagues (2016) provided multiple examples of decision models for foreclosure response that could be the basis for such an application. The Boston Data Portal (O'Brien 2018) is a mechanism for democratization of urban data. Morckel's work in analytic models to support interventions in shrinking cities and distressed communities offers promise for choosing local communities for novel interventions on the basis of predictors of housing abandonment (2013), and choosing parcels for acquisition, demolition, and/or re-use using suitability analysis (2017). There appear to be ample opportunities for implementation of PPGIS and integration into policy and planning practice in U.S. urban areas.

While principles for PPGIS application design are well represented in the research literature (Jankowski and Nyerges 2001; Jankowski 2011; Burnett 2018), we wish to emphasize principles for PPGIS use in the field. First, applications should be intuitive and not require extensive training (Aggett and McColl 2006). A facilitator or "concierge," in the spirit of community geography, can ensure that even the least tech-savvy community member can participate productively, although research suggests that direct interaction may promote more positive perceptions of the participatory planning process and the likelihood participants will make behavioral changes to implement new policies (Burnett 2020a). Second, organizations that host PPGIS projects should have the technical capacity, political savvy, and fundraising expertise to support resource-intensive spatial analytics efforts (Ellwood and Ghose 2001; Ghose 2011). Third, the PPGIS project experience should allow for ample collaborations, data sharing, and conversations, both in-person and remote, synchronously and asynchronously (Jankowski 2011; Burnett 2020a). Fourth, the PPGIS should support a diverse range of qualitative and quantitative decision-modeling tools and methods (Johnson et al. 2018). Last, the PPGIS should require only as much data as users can acquire and manipulate and take advantage of widely available technologies (Ghose 2017; Johnson 2015; Verplanke et al. 2016).

6.3 What Could It Look Like?

The notion of an "ideal" application to support spatial analysis and decision making, especially in a community planning context, has been a subject of research for many years (Klosterman 2001; Geertman 2002; Jankowski and Nyerges 2001; Burnett 2020b). Aggett and McColl (2006) summarize that a PPGIS could be designed to meet specific user needs according to four criteria: transparency, flexibility, ease of use, and ability to incorporate and communicate stakeholder interests. Of particular interest is the ability of a PPGIS tailored to the needs of shrinking cities and distressed communities, such as those described in chapter 3. Such a PPGIS should enable residents to formulate and solve a wide range of decision problems to support specific community-level development initiatives using multiple analytic methods, including those problems and solution methods presented in chapters 4 and 5.

Therefore, in addition to now-standard requirements that applications support multiple platforms, such as desktop PCs, laptop computers, tablets, and smartphones, and that applications provide detailed two-dimensional and three-dimensional representations of the study area for interactive data exploration using multiple data layers, we emphasize the following.

Our first design concern is that the application should support a rich interface for values and concerns elicitation, values structuring and objectives design, and problem identification. These are distinct concerns, though we choose to group them under the general rubric of problem structuring. As described by Jankowski (2011), "concerns" are specific statements of problems to be addressed, while "values" express generalized attitudes, inspired by concerns that motivate choices among specific alternatives. "Values structuring" and "objectives design" (Keeney 1992, 2007) enable stakeholders to draw connections between *objectives* that represent things we wish to achieve to a greater (maximize) or lesser (minimize) extent, *alternatives*, which can represent specific courses of action or desired outcomes, and *attributes*, which represent metrics by which level of achievement of particular objectives associated with certain alternatives may be measured in a precise way.

""Problem identification" is a term inspired by the literature on problem-structuring methods (Rosenhead and Mingers 2001), community-based operations research, and community operational research to denote the process by which a problem to be addressed can be defined for solution in terms of alternative models and associated solution methods. Types of problems generated through this process include multicriteria decision models (the primary focus of Jankowski and Nyerges 2001 and Aggett and McColl 2006) and multiobjective mathematical optimization models (the primary focus of our chapters 4 and 5). Others include collaborations for shared understandings of the problem context and consensus plans through interactive mapping described by Burnett (2020b), and applications of systems science principles such as "boundary critique" (e.g., see Midgley 2000) and "soft OR" methods such as soft systems methodology (e.g., see Mingers 2011) to generate enhanced understanding about problem contexts and solution possibilities. The "rich interface" we referred to above means that users should have the flexibility to define the problem they want to solve using graphical user interface tools that are easiest for them to master. While PPIS such as CommunityViz, Carticipe, and Maptionnaire may support discussions and surveys, it is less common for PPGIS to support a more comprehensive capability for problem structuring by diverse community members, locally and remotely, synchronously and asynchronously. That is one of the functionalities we want our desired PPGIS to incorporate.

Our second design concern is that the system should support actual solution of problems as defined by the problem structuring step. While many real-world problems can be expressed as relatively small lists of alternatives to be ranked using multicriteria decision models (MCDM; Jankowski and Nyerges 2001, Aggett and McColl 2006), other equally important real-world problems have so many potential alternatives that they can only be meaningfully expressed using the language of multiobjective mathematical optimization: decision variables, objectives, and constraints that generate multiple alternative solutions. Yet other problems can be resolved through voting, consensus, or soft OR methods. Such a wide range of solution approaches rooted in decision modeling is, however, entirely consistent with Geertman's (2002) notion of a PPGIS "toolbox," appropriately expanded. This solution step should also support intuitive, graphical investigation of solution characteristics: objective space versus decision space, in the case of multiobjective optimization (Cohen 1978); attribute values versus priorities (weights) placed on attributes, in the case of multicriteria decision models (e.g., see Malczewski 1999; Jankowski and Nyerges 2001).

Finally, the application should allow for robust, interactive sensitivity analysis, so that the user can easily assess the impact of changes in model assumptions (structural parameters, or presence/absence of constraints, in the case of multiobjective optimization, or changes in value functions or attribute weights, in the case of multicriteria decision models).

6.4 How Should We Design It?

PPGIS design best practices are based on community participation to identify functional requirements and information needs, organization analysis to assess technical, human, and community resources, joint assessment of appropriate technology level, size of groups who will use the application and nature of application usage (synchronous versus asynchronous), and software architecture. Jankowski and Nyerges's Enhanced Adaptive Structuration Theory 2 (EAST2; Jankowski and Nyerges 2001, 2003; Burnett 2019) provides a clear articulation of relationships among elements defining social and group concerns related to PPGIS design (referred to as "Convening Constructs"), those defining ways in which the PPGIS might be used in practice (referred to as "Process Constructs"), and those that represent outcomes related to process tasks and social impacts ("Outcome Constructs") (see figure 6.1). However, we believe that an explicit concern with the models for PPGIS provision and use and the political economy within which PPGIS will be deployed and used (Ghose 2017) will have the most immediate impact on whether a PPGIS application and related project will be successful.

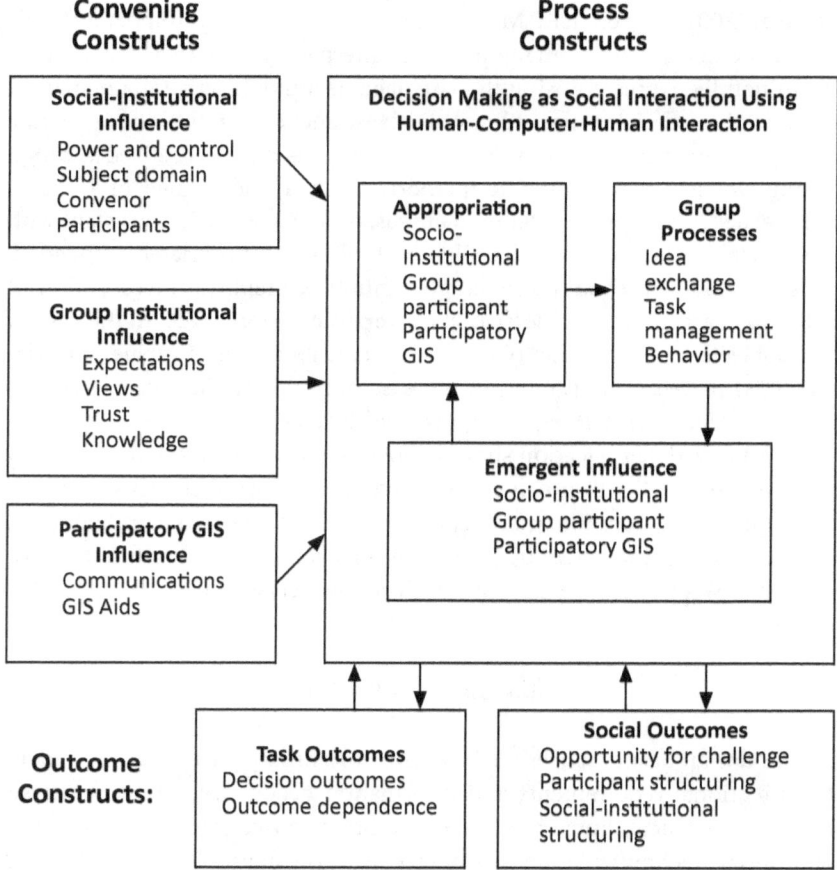

Figure 6.1. Diagram Representing Constructs, Aspects, Premises, and Relations (Arrows) between the Constructs Comprising the Enhanced Adaptive Structuration Theory 2 (EAST2) Framework. *Source:* Jankowski and Nyerges (2003).

That is, stakeholders seeking to design a PPGIS must perform two important tasks. They must choose between alternative models for PPGIS use in the field: community-based GIS; university-community partnerships; GIS facilities in universities and public libraries; map rooms through government GIS; Internet map servers; and neighborhood GIS centers. Any model chosen must account for power relationships between local organizations and city government, which often control access to spatial data and expertise. Stakeholders must also navigate power relationships between city agencies and funders that provide funding and access to data, technology and expertise, and community-based organizations sponsoring PPGIS-based initiatives that wish to speak for residents whose priorities may differ from those of their partners.

While the technology details of PPGIS design are beyond the scope of this book, the consensus of researchers appears to be that Web-based applications offer the greatest flexibility and ease of use, especially for remote and asynchronous participation, even in the face of unreliable access to high-speed internet access (Brown and Kyttä 2014; Ghose 2017). Such a design may be especially useful for remote and resource-poor environments where the digital divide may be greatest (Sieber 2006). Free or open-source GIS technologies, such as Quantum GIS (QGIS) (https://www.qgis.org/en/site/), Field Papers (http://fieldpapers.org/), Geographical Open Data Kit (http://geoodk.com/), and GeoPaparazzi (https://www.geopaparazzi.org/#/) may significantly reduce software development costs (Ghose 2017).

6.5 How Could It Be Used?

There are three primary dimensions of PPGIS use: local, versus remote; synchronous, versus asynchronous; and individual, versus group. For environments like shrinking cities and distressed communities, where access to technology and technical expertise may be limited, and community engagement, organizing, and advocacy is a central focus of redevelopment activities, we believe that a model of PPGIS use that is local, synchronous, and group based is most likely to support individual and group learning. Such an engagement mode can enable community residents, working with a skilled facilitator, to perform a number of critical learning and development tasks. Inspired by principles of community geography (Robinson et al. 2017), we discuss four of them here.

First, residents can learn about their communities through hands-on use of GIS tools and methods to create base maps that highlight variations in certain characteristics across communities and identifying concentrations or absences of resources and threats to well-being. Second, residents can compare, contrast, and validate their lived understanding of their communities with digital representations using qualitative GIS techniques such as mental mapping and maps that combine quantitative and qualitative data. Third, residents can engage in various forms of problem structuring that allow for interactions among participants, brainstorming to build and revise modeling constructs such as values structures and objectives, and discussions regarding the best way to represent a problem-solving opportunity using alternative decision-modeling frameworks. Last, residents can explore characteristics of problem solutions and propose sensitivity analyses.

For all of these tasks, an application feature that allows for threaded discussions, surveys and polling will enable participants to organize and preserve their discussions for future analysis, and to quantify important notions related to spatial data analysis, decision model design and implementation, and linkages between model outputs and policy and planning recommendations.

Of course, other modes of engagement—for example, remote, asynchronous, and individual—can also support community redevelopment initiatives. Two of us (Johnson and Hollander) have experience in distance learning and appreciate the flexibility this teaching mode provides. This is especially the case during the recent coronavirus epidemic. However, we realize that nothing can replace the experience of in-person, in-the-moment discussions that have the potential to change one's understanding of a community, of a problem, of a solution approach, of misunderstandings and biases. We assert that shared experiences of disadvantage, of oppression, and of barriers to opportunity that often characterize the lives of residents in shrinking cities and distressed communities can be transformed into recommendations, proposed initiatives, and principles for empowerment most directly through in-person, group-based, and technology-facilitated learning and engagement using PPGIS.

6.6 Will It Make a Difference?

Formal evaluations of PPGIS tend to focus on tools and technology, rather than outcomes of the participation process or longer-term community and social impacts (Brown and Kyttä 2014). An example of a tool- and technology-focused evaluation framework is that of Aggett and McColl (2006), whose decision support system evaluation framework encompasses utility assessments of specific application functionalities across Jankowski and Nyerges's three levels of DSS supports. Our focus in this section is rather on potential PPGIS impacts on social systems and local communities. Some dimensions along which these impacts could be measured include *good governance* (McCall 2003); *diversity in participation* (Radil and Jiao 2016); *empowerment* (Corbett and Keller 2005; Ghose 2011); *reductions in spatial conflict through stakeholder consensus-building* (Duval-Diop, Curtis, and Clark 2010), *organizational effectiveness* (Ghose 2017), and *technology acceptance and adoption* (Zhao and Coleman 2007). Along all of these dimensions, a proper evaluation should document amount of improvement along a particular dimension of impact associated with a particular intervention or application as compared to the status quo. We discuss these dimensions here.

McCall (2003) identifies accountability as an essential building block of *good governance* associated with community GIS applications. Accountability is defined as supporting higher-level good governance goals of legitimacy and participation; respect for human rights, empowerment, and equity; and competence, including efficiency (554). Improved governance can occur when participatory research is the basis for an intervention, and GIS is the technical tool. GIS tools to support participatory research include scenario development and innovative visualization to ensure exploration of decision spaces as opposed to simple prescriptions.

Diversity in participation refers to the range of backgrounds and perspectives of persons who are part of a PPGIS activity or initiative. Radil and Jiao (2016) show that researchers who seek local participation to identify strengths and weaknesses of a city through GIS-supported workshops may confront systemic biases that complicate analyses. One of these biases may be a belated recognition that participants reflect geographies of inequity, with more-affluent participants having higher rates of participation, as a result of proximity to study locations, which are sited in more privileged communities. Another may be systematic distinctions made by community members between what constitutes "strength" and "weakness" in community services and institutions that reflect perceptions of class or privilege.

Empowerment can be an amorphous concept. Corbett and Keller (2005) provide two related definitions relevant to PPGIS. They consider empowerment to be an increase in social influence or political power, while disempowerment is a decrease in social influence or political power. In turn, empowerment capacity refers to aspects of the deeper process of change in the internal condition of an individual or community that influences their empowerment. Ghose (2011) emphasizes the importance of empowerment of organizations that provide or support access to PPGIS in relation to institutions such as city agencies or funders that may limit availability of data, technical resources, or funding to the extent that community organizations support or oppose large policy and political concerns, for example, views on desired community development activities. All of these concepts can be quantified through surveys and field observations with community participants in a PPGIS intervention.

A PPGIS can lead to more sustainable solutions to spatial problems by supporting multi-*stakeholder consensus-building* regarding display and analysis of spatial attributes, identification of areas of conflict in objectives, and power relationships between community groups (Duval-Diop, Curtis, and Clark 2010). It can enhance *organizational effectiveness* through collaborative governance between community-based organizations, federal agencies, local planning agencies, and universities (Ghose 2011). However, this effectiveness is dependent on organizational factors such as organizational knowledge and experience, a network of collaborative relationships, organizational stability, and organizational priorities, strategies, and status (Elwood and Ghose 2004).

While PPGIS has the potential to balance transparency, flexibility, user-friendliness, and the ability to incorporate and communicate stakeholder interests (Aggett and McColl 2006), none of these beneficial outcomes can occur unless the application is actually incorporated into routine planning activities. Analysis of changes in ways people use information technology applications is the domain of human-computer interactions (HCI). One dimension of HCI research addresses how GIS facilitators affect participation rates (Haklay and Tobón 2005); another assesses changes in usability, interactivity, and visualization of PPGIS applications through measures of direct user interaction (Steinmann, Krek and Blaschke 2004); a third examines the impact of a tool's cost and measures of efficiency, interactivity, and connectivity on user satisfaction and level of learning. A comprehensive framework for measuring HCI in PPGIS is provided by the *Technology Acceptance Model* (Davis 1989). Zhao and Coleman (2007) apply the TAM to evaluate a PPGIS in terms of usefulness, ease of use, cost of entry, intended users, and satisfaction.

Overall, evaluation of the utility of PPGIS is complex. It requires an understanding of technical characteristics of the system, the social environment within which participants are drawn and that influences their attitudes about the problem to be solved and the tools used to solve the problem, and the nature of their intended interactions with the system. It also requires an understanding of the relationships between organizations that provide access to PPGIS and the political economy that determines whether PPGIS interventions improve the lives of individuals and the health of their neighborhoods.

6.7 Reflection

In chapter 2 we discussed the benefits and costs of models, data, and technologies associated with the big data and smart cities movements as they related to the needs of shrinking cities and distressed communities. A summary of these social benefits and costs is shown in table 6.1.

How do PPGIS for shrinking cities and distressed communities stack up?

Table 6.1. Benefits and Costs of Big Data/Smart Cities Innovations for Shrinking Cities and Distressed Communities

Benefits	Costs
• Quality of life • Community engagement • Web-supported democratic participation • Analytics and decision modeling • Civic games and simulations • Geodesign, geographic information systems, and participatory GIS • Community-based research and technology design • Community-engaged operations research and community data analytics • New models for researcher-community collaborations	• Political disengagement, social isolation, and unequal technology access of minority and underserved communities • Lack of recognition of privilege, inequity, and community exclusion in planning support technologies • Lack of trust • Unclear beneficiaries of big data and smart cities • Third spaces are not available to all • Excessive costs • Limited resources and technical capacity

Benefits

The impact on daily quality of life of PPGIS lies in the impact of recommendations generated by the system, not by use of the system, which may be infrequent and generally highly structured, for example, through the use of facilitators. PPGIS can support democratic participation, especially on the Web, if features such as online polling and surveys, as contained in Maptionnaire, are part of the application. Analytics and decision modeling are contained in CommunityViz, as well as Jankowski and Nyerges's GeoChoicePerspectives application (2001).

However, other PPGIS that emphasize collaboration and idea generation, such as Carticipe or Better Reykjavik, have few options for decision modeling. Few of the more widely available PPGIS discussed here engage civic games, though current research makes clear that games could be incorporated into GIS applications. Simulations, however, are an important part of CommunityViz's scenario creation features. As highly engineered professional-quality software, few widely available applications such as Maptionnaire or CommunityViz reflect principles of community-based research and technology design. PPGIS can certainly be integrated into community-engaged operations research and community data analytics initiatives; their data analytics capacity can support problem-structuring methods by helping users better understand the problem space prompting questions about what community attributes matter and how they can be measured. Finally, PPGIS can support new models for researcher-community collaborations since PPGIS can be used by community members and organizations independent of universities and researchers (Ghose 2017) and thus empower communities to formulate their own applied research questions.

Costs

PPGIS are well positioned to address concerns of political disengagement, social isolation, and unequal technology access, especially for minority and underserved communities. However, as Radil and Jiao (2016) show, without a deliberate effort to broaden participation in PPGIS, project outputs can simply reinforce perspectives and attitudes of more-privileged communities. If PPGIS are implemented with community-based organizations as full partners, and in recognition of a fiscally challenging neoliberal political economy in many cities (Ghose 2017), they have the potential to counter concerns of lack of recognition of privilege, inequity and community exclusion.

PPGIS can provide clear benefits to community residents of the big data and smart cities movements inasmuch as PPGIS can consume substantial amounts of data and use sophisticated technologies to provide quite detailed and useful perspectives on local communities. In contrast to many big data and smart cities initiatives, however, PPGIS can be designed to benefit community residents primarily, as opposed to government agencies, or private companies interested in user data. Although PPGIS, in its remote mode, can be used in third spaces, we feel that the greatest benefits of PPGIS come from synchronous group use with a facilitator. Usage in this way would require dedicated spaces, such as GIS facilities in universities and public libraries and neighborhood GIS centers (Ghose 2017) as well as specially designed community-based collaborative co-work and technology spaces, such as Boston's Fairmount Innovation Lab (http://fil594.org/). Direct and indirect costs of PPGIS design, development, implementation, use, and maintenance can be a concern. While Web services such as *Carticipe*, supported by the consultancy Repérage Urbain, and *Madam Mayor, I Have An Idea*, developed by the city of Paris, are free to end-users, feature-heavy applications such as CommunityViz and SeaSketch are available only to select organizations that have either purchased the product (CommunityViz) or have established partnerships with organizations that deploy the software as part of their mission (e.g., the Wiatt Institute, for SeaSketch). Finally, PPGIS, if implemented by mission-driven community-based organizations, have the potential to build technical capacity and access to data and analytical resources.

In summary, it appears that PPGIS can currently generate social benefits that exceed the costs. However, this conclusion relies on the work of community-based organizations with an advocacy, inclusion, engagement, and technology transfer/capacity building mission who are committed to using PPGIS to generate novel and potentially controversial conclusions, as opposed to ratifying decisions made at other levels of government.

6.8 Conclusion

In this chapter we have made a case for public participatory GIS as a software application supporting use across multiple modes, a toolbox providing a variety of resources for descriptive, exploratory, and prescriptive analysis, and a method for community-engaged planning and problem solving. We have argued that PPGIS—especially as extended according to the principles of community geography and incorporating principles of community-engaged operations research—is well suited to the needs of community members and the organizations that serve and represent them in shrinking cities and distressed communities.

We presented principles for an "ideal" PPGIS that could specifically meet the needs of underresourced communities exhibiting multiple measures of distress such as the three we have focused on in our case studies, and identified the many ways that such a PPGIS could make a difference in the lives of individuals and communities. We acknowledge, however, that a PPGIS that incorporates spatial learning, community discussions and participation, problem-structuring methods, a variety of decision-modeling applications, and creative exploration of alternative strategies arising from group consensus or decision models does not yet exist.

The principles for effective PPGIS are clear, but somewhat contradictory. Those that are especially relevant to planning and policy interventions in shrinking and distressed communities include spatial data exploration; community engagement through forums and surveys; problem-structuring methods; multiple decision-modeling applications; community learning through games, facilitated conversations, simulations, and other methods; creative exploration of solutions and recommendations generated by decision models or community consensus; and a connection between recommendations or consensus solutions generated by the PPGIS and courses for action as pursued by community-based organizations and/or government agencies. Is it really possible to combine all of these in a single application/method? It is unlikely that there will or even should be a one-size-fits-all PPGIS that can solve so many problems at once.

We feel that while a robust, extensible, and professional-quality IT application is essential for the success of a PPGIS initiative, it is even more important that the project be firmly rooted in principles of community engagement and empowerment, and local organization capacity-building regarding data, technology, analysis, and evidence-based advocacy. Otherwise, a PPGIS project could be at risk of representing a project that is not replicated and that generates findings that need not be heeded or recognized by a city government that generally controls access to data, technology, and financial resources.

CHAPTER 7

Lessons Learned

How Can Data, Models, and Technology Support Shrinking Cities and Distressed Communities?

7.1 Introduction

In the previous chapter we argued for the development of a public participatory geographic information system (PPGIS) that could meet the needs of communities facing sustained declines in population, economic activity, or resources, which we refer to as "shrinking cities and distressed communities." Such a system would support improvements in social and physical infrastructure through creative collection, visualization and analysis of local data, and formulation and solution of decision problems regarding the collection and use of public and private spaces. It would recognize the needs of these communities to use qualitative and quantitative data, decision models and information technology for planning, advocacy, and empowerment in ways potentially quite distinct from the needs and priorities of organizations and agencies that usually claim to speak for them or to act on their behalf.

This concluding chapter is a summary and synthesis of what we've learned, as well as a vision for data, models, and technologies to support communities and residents who face challenges to their very existence and who have not traditionally had the means to craft their own narratives and chart their own path forward using cutting-edge tools and methods.

This book's purpose has been to apply knowledge from multiple disciplines—urban planning, decision science, community development, geographic information systems and data analytics—to create a new way of understanding how data, models, and technologies can support local development in challenging environments. We've tried to question common assumptions that interventions inspired by the big data and smart cities movements can improve all urban communities, to draw portraits of three cities who face multiple measures of distress and decline that might benefit from our proposed interventions, to describe these interventions for two of these cities, and to present opportunities for local interventions rooted in public participatory GIS to support improvements that go beyond what we found in our field research.

We've learned quite a lot through our journey. In chapter 1 we provided a rationale for new research and practice in a domain that combines foci on shrinking cities and distressed communities, with an orientation toward prescriptive analysis to support local interventions. We provided rationales for our choice of three diverse shrinking cities for further study, and introduced a range of technologies, applications, and analytic methods that we use in empirical analysis throughout the book. In chapter 2 we reviewed a range of urban planning perspectives relevant to this book's focus. We showed that the case for investments in big data and smart city-related technologies in the context of shrinking cities and distressed communities is not as strong as many advocates would have us believe. We also argued that the success of such investments relies on principles of authentic public participation, flexibility in response to public criticism or increased understanding of best practices, ample access to human, financial, and technical resources and a thoroughgoing commitment to equity, inclusion, and diversity. In chapter 3 we profiled three cities—Baltimore, Flint, and Fall River—that vary in size, demography, and geography. This analysis reflected different aspects of shrinkage, decline, and distress in order to highlight a diversity regarding redevelopment goals, primary decision-making systems and processes, and future uses of land that may not support traditional residential development.

In chapter 4 we reviewed analytic strategies relevant to interventions in shrinking cities and distressed communities, and justified a focus on decision analytics. We applied principles of decision modeling to Fall River to show how one might develop a range of neighborhood-level investment strategies that maximize neighborhood satisfaction. These investment strategies account for residential versus nonresidential development, more- versus less-distressed neighborhoods, and neighborhoods that are likely to show increasing, decreasing, or roughly constant returns to scale in quality of life associated with different types of investments. In chapter 5 we addressed the more localized problem of acquisition, consolidation, and re-use of vacant and abandoned parcels in distressed communities to develop principles of decision model formulation using principles of value-focused thinking, and decision model solution using multiobjective optimization. We contrasted our approach to solving an explicit decision model with that of city planners who solve the same problem, but without an apparent awareness of quantifying objectives, decision alternatives, attributes and metrics, and tradeoffs. In chapter 6 we recognized the need for community engagement and technology-supported decision support systems, not present in the two previous chapters, to argue that interventions rooted in principles of public participatory geographic information systems may be best suited to meeting the needs of residents of shrinking cities and distressed communities for strategy design and local development.

In the remainder of this chapter we apply these results to address a broader set of questions related to supporting the development of cities that can better meet the needs of residents in communities that have been the focus of this book. These questions include: What can data, models and technology contribute to such communities? What are key principles regarding data, models, and technology that shrinking cities and distressed communities may consider for redevelopment and revitalization? What roles can stakeholders play? In these communities, what are primary barriers to data, models, and technology that may provide social and economic opportunities that more privileged communities may take for granted?

In proposing ways to address these questions, we emphasize a number of fundamental themes. First, *values are essential*. Inspired by the work of Keeney (1992) and Keisler and colleagues (2014), we believe that if researchers and practitioners don't identify the goals they wish to achieve and the objectives they wish to optimize in designing approaches to redevelopment and revitalization of shrinking cities and distressed communities, and if local stakeholders don't play a central role in identifying these goals and objectives, it is far less likely that any proposed intervention will be successful.

Second, we must *distinguish means from ends*. Data are crucial to understanding diverse aspects of communities, and systems and technologies can broaden the range of services that can be provided to communities, but why might we make these investments in data, models, and technologies? Who will benefit, and how, and how are these benefits likely to be distributed across stakeholder groups and geographies? Recent work by O'Brien (2018) and Gordon and Mihaldis (2016) remind us that data and technologies are only as useful as the ways that residents, with government and nonprofits, may collaborate to solve problems in creative ways. The most meaningful focus on data is not how "big" it is, but how we negotiate the tension between "data-driven" and "problem-driven" analysis.

Third, any intervention must be rooted in a commitment to *meaningful engagement of communities*. This phrase, adapted from principles of community operational research (Midgley, Johnson, and Chichirau, 2018), denotes that communities, more often the object of policies, plans, and interventions than the primary actor, must play a central role in agenda setting, problem formulation, systems development, and solution implementation to ensure successful outcomes.

Next, these investments must confront *administrative and technological barriers to application of decision analytics*: cities face real difficulties in the use of decision models and decision support systems to rigorously formulate, solve, and evaluate models for vacant land management. Last, these investments should embrace *thoughtfulness with uncertainty*: by expanding capacity to make better decisions, articulating core values and providing appropriate resources, residents of areas of interest for our research can learn, plan, build, and advocate to produce the livable communities they desire, in ways we may not anticipate or appreciate.

7.2 What Do We Need to Know to Help Communities Facing Shrinkage and Distress Thrive?

Cities and regions that wish to productively respond to trends of shrinkage and distress should balance a number of potentially conflicting priorities with limited public resources. They must meet residents' basic daily needs for shelter, physical safety, adequate nutrition, health, education, and employment; build social capacity for cooperation, access to opportunities, and advocacy for community improvement; provide supportive services, recreational outlets, and opportunities for cultural and artistic expression; enable resilience as well as adaptation in the face of uncertain future events, such as neighborhood change or extreme weather events; and enable residents to communicate their needs to government and nongovernmental organizations easily and without fear of retribution. Nowhere in this list have we mentioned data, models, or technology; these are means to more fundamental ends of an opportunity-rich and emotionally satisfying life. Still, they are essential to achieving these end-goals.

We believe that residents want to have a say in how government and private parties outside their communities can make investments in physical infrastructure. They want to decide what can be done not just with one or two vacant lots, but many vacant lots and abandoned housing across multiple communities. They want to make government and nonprofit service providers more responsive and accountable. They want to explore how different priorities associated with redevelopment and services can be balanced to best meet their needs. To do all of this, data, models, and technology can be transformed from the province of experts and those with specialized education into tools that allow diverse stakeholders to contribute equally to discussions about pathways to achieve the neighborhoods they will be proud to call home.

How can we decide what a city that successfully addresses the challenges of shrinkage and distress can look like, what it can do with and for residents, and how it can be experienced? This requires a commitment to discuss competing values that provide a framework for local development goals, and to creatively identify alternative paths to local development and change. It also requires a willingness of those with power, wealth, and influence to engage, share data and knowledge, and negotiate willingly and in good faith with residents. Finally, it requires all stakeholders to put equity, diversity, inclusion, and voice at the center of conversations about a community's future. Data, models, and technology can contribute to these goals by enabling residents to determine what counts in addressing local concerns, to agree how to collect and share qualitative and quantitative data that tell important stories about communities, to visualize communities as they exist now and how they could be, and to generate a range of alternative courses of action, each associated with differing priorities placed on goals of interest to different groups.

Of course, this world of the planner's imagination does not exist in most communities facing obstacles to opportunity, specifically shrinkage and distress—values underlying important decisions are hidden. In Boston, for example, a recent study of school assignment policies revealed unintended negative consequences for communities of color and low-income neighborhoods associated with an algorithm, originally marked as "objective," to assign students to schools (Buell 2018). In New York City, the ubiquitous LinkNYC data kiosks provide connectivity and mobile device charges, but also collect data from unsuspecting residents for purposes not readily explained (Buttar and Kalia 2017). In Puerto Rico, a lack of agreement about values has produced differing assessments among the federal government, local government, and researchers about the death toll from 2017's Hurricane Maria (Newkirk 2018). The smart city discourse points to data as the answer, but we have shown that more important are the values underlying that data. A city full of sensors and open data portals cannot be a place where better decisions are made, where residents feel they have a say over their lives and their communities, unless the values supporting those decisions are clear, explicit, and based on community input and dialogue.

Fortunately, we have seen reasons for hope in our book's case studies, and in our field research. In Flint, community engagement and active participation in planning has served as a counterweight to the widespread fear, distrust, and disruption of daily life associated with the state-imposed austerity regime implicated in the introduction of lead into tap water. In Baltimore, creative antivacancy and land-reuse policies and collaborations among anchor institutions in and near distressed communities offer opportunities to engage residents in the aftermath of demonstrations spurred by the death of Freddie Gray. In Fall River, large investments by that city's Office of Economic Development and a new emphasis on immigrant entrepreneurship may serve as a basis for revitalization.

7.3 Barriers to Best Uses of Data, Models, and Technology

There are numerous challenges to achieving the vision of values-focused, technology-aware, and locally engaged development in shrinking cities and distressed communities in the United States. Measures of income and wealth inequality have trended upward in recent years and for indicators like percentage share of total income of the very wealthiest individuals, are at levels not seen since the Great Depression (Institute for Policy Studies 2018). Poverty rates, while showing a decrease from a recent peak of 14.8 percent in 2014, have varied within a band of 11 to 15 percent for the past forty years (U.S. Census Bureau 2018). The global COVID-19 pandemic, which as of December 31, 2020, has resulted in over 82.6 million cases and 1.8 million deaths (*New York Times* 2020a), has inflicted immense damage on the United States. At the end of 2020, over 342,000 Americans have died due to the novel coronavirus, record levels of unemployment have resulted from widespread closures of local economies (*New York Times* 2020b), and social and economic inequality, already high before the pandemic, has played a role in disparities in infection and death rates by race and ethnicity (Mijs 2020). As a result, many low- and moderate-income families struggle to meet their basic needs and build their human and social capital. Such families and communities may have neither the time nor the resources to participate in engaging but time-consuming community development activities. It is hard for a planning process to be truly inclusive if residents in areas confronting shrinkage and distress are viewed by administrators and decision makers as sources of disruption and protest rather than as partners in development.

A neoliberal ideology that does not view access to basic urban services as a right, which advocates lowest-cost solutions as the only meaningful response (if they bother to consider meaningful responses at all) to problems facing populations who do not have access to many of these services, and puts a higher priority on the desires of higher-income and more-suburban voters than lower-income residents of urban communities will not be supportive of community engagement and creative uses of technology for local development. We saw the impacts of this ideology in our case study of Flint, and in our discussion of the barriers to community access to public participatory GIS in the United States (Ghose 2011, 2017).

A final barrier to creative and inclusive uses of data, models, and technology in shrinking cities and distressed communities is a pervasive conception of data and technology as most salient for commerce, entertainment, and surveillance. While Facebook has recently advertised the real-life beneficial impacts of responsible use of social media, there are very few widely available applications in the United States of citizen-focused technologies developed in Europe such as *Carticipe, Madame Mayor, I Have An Idea*, or *UrbanData2Decide* that could make data, models, and technology widely understood as a tool for engagement, empowerment, and advocacy in local planning.

We believe that addressing these fundamental concerns goes well beyond new decision models, innovative visualizations of alternative local development strategies, or new conceptions of public participatory GIS. Instead, what may be necessary is a commitment to inclusive and transparent governance, adequate funding for local initiatives, and recognition of structural barriers and historic inequalities. These sorts of changes require, once again, a new kind of values-focused planning consistent with the principles of collaborative planners (Innes and Booher 2004; Lane 2005; Ansell and Gash 2008) and community operational research (Midgley, Johnson, and Chichirau 2018).

7.4 Opportunities for Tech-Aware Development in Shrinking Cities and Distressed Communities

There are a number of ways in which creative use of data, models, and technology might make major contributions to more effective and inclusive planning in cities like those we have studies in this book. First, planners could benefit from *improved technical skills in decision science and information technology*. Results in chapter 5 made clear that a limited understanding of decision modeling by planners we worked with made it harder to generate sustainable solutions to the problem of vacant parcel acquisition and re-use that applied principles of evidence-based decision modeling. We are all instructors in or graduates of planning programs, and we know firsthand that required master's-level courses in decision modeling and analytics, and in information technology, are not as common as they could be. However, such courses should not be limited to methods and techniques: they should make values elicitation, problem structuring, systems thinking, and model-based problem solving central to their curricula.

Second, *people matter for effective planning support*. There should be a deep commitment to community engagement, participation, and empowerment, and a recognition of structural barriers, institutional bias, and practical impediments to building livable communities. We are encouraged by the many aspects of community-engaged planning taking place in Flint, but aware that without a substantial, long-term commitment to expensive investments in physical as well as social infrastructure, the long-term prospects for places like Flint are uncertain.

Third, *communities should be in the driver's seat*. In spite of the high level of technical training and commitment to principles of planning, responses to shrinkage, decline, and distress must put perspectives and values of residents of affected communities at the center of interventions. In a different context, an education activist has counseled a billionaire would-be social investor to approach new projects with "radical listening and radical humility." She continues:

Go to the communities, talk to parents, talk to children, talk to teachers and administrators and ask them: "What do you need? What are your hopes and dreams for education and for your children?" Because otherwise what will happen is that we're doing this to the community instead of for the community. (Goldstein 2018)

This principle seems particularly salient in the case of Baltimore.

Last, *stakeholders must identify tradeoffs and assumptions.* We believe that data, models, and technologies can enable communities to develop comprehensive plans that acknowledge difficult tradeoffs and varying assumptions about the ability of neighborhoods in shrinking cities to respond to different kinds of investments, but set a baseline for strategy design that goes beyond individual high-profile investments or charismatic political leaders. This seems relevant to cities facing challenges similar to those of Fall River.

7.5 Looking Forward

This book had its origins in conversations two of us (Michael and Justin) had a decade ago about ways that the disciplines of urban and community planning and decision sciences might be combined to generate new insights regarding local development. We understood that planning can generate rich insights about how and why neighborhoods grow, change, and sometimes shrink, and can provide tangible guidance on strategies to support new land uses and ways for residents to craft better lives in their neighborhoods. However, we also believed that the profession sometimes lagged in helping researchers and practitioners figure out exactly how to identify interventions in communities that could be seen as "optimal," or most preferred, or a verifiable improvement over the status quo, reflecting quantifiable tradeoffs between multiple competing objectives and sometimes-contested notions of values. We understood that decision sciences can use models, usually quantitative in nature, to solve cognitively challenging problems in diverse domains of public affairs and commerce in the tradition of descriptive, predictive, and prescriptive analytics. However, there were unmet opportunities for these models to be better aligned with values that motivate the need for interventions, and to be better motivated with potentially beneficial social outcomes that can be long term in nature, as opposed to shorter-term outcomes associated with efficiency gains. We thought that the problem of shrinking cities, declining regions, and distressed communities, then as now a rich area of inquiry and practice across developed countries, might be a promising application area for these two disciplines. However, we realized that these two traditions had interacted for many years, without a common understanding of how to leverage the strengths of both in ways recognized by training programs or in the field.

As we continued to work together, we also realized that an emerging context for our work, the big data and smart cities movements, raised more intriguing questions about whether and how data, models, and technologies could provide new ways for communities affected by shrinkage and decline—not just the more affluent communities that could make best use of various new technologies services for increased productivity and recreation—to have a real say over the future of their communities. We understood that well-established communities of research and practice in planning support systems, spatial analysis, and smart cities offered many promising areas for inquiry. However, there did not seem to be a strong understanding of how notions of values, local engagement, and critical perspectives could result in new kinds of applications especially well-suited for the needs of underserved and marginalized urban communities—the ones most adversely affected by issues of shrinkage, decline, and distress. We understood that creative use of geographic information systems could enable stakeholders with diverse levels of technical training to represent challenges their communities face through map-making and spatial analysis. However, we believe that we have not tapped the full potential of critical approaches to geography, such as critical cartography, critical GIS, and creative spatial visualizations that engage diverse stakeholders (e.g., see Kollektiv Orangotango+ 2019; Krygier and Wood 2016).

Through an exploratory study of decision modeling for neighborhood-based redeveloping in the smaller shrinking city of Fall River, and a funded study of decision modeling for vacant land acquisition and redevelopment in Baltimore, we developed a more comprehensive approach to model building and design of local interventions. These efforts embraced quantitative and qualitative data, problem-structuring methods, spatial analysis, and planning support systems that we believe offers new insights to scholars, practitioners, and community-based stakeholders reflecting diverse disciplinary and knowledge traditions.

Some of our recent work reinforces these themes in ways relevant to our case study cities of Flint, Fall River, and Baltimore. A study of the intersections between urban planning and operations research/analytics over forty years has revealed that a prospective and prescriptive approach to planning that embraces qualitative operations research methods can help researchers and practitioners develop effective interventions that are equitable and that reflect the concerns of community members and community-serving organizations (Fabusuyi and Johnson 2020). A class taught by one of us (Johnson) with the mayor's office of the city of Boston has addressed issues of vacancy, eviction and displacement associated with changing communities (Johnson 2018b). One student-run project to assess the level of community engagement in a recent city-wide planning process revealed that engaging residents as substantive partners to learn what our communities can look like, and do for residents, requires a real commitment to transparency, accessibility, and critical perspectives. Another project to learn how new residents of gentrifying neighborhoods could better understand a positive role they could play in community transformation helped us understand that working with neighborhoods most affected by issues of decline and distress requires imaginative ways for ordinary residents to help define problems, collect data, and devise novel solutions distinct from those planners might use. In addition, a study by one of us (Burnett) regarding use of public participatory GIS for campus planning has revealed to us new opportunities to combine surveys, spatial data knowledge creation, and decision modeling in a Web-based PPGIS to generate novel insights by community members regarding options for community development (Burnett 2019).

These recent and ongoing projects have reinforced insights that we hope resonate with you as well. Data, models, and technology are important; without them we can't visualize a new future or figure out how to bring it into being. But even more important are values: principles that support interventions that can enable residents of struggling communities to assert ownership of new ideas for local development. These ideas, coming from community members who are experts on their own experiences, can help other experts—planners, decision scientists, information technologists—to think differently about how to generate and apply knowledge for community development.

Works Cited

Abbey-Lambertz, Kate. "These Are The 10 Most Livable Cities In The World." *Huffington Post*, 19 August 2016. https://www.huffingtonpost.com/entry/most-livable-cities-2016_us_57b5f32ce4b0b51733a1dd55

Ackermann, Fran. 2012. "Problem Structuring Methods 'in the Dock': Arguing the Case for Soft OR." *European Journal of Operational Research* 219 (3): 652–658. https://doi.org/10.1016/j.ejor.2011.11.014

Aggett, Graeme, and McColl, Chris. 2006. "Evaluating Decision Support Systems for PPGIS Applications." *Cartography and Geographic Information Science* 33 (1): 77–92. https://doi.org/10.1559/152304006777323163

Agyeman, Julian. 2005. *Sustainable Communities and the Challenge of Environmental Justice*. New York: NYU Press.

Al-Kodmany, Kheir. 2012. "Utilizing GIS in Nonprofit Organizations for Urban Planning Applications: Experiences from the Field." *Journal of Geographic Information System* 04 (04): 279–297. https://doi.org/10.4236/jgis.2012.44034

Albright, S. Christian, and Winston, Wayne L. 2015. *Business Analytics: Data Analysis and Decision Making*, 5th ed. Stamford, CT: Cengage Learning.

Alexander, Ernest R. 2000. "Rationality Revisited: Planning Paradigms in a Post-Postmodernist Perspective." *Journal of Planning Education and Research*, 19(3): 242–256. https://doi.org/10.1177/0739456X0001900303

Ali, Arshad A. 2016. "Citizens under Suspicion: Responsive Research with Community under Surveillance." *Anthropology & Education Quarterly* 47: 78–95. https://doi.org/10.1111/aeq.12136

Allen, David W., and Coffey, Jeffery M. 2010. *GIS Tutorial 3: Advanced Workbook*. Redlands, CA: Esri Press.

Allen, David W. 2013. *GIS Tutorial 2: Spatial Analysis Workbook*. Redlands, CA: Esri Press. https://esripress.esri.com/bookResources/index.cfm?event=catalog.book&id=19

Ansell, Chris, and Gash, Alison. 2008. "Collaborative Governance in Theory and Practice." *Journal of Public Administration Research and Theory* 18 (4): 543–571. https://doi.org/10.1093/jopart/mum032

Appel, Sheila U., Botti, Derek, Jamison, James, Plant, Leslie, Shyr, Jing Y., and Varshney, Lav R. 2014. "Predictive Analytics Can Facilitate Proactive Property Vacancy Policies for Cities." *Technological Forecasting and Social Change* 89 (November): 161–173. https://doi.org/10.1016/j.techfore.2013.08.028

Ardron, Jeff A., Possingham, Hugh P., and Klein, Carissa J. 2013. "Marxan Good Practices Handbook, Version 2." Victoria, British Columbia, Canada. http://pacmara.org/wp-content/uploads/2018/05/Marxan-Good-Practices-Handbook-v2-2013.pdf

Arnstein, Sherry R. 1969. "A Ladder Of Citizen Participation." *Journal of the American Institute of Planners* 35 (4): 216–224. https://doi.org/10.1080/01944 366908977225

Atkinson, Scott. "In Flint Neighborhood, Vacant Lots Will Soon Bear Fruit." *Next City*, 20 July 2017a. https://nextcity.org/daily/entry/eastside-flint-greenspace community-garden

Atkinson, Scott. "Flint Market Will Put Good Food, Ownership in Hands of Residents." *Next City*, 13 July 2017c. https://nextcity.org/daily/entry/flint-food-co-op-ownership-residents

Atkinson, Scott. "Flint Mapping Makes City Planning a Team Effort." *Next City*, 4 August 2017b. https://nextcity.org/daily/entry/flint-mapping-neighborhood-inventory-project-grants

Attorney General of Massachusetts. "AG Coakley, Mayor Flanagan, and Local Officials Tour Rehabbed Abandoned Property in Fall River." 12 July 2012.

Baibarac, Corelia Elena. 2014. "The 'Urban Spacebook' Experimental Process: Co-designing a Platform for Participation." *The Journal of Community Informatics* 10 (3).

Balassiano, Katia, and Seeger, Christopher. 2014. "Empowering Newcomers with Low-Tech Workshops and High-Tech Analyses." *The Journal of Community Informatics* 10 (3).

Baltimore City Department of Planning. 2012. "The Baltimore City Growing Green Initiative."

Baltimore City Planning Commission. 2013. *Homegrown Baltimore: Grow Local—Baltimore City's Urban Agriculture Plan*. Baltimore: Office of Sustainability and City of Baltimore Department of Planning.

Baltimore Housing. n.d. "From Vacants to Value: Creating Value by Rehabbing Vacant Homes and Reclaiming Blighted Blocks." Baltimore.

Banister, Jon. "Amazon Plans to Begin Work on HQ2 Development This Month." *Bisnow* 15 January 2020. https://www.bisnow.com/washington-dc/news/economic-development/amazon-plans-to-begin-work-on-hq2-development-this-month-102548

Bartholomew, Keith. 2007. "Land Use-Transportation Scenario Planning: Promise and Reality." *Transportation* 34 (4): 397–412.

Bartlett, Darius, and Celliers, Louis. 2016. "Geoinformatics for Marine and Coastal Management." In *Geoinformatics for Marine and Coastal Management*, 1–413. CRC Press. https://doi.org/10.1201/9781315181523

Bayram, Armagan, Solak, Senay, and Johnson, Michael. 2014. "Stochastic Models for Strategic Resource Allocation in Nonprofit Foreclosed Housing Acquisitions." *European Journal of Operational Research* 233 (1): 246–262. https://doi.org/10.1016/j.ejor.2013.08.040

Beauregard, Robert A. 1984. "Making Planning Theory: A Retrospection." *Urban Geography* 5 (3): 255–261.

Beauregard, Robert A. "Urban Population Loss in Historical Perspective: United States, 1820–2000." *Environment and Planning A: Economy and Space* 41, no. 3 (2009): 514–528.

Beauregard, Robert A. 2003. *Voices of Decline: The Postwar Fate of U.S. Cities*, 2nd ed. New York: Routledge.

Bilandzic, Mark, and Venable, John R. 2011. Towards Participatory Action Design Research and Design Science Research Methods for Urban Informatics. *The Journal of Community Informatics* 7 (3).

Bischoff, Kendra, and Reardon, Sean F. 2014. "Residential Segregation by Income, 1970–2009." In J. Logan (ed.), *Diversity and Disparities: America Enters A New Century*. New York: The Russell Sage Foundation, 208–233.

Blakely, Edward. 1994. *Planning Local Economic Development: Theory and Practice*, 2nd ed. Thousand Oaks, CA: Sage.

Blessett, Brandi L. 2011. *Dispersion or Re-Segregation: A Spatial and Temporal Analysis of Public Policies and Their Impact on Urban African American Mobility*. Norfolk, VA: Old Dominion University.

Bluestone, Barry, and Harrison, Bennett. 1982. *The Deindustrialization of America: Plant Closings, Community Abandonment, and the Dismantling of Basic Industries*. New York: Basic Books.

Boardman, Anthony E., Greenberg, David H., Vining, Aidan R., and Weimer, David L. 2017. *Cost-Benefit Analysis: Concepts and Practice*. Cambridge: Cambridge University Press.

Borchers, Callum. "Corruption Trial Of Former Fall River Mayor Jasiel Correia Delayed 4 Months." *WBUR*, 6 April 2020. https://www.wbur.org/news/2020/04/06/jasiel-correia-corruption-trial-delayed-coronavirus

Boston Area Research Initiative. Boston Data Portal, 2018. https://cssh.northeastern.edu/bostonarearesearchinitiative/boston-data-portal

Bowie, Janice, Farfel, Mark, and Moran, Heather. 2005. "Community Experiences and Perceptions Related to Demolition and Gut Rehabilitation of Houses for Urban Redevelopment." *Journal of Urban Health* 82: 532–542.

Boyd, Danah, and Crawford, Kate. 2011. "Six Provocations for Big Data." In *A Decade in Internet Time: Symposium on the Dynamics of the Internet and Society*.

Bradbury, Katherine L., Downs, Anthony, and Small, Kenneth A. 1982. *Urban Decline and the Future of American Cities*. Washington, DC: Brookings Institution.
Bradley, Bill. "Despite Bankruptcy, Development Soldiers on in Detroit's Downtown Core." *Next City*, 24 July 2013. http://nextcity.org/daily/entry/despite-bankruptcy-development-soldiers-on-in-detroits-downtown-core
Brail, Richard K. 2008. *Planning Support Systems for Cities and Regions*. Hollis, NH: Lincoln Institute of Land Policy.
Brown, Greg, and Kyttä, Marketta. 2014. "Key Issues and Research Priorities for Public Participation GIS (PPGIS): A Synthesis Based on Empirical Research." *Applied Geography* 46: 122–136. https://doi.org/10.1016/j.apgeog.2013.11.004
Brown, Greg. 2012. "Public Participation GIS (PPGIS) for Regional and Environmental Planning: Reflections on a Decade of Empirical Research." *URISA Journal* 24 (2): 7–18.
Brown, Greg. 2015. "Engaging the Wisdom of Crowds and Public Judgement for Land Use Planning Using Public Participation Geographic Information Systems." *Australian Planner* 52 (3): 199–209. https://doi.org/10.1080/07293682.2015.1034147
Buckley, Cara. "On a Magazine's List of the City's 'Most Livable Neighborhoods,' a Few Surprises." *The New York Times*, 12 April 2010. https://www.nytimes.com/2010/04/13/nyregion/13greenpoint.html
Buell, Spencer. 2018. "An Algorithm 'Diminished Integration' at Boston Schools, a Report Found." *Boston Magazine* 17 July 2018. https://www.bostonmagazine.com/education/2018/07/17/boston-schools-integration-report
Bullard, Robert D., and Wright, Beverly H. 1990. "The Quest for Environmental Equity: Mobilizing the Black Community for Social Change." *Race, Poverty & the Environment* 1 (2): 3–17.
Bullard, Robert D. 1994. "Grassroots Flowering: The Environmental Justice Movement Comes of Age." *The Amicus Journal* 16: 32–37.
Burnett, Charla M. 2018. "Democratizing the Decision-Making Process: Methods Approach to Comparative Public Participatory Geographic Information Systems." *University of Massachusetts Boston Dissertation Proposal*.
Burnett, Charla M. 2019. "Mapping Green Spaces on College Campuses Using Participatory GIS: A Model for Managing Multi-Stakeholder Perspectives." *Mimeo*. Boston.
Burnett, Charla M. 2020. Incorporating the Participatory Process in the Design of Geospatial Support Tools: Lessons Learned from SeaSketch. *Environmental Modelling & Software* 127 (May): 104678. https://doi.org/10.1016/j.envsoft.2020.104678
Burnett, Charla M. 2020. "Surveying Emotions in Participatory Geographic Information Systems: Feedback from SeaSketch Users." Boston, MA.
Buttar, Shahid, and Kalia, Amul. 2017. "LinkNYC Improves Privacy Policy, Yet Problems Remain." *Electronic Frontier Foundation*. https://www.eff.org/deeplinks/2017/09/linknyc-improves-privacy-policy-yet-problems-remain

Campanella, Thomas. 2011. "Jane Jacobs and the Death and Life of American Planning." *Places Journal* (April).
Carver, Steve. 2003. The Future of Participatory Approaches Using Geographic Information: Developing a Research Agenda for the 21st Century. *URISA Journal* 15(1): 61–71.
Catsaros, Christophe. "Les flux de réfugiés vont-ils changer les villes?" *Le Temps*, 13 Septembre 2015. https://blogs.letemps.ch/christophe-catsaros/2015/09/13/les-flux-de-refugies-vont-ils-changer-les-villes
Caulkins, Jonathan P., Yegorov, Yuri, Feichtinger, Gustav, Grass, Dieter, Johnson, Michael, and Tragler, Gernot. 2005. "Placing the Poor While Keeping the Rich in Their Place." *Demographic Research* 13: 1–34. https://doi.org/10.4054/DemRes.2005.13.1
Centers for Disease Control and Prevention. "Strategies for Reducing Health Disparities—Selected CDC-Sponsored Interventions, United States, 2016." *Morbidity and Mortality Weekly*, 12 February 2016. https://www.cdc.gov/mmwr/volumes/65/su/pdfs/su6501.pdf
Čerić, Vlatko. 1991. "Rational Analysis for a Problematic World: Problem Structuring Methods for Complexity, Uncertainty and Conflict." *European Journal of Information Systems* 1 (1): 75–76. https://doi.org/10.1057/ejis.1991.10
Chang, Virginia W., Hillier, Amy E., and Mehta, Neil K. 2009. "Neighborhood Racial Isolation, Disorder and Obesity." *Social Forces* 87 (4): 2063–2092.
Chin, Alan. "Amid Baltimore Protests, These Residents Held a Town Meeting on the Street." *Next City*, 29 April 2015. https://nextcity.org/daily/entry/photos-baltimore-protests-residents-hold-town-meeting-on-street
Chorianopoulos, Konstantinos. 2014. "Community-based Pedestrian Mapmaking." *The Journal of Community Informatics* 10 (3): 1–8.
Christopher, Martin. 2016. *Logistics and Supply Chain Management*, 5th ed. Edinburgh Gate, UK: Pearson Education, Ltd.
City of Baltimore. 2010. "Purpose and Methodology." https://archive.baltimorecity.gov/Default.aspx?TabID=1039
City of Baltimore. 2009. *Live Earn Play Learn: City of Baltimore Comprehensive Master Plan*. Baltimore: Department of Planning.
City of Baltimore. n.d. *Vacants to Value*. Baltimore: Housing Authority of Baltimore City and Department of Housing and Community Development.
Clagett, Virginia P. 2003. "House Bill 424: Baltimore City—Condemnation and Immediate Possession and Title of Distressed Property." *University of Baltimore Journal of Environmental Law* 11: 71–74.
Clark, Anna. 2018. *The Poisoned City: Flint's Water and the American Urban Tragedy*. New York: Metropolitan Books.
Clark, William A. V. 1989. "Residential Segregation in American Cities: Common Ground and Differences in Interpretation." *Population Research and Policy Review* 8 (2): 193–197.

Cohen, James R. 2001. "Abandoned Housing: Exploring Lessons from Baltimore." *Housing Policy Debate* 12 (3): 415–448.
Cohon, Jared L. 1978. *Multiobjective Programming and Planning. Mathematics in Science and Engineering 140*. New York: Academic Press.
Coibion, Olivier, Gorodnichenko, Yuriy, Kudlyak, Marianna, and Mondragon, John. "Greater Inequality and Household Borrowing? New Evidence from Household Data." *Vox*, 2014. https://voxeu.org/article/inequality-and-household-debt-new-evidence
Collette, Yann, and Siarry, Patrick. 2013. *Multiobjective Optimization: Principles and Case Studies*. New York: Springer Science & Business Media.
Commonwealth of Massachusetts. 2018. "Environmental Justice Communities in Massachusetts." Mass.gov. https://www.mass.gov/info-details/environmental-justice-populations-in-massachusetts
Conrad, Elisabeth, Cassar, Louis F., Christie, Mike, and Fazey, Ioan. 2011. "Hearing but Not Listening? A Participatory Assessment of Public Participation in Planning." *Environment and Planning C: Government and Policy* 29 (5): 761–782. https://doi.org/10.1068/c10137
Cope, Meghan, and Elwood, Sarah. 2009. *Qualitative GIS: A Mixed Methods Approach*. Thousand Oaks, CA: Sage.
Corbett, Jon M., and Keller, C. Peter. 2005. "An Analytical Framework to Examine Empowerment Associated with Participatory Geographic Information Systems (PGIS)." *Cartographica: The International Journal for Geographic Information and Geovisualization* 40 (4): 91–102. https://doi.org/10.3138/J590-6354-P38V-4269
Corburn, Jason. 2003. "Bringing Local Knowledge into Environmental Decision Making." *Journal of Planning Education and Research* 22 (4): 420–33.
Craig, William J., Harris, Trevor M., and Weiner, Daniel. 2002. *Community Participation and Geographical Information Systems*. London: Taylor and Francis.
Cranshaw, Justin, Toch, Eran, Hong, Jason, Kittur, Aniket, and Sadeh, Norman. 2010. "Bridging the Gap Between Physical Location and Online Social Networks." *Proceedings of the 12th ACM International Conference on Ubiquitous Computing*, 119–128.
Culhane, Dennis P., and Hillier, Amy E. 2001. "Comment on James R. Cohen's 'Abandoned Housing: Exploring Lessons from Baltimore.'" *Housing Policy Debate* 12 (3): 449–455.
Cullingworth, J. Barry, and Caves, Robert W. 2003. *Planning in the USA: Policies, Issues, and Processes*. London & New York: Routledge.
Cuppen, Eefje. 2012. "Diversity and Constructive Conflict in Stakeholder Dialogue: Considerations for Design and Methods." *Policy Sciences* 45 (1): 23–46.
Davenport Whiteman, Eliza. 2014. *Decision-Making Strategies for Vacant Lot Reuse in Baltimore, Maryland*. Medford, MA: Tufts University.
Davidoff, Paul. 1965. Advocacy and Pluralism in Planning. *Journal of the American Institute of Planners* 31 (4): 331–228.

Davis, Fred D. 1989. Perceived Usefulness, Perceived Ease of Use, and User Acceptance of Information Technology. *MIS Quarterly* 13(3): 319–340. https://doi.org/10.2307/249008

Dear, Michael, and Flusty, Steven. 1998. "Postmodern Urbanism." *Annals of the Association of American Geographers* 88: 50–72.

DeLessio, Joe. "New York's New Public Wi-Fi Kiosks Are Spying on You, Says Civil-Liberties Group." *New York Magazine*, 18 March 2016. http://nymag.com/daily/intelligencer/2016/03/nyclu-raises-linknyc-privacy-concerns.html

Demetriou, Demetris, Stillwell, John, and See, Linda. 2012. "An Integrated Planning and Decision Support System (IPDSS) for Land Consolidation: Theoretical Framework and Application of the Land-Redistribution Modules." *Environment and Planning B: Planning and Design* 39 (4): 609–628. https://doi.org/10.1068/b37075

Desai, Anand. 2012. *Simulation for Policy Inquiry*. New York: Springer.

Desmond, Matthew. 2016. *Evicted: Poverty and Profit in the American City*. New York: Crown Publishers.

Detroit Future City. 2012. *Detroit Future City: 2012 Detroit Strategic Framework Plan*. Detroit, MI: Inland Press.

Detroit Future City. 2015. "Working with Lots: A Field Guide." Accessed May 28, 2020. https://dfc-lots.com/assets/construction-packages/DFC_Field_Guide_Web-1.pdf

Dewar, Margaret and Manning Thomas, June (Eds.). 2012. *The City after Abandonment*. Philadelphia: University of Pennsylvania Press.

Dias, Elizabeth, Eligon, John. and Oppel Jr., Richard A. 2018. "Arrests, Outrageous to Some, Are Everyday Life for Others." *The New York Times*, 17 April 2018. https://www.nytimes.com/2018/04/17/us/starbucks-arrest-philadelphia.html

Do, D. Phuong, Frank, Reanne, Zheng, Cheng, and Iceland, John. 2017. "Hispanic Segregation and Poor Health: It's Not Just Black and White." *American Journal of Epidemiology* 186 (8): 990–999.

Dovey, Rachel. "State Takeover of Flint Is (Mostly) Done." *Next City*, 25 January 2018. https://nextcity.org/daily/entry/state-takeover-of-flint-is-mostly-done

Dubb, Steve. "Baltimore Confronts Enduring Racial Health Disparities." *Nonprofit Quarterly*, 22 November 2017. https://nonprofitquarterly.org/2017/11/22/baltimore-confronts-enduring-racial-health-disparities

Dubb, Steve. 2018. "In Baltimore, Johns Hopkins Seeks to Be a Good Neighbor." *Nonprofit Quarterly*, 14 May 2018. https://nonprofitquarterly.org/2018/05/14/baltimore-johns-hopkins-seeks-good-neighbor

DuBow, Wendy M., and Litzler, Elizabeth. 2019. "The Development and Use of a Theory of Change to Align Programs and Evaluation in a Complex, National Initiative." *American Journal of Evaluation* 40 (2): 231–248. https://doi.org/10.1177/1098214018778132

Dulin-Keita, Akilah, Kaur Thind, Herpreet, Affuso, Olivia, and Baskin, Monica L. 2013. The Associations of Perceived Neighborhood Disorder and Physical

Activity with Obesity among African American Adolescents. *BMC Public Health* 13, 440. https://doi.org/10.1186/1471-2458-13-440

Duval-Diop, Dominique, Curtis, Andrew, and Clark, Annie. 2010. "Enhancing Equity with Public Participatory GIS in Hurricane Rebuilding: Faith Based Organizations, Community Mapping, and Policy Advocacy." *Community Development* 41 (1): 32–49. https://doi.org/10.1080/15575330903288854

Economic Innovation Group. 2018. "From Great Recession to Great Reshuffling: Charting a Decade of Change Across American Communities." *Prepared by Kenan Fikri and John Lettieri*. https://eig.org/wp-content/uploads/2018/10/2018-DCI.pdf

The Economist. "Rus in urbe redux." 30 May 2015. https://www.economist.com/international/2015/05/30/rus-in-urbe-redux

Eden, Colin, and Ackerman, Fran. 2004. "Use of 'Soft OR' by Clients: What Do They Want From Them?" In M. Pidd (ed.), *Systems Modelling: Theory and Practice*, 146–163. Chichester, UK: Wiley.

Edsforth, Ronald William. 1982. *A Second Industrial Revolution: The Transformation of Class, Culture, and Society in Twentieth-Century Flint, Michigan*. East Lansing, MI: Michigan State University.

Egan, Timothy. "Ruling Sets Off Tug of War Over Private Property." *The New York Times*, 30 July 2005. http://www.nytimes.com/2005/07/30/us/ruling-sets-off-tug-of-war-over-private-property.html

Ehrgott, Matthias. 2005. *Multiple Criteria Optimization*, 2nd ed. Berlin: Springer.

Ehrgott, Matthias, and Gandibleux, Xavier. 2002. "Multiple Criteria Optimization: State of the Art Annotated Bibliographic Surveys." In Matthias Ehrgott and Xavier Gandibleux (eds.), *Multiple Criteria Optimization*, International Series in Operations Research & Management Science, 52: 496. https://doi.org/10.1007/b101915

Eicher, Caitlin, and Kawachi, Ichiro. 2011. "Social Capital and Community Design," in *Making Healthy Places: Designing and Building for Health, Well-Being, and Sustainability*. Washington, DC: Island Press.

Eiselt, H. A., and Sandblom, Carl-Louis. 2004. *Decision Analysis, Location Models, and Scheduling Problems*. Berlin: Springer.

El Nasser, Haya. "Sunburnt Cities Have a Shot to Control Growth." *USA Today*, 8 March 2011. https://usatoday30.usatoday.com/money/economy/housing/2011-03-08-sunburnt08_CV_N.htm

Elwood, Sarah, and Ghose, Rina. 2001. "PPGIS in Community Development Planning: Framing the Organizational Context." *Cartographica* 38 (3–4): 19–33. https://doi.org/10.3138/R411-50G8-1777-2120

Eversley, Melanie. "One Year Later, Baltimore Still Reeling from Freddie Gray Death, Riots." *USA Today*, 18 April 2016. https://www.usatoday.com/story/news/2016/04/18/oneyear-later-baltimore-still-reeling-freddie-gray-death-riots/83181808

Fabusuyi, Tayo. 2018. "Is Crime a Real Estate Problem? A Case Study of the Neighbourhood of East Liberty, Pittsburgh, Pennsylvania." *European Journal of Operational Research* 268 (3): 1050–1061.

Fabusuyi, Tayo, and Johnson, Michael. 2019. "Urban Planning & Operations Research: A Review and Critique." *Available at SSRN 3503450. Working paper.*

Fainstein, Susan S. 2010. *The Just City*. Ithaca, NY: Cornell University Press.

Fainstein, Susan S. 2000. "New Directions in Planning Theory." *Urban Affairs Review* 35 (4): 451–478.

Fainstein, Susan S. 2014. The Just City. *International Journal of Urban Sciences* 18 (1): 1–18.

Fallows, James, and Fallows, Deborah. 2018. *Our Towns: A 100,000-Mile Journey into the Heart of America*. New York: Pantheon Books.

Farquhar, Stephanie E. 2012. *Making a University City: Cycles of Disinvestment, Urban Renewal and Displacement in East Baltimore*. Baltimore: Johns Hopkins University Press.

Fernández Campbell, A. "Do Parts of the Rust Belt 'Need to Die Off'?" *The Atlantic*, 20 July 2016. http://www.theatlantic.com/business/archive/2016/07/rust-belt-survival/492155

Fischer, Frank, and Forester, John. 1993. *The Argumentative Turn in Policy Analysis and Planning*. Durham, NC: Duke University Press.

Fitzsimmons, James A., Fitzsimmons, Mona J., and Bordoloi, Sanjeev. 2014. *Service Management: Operations, Strategy, Information Technology*, 8th ed. New York: McGraw Hill Irwin.

Florida, Richard. "How 'Not' to Save Neighborhoods." *The New York Times*, 1 June 2011. https://www.nytimes.com/roomfordebate/2011/03/28/the-incredible-shrinking-city/how-not-to-save-neighborhoods

Foreman, Benjamin, and Larson, Sandra. 2014. "Going for Growth: Promoting Immigrant Entrepreneurship in Massachusetts Gateway Cities." MassINC Gateway Cities Innovation Institute. https://www.mapc.org/wp-content/uploads/2017/09/B19-Mills-to-Main-Streets-MassINC-Immigrant-Entreprenurship-Report.pdf

Forester, John. 1999. *The Deliberative Practitioner: Encouraging Participatory Planning Processes*. Cambridge, MA: MIT Press.

Forgionne, Guisseppi A. 1991. "HANS: A Decision Support System for Military Housing Managers." *Interfaces* 21 (6): 37–51. https://doi.org/10.1287/inte.21.6.37

Forgionne, Guisseppi A., and Frager, Yehuda S. 1998. "The US Army Relies on Decision Support Systems in Allocating Housing Resources." *Interfaces* 28 (2): 72–79. https://doi.org/10.1287/inte.28.2.72

Fortin, Jacey. "Mayor of Fall River Is Ousted and Re-elected at the Same Time." *The New York Times*, 13 March 2019. https://www.nytimes.com/2019/03/13/us/jasiel-correia-mayor-fall-river.html

Franco, L. Alberto, and Montibeller, Gilberto. 2010. "Facilitated Modelling in Operational Research." *European Journal of Operational Research* 205 (3): 489–500. https://doi.org/10.1016/j.ejor.2009.09.030

Frank, Thomas. "Why Have Democrats Failed in the State Where They're Most Likely to Succeed?" *The Nation*, 29 March 2016a. https://www.thenation.com/article/archive/why-have-democrats-failed-in-the-state-where-theyre-most-likely-to-succeed

Frank, Thomas. 2016b. *Listen, Liberal: Or, What Ever Happened to the Party of the People?* New York: Macmillan.

Frey, William H. 2017. "City Growth Dips Below Suburban Growth, Census Shows." *The Brookings Institution*. https://www.brookings.edu/blog/the-avenue/2017/05/30/city-growth-dips-below-suburban-growth-census-shows

Friedman, Eric. 2003. "Vacant Properties in Baltimore: Strategies for Reuse." Submission for the Abell Foundation Award in Urban Policy, 2003. https://www.abell.org/sites/default/files/files/2003%20Friedman.pdf

Frontline Systems. 2011. "Premium Solver Pro Version 11.5.2.0." http://www.solver.com/premium-solver-pro

Frontline Systems. 2015. "Excel Solver–Integer Programming." https://www.solver.com/excel-solver-integer-programming

Fullilove, Mindy Thompson. 2001. Root Shock: The Consequences of African American Dispossession. *Journal of Urban Health* 78 (1): 72–80. https://doi.org/10.1093/jurban/78.1.72

Gabriel, Steven A., Faria, José A., and Moglen, Glenn E. 2006. "A Multiobjective Optimization Approach to Smart Growth in Land Development." *Socio-Economic Planning Sciences* 40 (3): 212–248. https://doi.org/10.1016/j.seps.2005.02.001

Gallagher, John. "Plan to Save Detroit Unveiled: Vision for a Smaller, Stronger Motor City." *Detroit Free Press*, 8 January 2013. https://www.detroityes.com/mb/showthread.php?15355-Urban-Plans-spend-two-years-studying-Detroit-and-talking-with-over-30-000-residents

Galster, George. 2017. "Why Shrinking Cities Are Not Mirror Images of Growing Cities: A Research Agenda of Six Testable Propositions." *Urban Affairs Review* 55 (2017): 355–372.

Ganning, Joanna P., and Tighe, J. Rosie. 2018. Moving toward a Shared Understanding of the U.S. Shrinking City. *Journal of Planning Literature*. https://doi.org/10.1177/0739456X18772074

Gans, Herbert J. 1982. *The Urban Villagers: Group and Class in the Life of Italian-Americans*. Updated and Expanded Edition. New York: Free Press.

Gardner, Rachele, Snyder, William M., and Zugay, Ayda. 2019. Amplifying Youth Voice and Cultivating Leadership through Participatory Action Research. *Education Policy Analysis Archives* 27 (54). https://doi.org/10.14507/epaa.27.2621

Garrow, Eve E. 2015. "Racial and Ethnic Composition of the Neighborhood and the Disbanding of Nonprofit Human Service Organizations." *Du Bois Review: Social Science Research on Race* 12: 161–185.

Garvin, Eugenia, Branas, Charles, Keddem, Shimrit, Sellman, Jeffrey, and Cannuscio, Carolyn. 2013. "More Than Just an Eyesore: Local Insights and Solutions on Vacant Land and Urban Health." *Journal of Urban Health* 90 (3): 412–426.

Gay Stolberg, S. "Baltimore Enlists National Guard and a Curfew to Fight Riots and Looting." *The New York Times*, 27 April 2015. https://www.nytimes.com/2015/04/28/us/baltimore-freddie-gray.html

Gaynor, Tia. 2017. "A Primer for Effective and Meaningful Social Equity Measurement." *PA Times*. March 7, 2017. https://patimes.org/primer-effective-meaningful-social-equity-measurement

Geers, Glenn, and Economou, Dean. 2014. "Computable Livability." In *National Science Foundation Workshop on Big Data and Urban Informatics*, Chicago. https://www.researchgate.net/publication/280034988_Computable_Liveability

Geertman, Stan, Ferreira, Joseph, Goodspeed, Robert, and Stillwell, John C. H. (eds.) 2015. *Planning Support Systems and Smart Cities*. New York: Springer.

Geertman, Stan. 2002. "Participatory Planning and GIS: A PSS to Bridge the Gap." *Environment and Planning B: Planning and Design* 29 (1): 21–35. https://doi.org/10.1068/b2760

Ghose, Rina. 2001. "Use of Information Technology for Community Empowerment: Transforming Geographic Information Systems into Community Information Systems." *Transactions in GIS* 5 (2): 141–163. https://doi.org/10.1111/1467-9671.00073

Ghose, Rina. 2011. "Politics and Power in Participation and GIS Use for Community Decision Making." In *The SAGE Handbook of GIS and Society*, 423–438. London: Sage. https://doi.org/10.4135/9781446201046.n22

Ghose, Rina. 2017. "Public-Participation GIS." In *International Encyclopedia of Geography: People, the Earth, Environment and Technology*, 1–11. Oxford, UK: John Wiley & Sons, Ltd. https://doi.org/10.1002/9781118786352.wbieg1155

Gilbert, Kenneth C., Holmes, David D., and Rosenthal, Richard E. 1985. "A Multiobjective Discrete Optimization Model for Land Allocation." *Management Science* 31 (12): 1509–1522. https://doi.org/10.1287/mnsc.31.12.1509

Gilman, Theodore J. 1997. "Urban Redevelopment in Omuta, Japan, and Flint, Michigan: A Comparison". In P. P. Karan, Kristin Stapleton (eds.), *The Japanese City*. Lexington: University Press of Kentucky, 176–220.

Gioielli, Robert. 2010. " 'We Must Destroy You to Save You': Highway Construction and the City as a Modern Commons." *Radical History Review* 109: 62–82.

Glaeser, Edward L., Kominers, Scott Duke, Luca, Michael, and Naik, Nikhil. 2015. *Big Data and Big Cities: The Promises and Limitations of Improved Measures of Urban Life*. Cambridge, MA: National Bureau of Economic Research.

Glanz, Karen, Rimer, Barbara K., and Viswanath, Kasisomayajula. 2008. *Health Behavior and Health Education: Theory, Research and Practice*, 4th ed. San Francisco: Jossey-Bass.

Gleeson, Michael E. 1985. "Estimating Housing Mortality from Loss Records." *Environment and Planning A: Economy and Space* 17 (5): 647–659. https://doi.org/10.1068/a170647

Glink, I. 2015. "The Fastest-Shrinking Cities in America, 2015." Yahoo Real Estate. https://www.yahoo.com/news/the-fastest-shrinking-cities-in-america-2015-005602170.html

Göçmen, Z. Aslıgül, and Ventura, Stephen J. 2010. "Barriers to GIS Use in Planning." *Journal of the American Planning Association* 76 (2): 172–183.

Goldberg, Grace E., and McClintock, William J. 2015. "Integrated Participation Tools Facilitate Science-Based Spatial Planning With a Web-Based GIS." In *12th International Symposium for GIS and Computer Cartography for Coastal Zones Management*. Western Cape, South Africa.

Goldberg, Grace, Hastings, Sean, and McClintock, Will. 2018. "SeaSketch for Safe Passage: Collaborative Mapping Helps Conflicting Marine Interests Work Towards Shared Goals." *Proceedings of the Marine Safety & Security Council, the Coast Guard Journal of Safety at Sea* 75 (2): 77–81.

Goldkamp, Joseph. 2016. "Exploring the Core of Baltimore: Does It Produce the Change It Hopes to Be?" *Nonprofit Quarterly* (October). https://nonprofitquarterly.org/2016/10/12/exploring-core-baltimore-produce-change-hopes

Goldsmith, Stephen, and Crawford, Susan. 2014. *The Responsive City: Engaging Communities Through Data-Smart Governance*. New York: John Wiley & Sons.

Goldstein, Dana. 2018. "Jeff Bezos Cites a Big Number, but Few Details, in Plan for Low-Income Montessori Preschools." *The New York Times*. 21 September 2018. https://www.nytimes.com/2018/09/21/us/bezos-montessori-preschool.html

Goldstein, Ira. 2011. "Market-Value Analysis: A Data-Based Approach to Understanding Urban Housing Markets." In Matt Lambert and Jane Humphreys (eds.), *Putting Data to Work: Data-Driven Approaches to Strengthening Neighborhoods*, Board of Governors of the Federal Reserve System, 49–60. http://www.federalreserve.gov/communitydev/files/data-driven-publication-20111212.pdf

Gomez, Marisela B., and Muntaner, Carles. 2005. "Urban Redevelopment and Neighborhood Health in East Baltimore, Maryland: The Role of Communitarian and Institutional Social Capital." *Critical Public Health* 15 (2): 83–102.

Gomez, Marisela B. 2012. *Race, Class, Power, and Organizing in East Baltimore: Rebuilding Abandoned Communities in America*. Lanham, MD: Lexington Books.

Goodchild, Michael F. 2010. "Towards Geodesign: Repurposing Cartography and GIS?" *Cartographic Perspectives* 66: 7–21.

Goodyear, Sarah. 2018. "3-1-1: A City Services Revolution." *CityLab*. https://www.citylab.com/city-makers-connections/311

Gordon, Eric, and Mihaildis, Paul. 2016. *Civic Media: Technology, Design, Practice*. Cambridge, MA: MIT Press.

Gordon, Eric, and Walter, Steven. 2016. "Meaningful Inefficiencies: Resisting the Logic of Technological Efficiency in the Design of Civic Systems." In E. Gordon and P. Mihaildis (eds.), *Civic Media: Technology, Design, Practice*. Cambridge, MA: MIT Press, 243–266.

Gordon, Eric, Baldwin-Philippi, Jesse, and Balestra, Martina. 2013. *Why We Engage: How Theories of Human Behavior Contribute to Our Understanding of Civic Engagement in a Digital Era*. The Berkman Center for Internet & Society, Harvard University.

Gordon, Eric, Schirra, Steven, and Hollander, Justin. 2011. "Immersive Planning: A Conceptual Model for Designing Public Participation with New Technologies." *Environment and Planning B: Planning and Design* 38: 505–519.

Gordon, Eric, and Mihaildis, Paul. 2016. *Civic Media: Technology, Design, Practice*. Cambridge, MA: MIT Press.

Gordon, Eric, and Walter, Stephen. 2019. "Meaningful Inefficiencies: Resisting the Logic of Technological Efficiency in the Design of Civic Systems." In René Glas, Sybille Lammes, Michiel de Lange, Joost Raessens, and Imar de Vries (eds.), *The Playful Citizen*. Amsterdam: Amsterdam University Press, 310–334.

Gorr, Wilpen L., and Kurland, Kristin S. 2013. "GIS Tutorial 1: Basic Workbook. Redlands." Redlands, CA: Esri Press.

Gratz, Roberta Brandes. "Saving Shrinking Cities." *Huffington Post*, 4 August 2010. https://www.huffpost.com/entry/saving-shrinking-cities_b_670389

Greater Baltimore Committee and Baltimore Metropolitan Council. *2018 Greater Baltimore State of the Region Report*. https://gbc.org/wp-content/uploads/2018/05/2018-State-of-the-Region-Report-GBC-BMC-FINAL.pdf

Grinberger, A. Yair, Lichter, Michal, and Felsenstein, Daniel. 2015. "Simulating Urban Resilience: Disasters, Dynamics and (Synthetic) Data." In S. Geertman, J. Ferreira, R. Goodspeed, and J. Stillwell (eds.), *Planning Support Systems and Smart Cities*. Cham, Swizerland: Springer, 99–119.

Großmann, Katrin, Bontje, Marco, Haase, Annegret, and Mykhnenko, Vlad. 2013. "Shrinking Cities: Notes for the Further Research Agenda." *Cities* 35: 221–225.

Grubesic, Tony, and Murray, Alan. 2010. "Methods to Support Policy Evaluation of Sex Offender Laws." *Papers in Regional Science* 89 (3): 669–684. https://doi.org/10.1111/j.1435-5957.2009.00270.x

Haklay, Mordechai, and Tobón, Carolina. 2003. "Usability Evaluation and PPGIS: Towards a User-Centred Design Approach." *International Journal of Geographical Information Science* 17 (6): 577–592. https://doi.org/10.1080/1365881031000114107

Hall, Stuart. 1997. "The Local and the Global: Globalization and Ethnicity," in Anthony D. King (ed.), *Culture, Globalization and the World-System: Contemporary Conditions for the Representation of Identity*. Minneapolis: University of Minnesota Press.

Hamilton, Steve, and Zhu, Ximon. 2017. "Funding and Financing Smart Cities." *Deloitte Center for Government Insights*. https://www2.deloitte.com/content/dam/Deloitte/us/Documents/public-sector/us-ps-funding-and-financing-smart-cities.pdf

Hammer, Janet, and Pivo, Gary. 2017. "The Triple Bottom Line and Sustainable Economic Development Theory and Practice." *Economic Development Quarterly* 31 (1): 25–36. https://doi.org/10.1177/0891242416674808

Hampton, Keith Neil, and Wellman, Barry. 2003. "Neighboring in Netville: How the Internet Supports Community and Social Capital in a Wired World." *City & Community* 2 (4): 277–311.

HarassMap. 2014. "Towards a Safer City–Sexual Harassment in Greater Cairo: Effectiveness of Crowdsourced Data." https://harassmap.org/storage/app/media/uploaded-files/Towards-A-Safer-City_executive-summary_EN.pdf

Hargittai, Eszter, and Hinnant, Amanda. 2008. "Digital Inequality: Differences in Young Adults' Use of the Internet." *Communication Research* 35 (5): 602–621.

Harris, David. "Flint's East Side Bears Worst Arson Scars: 'They Burned the Whole Block.'" *MLive*, 8 January 2011. https://www.mlive.com/news/flint/index.ssf/2011/01/flints_east_side_bears_worst_a.html

Harris, Fred, and Curtis, Alan. 2018. *Healing Our Divided Society: Investing in America Fifty Years after the Kerner Report*. Philadelphia: Temple University Press.

Hasegawa, Yoko, Sekimoto, Yoshihide, Seto, Toshikazu, and Fukushima, Yuki. 2015. "How Will Compact City Affect Me? Urban Planning Simulation for Citizens." In J. Ferreira and R. Goodspeed (eds.), *Proceedings of the 14th International Conference on Computers in Urban Planning and Urban Management: Planning Support Systems and Smart Cities*. Cambridge, MA: MIT Press.

Healey, Patsy. 1999. *Collaborative Planning: Shaping Places in Fragmented Societies*. Basingstoke, Hampshire & New York: Palgrave Macmillan.

Heckert, Megan, and Mennis, Jeremy. 2012. "The Economic Impact of Greening Urban Vacant Land: A Spatial Difference-In-Differences Analysis." *Environment and Planning A: Economy and Space* 44 (12): 3010–3027. https://doi.org/10.1068/a4595

Heim LaFrambois, Megan E., Park, Yunmi, and Yurcuba, Daniel. 2019. "How Shrinking Cities Plan for Change: Comparing Population Projections and Planning Strategies in Depopulating U.S. Cities." *Journal of Planning Education and Research*. Published online June 23, 2019. https://doi.org/10.1177/0739456X19854121

Herald News. "Thriving Textile Industry Made Village a Boom Town." *Fall River, MA Herald News*, 17 October 1978a. https://www.sailsinc.org/durfee/thriving.pdf

Herald News. "Fall River Line Had a Style All Its Own." *Fall River, MA Herald News*, 17 October 1978b. https://www.sailsinc.org/durfee/frlinehadastyle.pdf

Herald News. "1928 Fire Destroyed Much of Downtown." *Fall River, MA Herald News*, 17 October 1978c. https://www.sailsinc.org/durfee/1928fire.pdf

Highsmith, Andrew R. 2009. "Demolition Means Progress: Urban Renewal, Local Politics, and State-Sanctioned Ghetto Formation in Flint, Michigan." *Journal of Urban History* 35 (3): 348–368.

Hinds, Michael Decourcy. "Baltimore's Story of City Homesteading." *The New York Times*, 16 January 1986. https://www.nytimes.com/1986/01/16/garden/baltimore-s-story-of-city-homestaeding.html

Hirokawa, Randy Y, and Poole, Marshall Scott. 1996. *Communication and Group Decision Making*. Thousand Oaks, CA: Sage.

Hoch, Charles. 1996. "A Pragmatic Inquiry About Planning and Power," in Seymour J. Mandelbaum, Luigi Mazza, and Robert W. Burchell (eds.), *Explorations in Planning Theory. Center for Urban Policy Research*. New Brunswick, NJ: Transaction Publishers, 30–44.

Hollander, Justin B. 2018. *A Research Agenda for Shrinking Cities*. Cheltenham, UK: Edward Elgar Publishing, Ltd.

Hollander, Justin B., and Nemeth, Jeremy. 2011. "The Bounds of Smart Decline: A Foundational Theory for Planning Shrinking Cities." *Housing Policy Debate* 21 (3): 349–367.

Hollander, Justin B. 2010. "Can a City Successfully Shrink? Evidence from Survey Data on Neighborhood Quality." *Urban Affairs Review* 47 (1): 129–141.

Hollander, Justin B. 2009. *Polluted and Dangerous: America's Worst Abandoned Properties and What Can Be Done About Them*. Lebanon, NH: University Press of New England.

Hollander, Justin B., Pallagst, Karina, Schwarz, Terry, and Popper, Frank J. 2009. "Planning Shrinking Cities. Progress in Planning." *Special Issue: Emerging Research Areas* 72 (4): 223–232.

Hollander, Justin B. 2011. *Sunburnt Cities: The Great Recession, Depopulation and Urban Planning in the American Sunbelt*. New York: Routledge.

Hollander, Justin B. 2010. "Moving Toward a Shrinking Cities Metric: Analyzing Land Use Changes Associated with Depopulation in Flint, Michigan." *SSRN Electronic Journal* 12 (1): 133–151. https://doi.org/10.2139/ssrn.1585405

Hoover, Edgar Malone, and Vernon, Raymond. 1962. *Anatomy of a Metropolis*. New York: Doubleday.

Imagine Flint. Master Plan for a Sustainable Flint. Produced by Houseal Lavigne Associates, 2013a.

Imagine Flint. Master Plan for a Sustainable Flint: Summary of Goals and Objectives. Produced by Houseal Lavigne Associates, 2013b.

Innes, Judith E., and Booher, David E. 2004. "Reframing Public Participation: Strategies for the 21st Century." *Planning Theory & Practice* 5 (4): 419–436.

Innes, Judith E., and Booher, David E. 2010. *Planning with Complexity: An Introduction to Collaborative Rationality for Public Policy*. New York: Routledge.

Innes, Judith E., and Booher, David E. 2004. "Reframing Public Participation: Strategies for the 21st Century." *Planning Theory and Practice* 5 (4): 419–436. https://doi.org/10.1080/1464935042000293170

Institute for Policy Studies. "Income Inequality." *Inequality.org*, 2018a. https://inequality.org/facts/income-inequality

Institute for Policy Studies. "Wealth Inequality." *Inequality.org*, 2018b. https://inequality.org/facts/wealth-inequality

Institute for Policy Studies. "Inequality and Health." *Inequality.org*, 2018c. https://inequality.org/facts/inequality-and-health

Jackson, Kenneth T. 1985. *Crabgrass Frontier: The Suburbanization of the United States*. New York: Oxford University Press.

Jacobs, Jane. 1984. *Cities and the Wealth of Nations: Principles of Economic Life*. New York: Vintage Books.

Jacobs, Scott, Dyson, Brian, Shuster, William D., and Stockton, Tom. 2017. "A Structured Decision Approach for Integrating and Analyzing Community Perspectives in Re-Use Planning of Vacant Properties in Cleveland, Ohio." *Urban Land Use* 6 (1): 163–188. https://doi.org/10.1201/9781315365794-8

Jacobson, Joan. 2015. "Vacants to Value: Baltimore's Bold Blight-Elimination Effort Is Making Modest Progress despite Limited Renovation Funds and Questionable Accounting." *The Abell Report* 28 (5). http://www.abell.org/sites/default/files/files/cd-vacants2-value1115.pdf

Jankowski, Piotr, and Nyerges, Timothy L. 2003. "Toward a Framework for Research on Geographic Information-Supported Participatory Decision-Making." *URISA Journal* 15 (1): 9–17. http://faculty.washington.edu/nyerges/urisa.pdf%5Cn-http://www.urisa.org/files/Jankowskivol15apa1.pdf

Jankowski, Piotr and Timothy Nyerges. 2001. *GIS for Group Decision Making*. London: CRC Press. https://doi.org/10.4324/9780203484906

Jankowski, Piotr. 2011. "Designing Public Participation Geographic Information Systems." In *The SAGE Handbook of GIS and Society*, 347–360. London: Sage. https://doi.org/10.4135/9781446201046.n18

Jasinski, Peter. "Amazon in Fall River Reports Creating Double the Jobs It Promised." *South Coast Today*, 8 July 2019. https://www.southcoasttoday.com/news/20190708/amazon-in-fall-river-reports-creating-double-jobs-it-promised

Johansen, Rachel, Neal, Zachary, and Gasteyer, Stephen. 2015. "The View From a Broken Window: How Residents Make Sense of Neighborhood Disorder in Flint." *Urban Studies* 52 (16): 3054–3069.

Johnson, Michael P. 2005. "Spatial Decision Support for Assisted Housing Mobility Counseling." *Decision Support Systems* 41 (1): 296–312. https://doi.org/10.1016/j.dss.2004.08.013

Johnson, Michael P. 2006. "Single-Period Location Models for Subsidized Housing: Project-Based Subsidies." *Socio-Economic Planning Sciences* 40 (4): 249–274. https://doi.org/10.1016/j.seps.2004.11.001

Johnson, Michael P. 2007. "Planning Models for the Provision of Affordable Housing." *Environment and Planning B: Planning and Design* 34 (3): 501–523. https://doi.org/10.1068/b31165

Johnson, Michael P. 2011. "Housing and Community Development." In *Wiley Encyclopedia of Operations Research and Management Science*. New York: Wiley Online Library.

Johnson, Michael P. 2012. "Community-Based Operations Research: Introduction, Theory, and Applications." In *Community-Based Operations Research*. New York: Springer, 3–36.

Johnson, Michael P. 2012a. "Decision Models for Housing and Community Development," in A. Carswell (ed.), *The Encyclopedia of Housing*. Los Angeles: Sage.

Johnson, Michael P. 2015. "Data, Analytics and Community-Based Organizations: Transforming Data to Decisions for Community Development." *I/S: A Journal of Law and Policy for the Information Society* 11: 49–96.

Johnson, Michael P. 2011. "Housing and Community Development," in J. Cochran (ed.), *Wiley Encyclopedia of Operations Research and Management Science*. New York: Wiley.

Johnson, Michael P. 2015. "Researching What Matters With Community Members: Session Introduction," Data Day, Boston, 26 June 2015. https://works.bepress.com/michael_johnson/64

Johnson, Michael P. 2015a. "Data, Analytics and Community-Based Organizations: Transforming Data to Decisions for Community Development." *I/S: A Journal of Law and Policy for the Information Society*: Big Data Future Part Two 11: 49–96.

Johnson, Michael P. 2018a. "Community-Engaged Operations Research: Localized Interventions, Appropriate Methods, Social Impact." Presented at Massachusetts Institute of Technology, Operations Research Center, IAP Seminar, "Operations Research for Social Good," 29 January 2018. https://works.bepress.com/michael_johnson/96

Johnson, Michael P. 2018b. "Course Syllabus: HONORS 490 Mayor's Symposium: Housing in a Changing City." Boston: University of Massachusetts Boston. http://works.bepress.com/michael_johnson/97

Johnson, Michael P., and Chichirau, George. 2020. "Diversity, Equity and Inclusion in Operations Research and Analytics: A Research Agenda for Scholarship, Practice and Service." In Druehl and Elmaghraby (eds.), *Tutorials in Operations Research 2020: Pushing the Boundaries: Frontiers in Impactful OR/OM*

Research. Catonsville, MD: The Institute for Operations Research and the Management Sciences, 1–38. doi: 10.1287/educ.2020.0214.

Johnson, Michael P., Drew, Rachel Bogardus, Keisler, Jeffrey M., and Turcotte, David A. 2012. "What Is a Strategic Acquisition? Decision Modeling in Support of Foreclosed Housing Redevelopment." *Socio-Economic Planning Sciences* 46 (3): 194–204. https://doi.org/10.1016/j.seps.2012.05.002

Johnson, Michael P., and Hollander, Justin. 2014. *Baltimore Vacant Lot Redevelopment Project: Final Report*. With Rohman, Hanaa Abhdel, Bahirwani, Suveer, Ciurzak, Peter, Engel, Albert, Keeny, Kristine, Lambergs, Elza, Levine, Annie, Tu, Jingyu, Whiteman, Eliza, Hughes, Merritt, Lee, Hyun-Jung, and Usidame, Omonukola (Buki). Baltimore: City of Baltimore Department of Planning.

Johnson, Michael P., Hollander, Justin, and Hallulli, Alma. 2014. "Maintain, Demolish, Re-Purpose: Policy Design for Vacant Land Management Using Decision Models." *Cities* 40 (October): 151–162. https://doi.org/10.1016/j.cities.2013.05.005

Johnson, Michael P., Hollander, Justin B., and Davenport Whiteman, Eliza. 2015. "Data and Analytics for Neighborhood Development: Smart Shrinkage Decision Modeling in Baltimore, Maryland." In S. Geertman, J. Ferreira, R. Goodspeed, and J. Stillwell (eds.), *Planning Support Systems and Smart Cities*. Switzerland: Springer, 61–76.

Johnson, Michael P., Keisler, Jeffrey M., Solak, Senay, Turcotte, David A., Bayram, Armagan, and Drew, Rachel Bogardus. 2015. *Decision Science for Housing and Community Development: Localized and Evidence-Based Responses to Distressed Housing and Blighted Communities*. New York: John Wiley & Sons.

Johnson, Michael P., Ladd, Helen F., and Ludwig, Jens. 2002. "The Benefits and Costs of Residential Mobility Programmes for the Poor." *Housing Studies* 17 (1): 125–138. https://doi.org/10.1080/02673030120105947

Johnson, Michael P., and Midgley, Gerald. (eds.) 2018. "Community Operational Research: Innovations, Internationalization and Agenda-Setting Applications." *European Journal of Operational Research* 268 (3).

Johnson, Michael P., Midgley, Gerald, and Chichirau, George. 2018. "Emerging Trends and New Frontiers in Community Operational Research." *European Journal of Operational Research* 268 (3): 1178–1191. https://doi.org/10.1016/j.ejor.2017.11.032

Johnson, Michael P., Midgley, Gerald, Wright, Jason, and Chichirau, George. 2018. "Community Operational Research: Innovations, Internationalization and Agenda-Setting Applications." *European Journal of Operational Research* 268 (3): 761–770. https://doi.org/10.1016/j.ejor.2018.03.004

Jutraž, Anja, and Zupančič, Tadeja. 2015. "Virtual Worlds as Support Tools for Public Engagement in Urban Design." In S. Geertman, J. Ferreira, R. Goodspeed, and J. Stillwell (eds.), *Planning Support Systems and Smart Cities*. Cham, Swizerland: Springer, 391–408.

Karoub, Jeff. "After Detroit, Another City Ponders Bankruptcy." *KSL.com*, 8 July 2014. https://www.ksl.com/?nid=151&sid=30627642

Kaufman, Rachel. "Baltimore Anchor Institutions Work Together on Blight." *Next City*, 7 October 2016. https://nextcity.org/daily/entry/baltimore-anchor-institutions-blight

Kawachi, Ichiro, Subramanian, S. V., and Kim, Daniel. 2008. "Social Capital and Health," in I. Kawachi, S. V. Subramanian, and D. Kim (eds.), *Social Capital and Health*. New York: Springer, 1–26.

Keeney, Ralph L. 1992. *Value-Focused Thinking: A Path to Creative Decision Analysis*. Cambridge MA: Harvard University Press.

Keeney, Ralph L. 1996. "Value-Focused Thinking: Identifying Decision Opportunities and Creating Alternatives." *European Journal of Operational Research* 92 (3): 537–549. https://doi.org/10.1016/0377-2217(96)00004-5

Keeney, Ralph L. 2007. "Developing Objectives and Attributes." In *Advances in Decision Analysis: From Foundations to Applications*, 104–128. https://doi.org/10.1017/CBO9780511611308.008

Keisler, Jeffrey, Turcotte, David A., Drew, Rachel, and Johnson, Michael P. 2014. "Value-Focused Thinking for Community-Based Organizations: Objectives and Acceptance in Local Development." *EURO Journal on Decision Processes* 2 (3–4): 221–256. https://doi.org/10.1007/s40070-014-0032-y

Kim, Gunwoo. 2016. "The Public Value of Urban Vacant Land: Social Responses and Ecological Value." *Sustainability (Switzerland)* 8 (5): 486. https://doi.org/10.3390/su8050486

Kim, Joongsub, and Lerine Steenkamp, Annette. 2013. "Analysis of Smart City Models and the Four-Foci Taxonomy for Smart City Design." The Visibility of Research: Architectural Research Conference, 638–649.

Kinney, Rebecca J. 2016. *Beautiful Wasteland: The Rise of Detroit as America's Postindustrial Frontier*. Minneapolis: University of Minnesota Press.

Klosterman, Richard E. 1997. "Planning Support Systems: A New Perspective on Computer-Aided Planning." *Journal of Planning Education and Research* 17 (1): 45–54. https://doi.org/10.1177/0739456X9701700105

Klosterman, Richard E. 2001. "Planning Support Systems: A New Perspective on Computer-aided Planning." In R. K. Brail and R. E. Klosterman (eds.), *Planning Support Systems: Integrating GIS, Models and Visualization Tools*. Redlands, CA: Esri Press, 1–24.

Kollektiv Orangotango+ (Ed.). 2019. *This Is Not An Atlas: A Global Collection of Counter-Cartographies*. Bielefeld, Germany: Transcript-Verlag.

Kopp, John. "Business Insider Sees Evidence Piling Up for this Amazon HQ2 Site." *Philly Voice*, 30 March 2018.

Krivo, Lauren J., Peterson, Ruth D., and Kuhl, Danielle C. 2009. Segregation, Racial Structure, and Neighborhood Violent Crime. *American Journal of Sociology* 114 (6): 1765–1802.

Krohe, James, Jr. 2011. "The Incredible Shrinking City." *Planning* 77 (9): 10–15.

Kromer, John. 2002. "Vacant-Property Policy and Practice: Baltimore and Philadelphia." The Brookings Institution Center on Urban and Metropolitan Policy. October 2002. https://www.brookings.edu/research/vacant-property-policy-and-practice-baltimore-and-philadelphia

Krygier, John, and Wood, Denis. 2016. *Making Maps: A Visual Guide to Map Design for GIS*. New York: Guilford Press.

Kumar, Rajeev, Joshi, Ashwin H., Banka, Krishna K., and Rockett, Peter I. 2008. "Evolution of Hyperheuristics for the Biobjective 0/1 Knapsack Problem by Multiobjective Genetic Programming." In *Proceedings of the 10th Annual Conference on Genetic and Evolutionary Computation*, 1227–1234.

Kwartler, Michael, and Bernard, Robert N. 2001. "CommunityViz: An Integrated Planning Support System." In *Planning Support Systems Integrating Geographic Information Systems Models and Visualization Tools*, 285–308.

Kyem, Peter A. Kwaku. 2000. "Embedding GIS Applications into Resource Management and Planning Activities of Local and Indigenous Communities." *Journal of Planning Education and Research* 20 (2): 176–186. https://doi.org/10.1177/0739456X0002000204

Kyem, Peter A. Kwaku. 2004. "Of Intractable Conflicts and Participatory GIS Applications: The Search for Consensus amidst Competing Claims and Institutional Demands." *Annals of the Association of American Geographers* 94 (1): 37–57. https://doi.org/10.1111/j.1467-8306.2004.09401003.x

Lane, Marcus B. 2005. "Public Participation in Planning: An Intellectual History." *Australian Geographer* 36 (3): 283–299. https://doi.org/10.1080/00049180500325694

Langdon, Philip. 2005. "Eminent Domain Goes to Court." *Planning* 71 (4): 12–15.

Larson, Richard C., and Odoni, Amedeo R. *Urban Operations Research*, 2nd ed. Charlestown, MA: Dynamic Ideas, 2007.

Larson, Sandra. "Silo-Busting Data Analytics Help Mass. Cities Tackle Vacant Properties." *NextCity*, 14 October 2016. https://nextcity.org/daily/entry/blight-data-tools-mass-cities-vacant-properties

Leclerc, Philip D., McLay, Laura A., and Mayorga, Maria E. 2012. "Modeling Equity for Allocating Public Resources." In *International Series in Operations Research and Management Science*, 167: 97–118. New York: Springer. https://doi.org/10.1007/978-1-4614-0806-2_4

LeDuff, Charlie. "Riding Along With the Cops in Murdertown, U.S.A." *The New York Times*, 15 April 2011. https://www.nytimes.com/2011/04/17/magazine/mag-17YouRhere-t.html

Lee, David, Alvarez Felix, Jesus Ricardo, He, Shan, Offenhuber, Dietmar, and Ratti, Carlo. 2015. "CityEye: Real-Time Visual Dashboard for Managing Urban Services and Citizen Feedback Loops." In J. Ferreira and R. Goodspeed (eds.), *Proceedings of the 14th International Conference on Computers in Urban Planning and Urban Management: Planning Support Systems and Smart Cities*. Cambridge, MA: Massachusetts Institute of Technology.

Lefebvre, Henri. 1996. *Writings on Cities*. New York: Blackwell.

Liberatore, Matthew J., and Luo, Wenhong. 2010. "The Analytics Movement: Implications for Operations Research." *Interfaces* 40 (4): 313–324. https://doi.org/10.1287/inte.1100.0502

Lieb, Emily. 2010. *Row House City: Unbuilding Residential Baltimore, 1940–1980*. New York: Columbia University Press.

Lieske, Scott N., Martin, Kari, Grant, Ben, and Baldwin, Claudia. 2015. "Visualization Methods for Linking Scientific and Local Knowledge of Climate Change Impacts," in S. Geertman, J. Ferreira, R. Goodspeed, and J. C. H. Stillwell (eds.), *Planning Support Systems and Smart Cities*. New York: Springer, 373–389.

Lipsitz Flippin, Alexis. "Baltimore City Council Hears Testimony on 'Complete Streets' Bill." *Next City*, 26 April 2018. https://nextcity.org/daily/entry/baltimore-city-council-hears-testimony-on-complete-streets-bill

Logan, John R. 2013. "The Persistence of Segregation in the 21st Century Metropolis." *City Community* 12 (2).

Logan, John R., Xu, Zengwang, and Stults, Brian J. 2012. *Census Geography: Bridging Data for Census Tracts across Time*. Providence, RI: Spatial Structures in the Social Sciences, Brown University.

Logan, John R., and Molotch, Harvey L. 1987. *Urban Fortunes: The Political Economy of Place*. 20th anniversary edition. Berkeley, CA: University of California Press.

Logan, John R., and Stults, Brian J. 2011. "The Persistence of Segregation in the Metropolis: New Findings from the 2010 Census." *Census Brief prepared for Project US2010*.

Lucas, Kim. Personal conversation. Mayor's Office of New Urban Mechanics, City of Boston, June 22, 2018.

Lykes, M. Brinton, and Mallona, Amelia. 2008. "Towards Transformational Liberation: Participatory and Action Research and Praxis." In Peter Reason and Hilary Bradbury (eds.), *The SAGE Handbook of Action Research and Participative Inquiry and Practice*. Los Angeles: Sage, 107–120.

Malczewski, Jacek. 1999. *GIS and Multicriteria Decision Analysis*. New York: John Wiley & Sons.

Mallach, Alan. 2012. "Laying the Groundwork for Change: Demolition, Urban Strategy, and Policy Reform." Washington DC. https://www.brookings.edu/research/laying-the-groundwork-for-change-demolition-urban-strategy-and-policy-reform

Mallach, Alan, and Brachman, Lavea. 2013. *Regenerating America's Legacy Cities*. Cambridge, MA: Lincoln Institute of Land Policy.

Mallach, Alan. 2008. "Managing Neighborhood Change A Framework for Sustainable and Equitable Revitalization." Montclair, NJ. http://www.nhi.org/pdf/ManagingNeighborhoodChange.pdf

Mantaay, Juliana, and Ziegler, John. 2006. *GIS for the Urban Environment*. Redlands, CA: Esri Press.

Manville, Michael, and Kuhlmann, Daniel. 2016. "The Social and Fiscal Consequences of Urban Decline: Evidence from Large American Cities, 1980–2010." *Urban Affairs Review* 54 (3): 451–489.

Marine Planning Partnership for the North Pacific Coast. 2015. "North Coast Marine Plan." http://mappocean.org/wp-content/uploads/2016/07/Marine-Plan_NorthCoast_WebVer_20151207_corrected.pdf

Marsh, Michael T., and Schilling, David A. 1994. "Equity Measurement in Facility Location Analysis: A Review and Framework." *European Journal of Operational Research* 74 (1): 1–17. https://doi.org/10.1016/0377-2217(94)90200-3

Maryland Attorney General. n.d. "State Attorneys General Mortgage Servicing Settlement."

Massachusetts Institute for a New Commonwealth. 2007. *Massachusetts Gateway Cities: Lessons Learned and an Agenda for Renewal*. Boston: MassINC and The Brookings Institution.

MassINC "Taking Matters into Their Own Hands." *The Gateway Cities Journal*, 4 January 2018. https://massinc.org/2018/01/04/taking-matters-into-their-own-hands

MassINC. "Profile: City of Fall River." https://2gaiae1lifzt2tsfgr2vil6c-wpengine.netdna-ssl.com/wp-content/uploads/2015/09/Fall-River-profile.ashx_.pdf

MassINC. "Program Overview: About the Gateway Cities." 2012. https://massinc.org/our-work/policy-center/gateway-cities/about-the-gateway-cities

Matthews, Rick A. 1997. *What's Good for G.M . . . Deindustrialization and Crime in Four Michigan Cities, 1975–1983*. Kalamazoo, MI: Western Michigan University Press.

May, George S. 1965. *Michigan: A History of the Wolverine State*. Grand Rapids, MI: William B. Eerdmans Publishing Company.

Mayorga, Edwin. 2014. "Toward Digital, Critical, Participatory Action Research: Lessons from the #BarrioEdProj." *The Journal of Interactive Technology and Pedagogy* 5 (June). https://jitp.commons.gc.cuny.edu/toward-digital-critical-participatory-action-research

McAfee, Andrew, and Brynjolfsson, Erik. 2012. "Big Data: The Management Revolution." *Harvard Business Review* 90 (10): 4.

McCall, Michael K. 2003. "Seeking Good Governance in Participatory-GIS: A Review of Processes and Governance Dimensions in Applying GIS to Participatory Spatial Planning." *Habitat International* 27 (4): 549–573. https://doi.org/10.1016/S0197-3975(03)00005-5

McCall, Michael K. 2017. "Urban PGIS: PGIS, PPGIS, Participatory Mapping in the Urban Context Utilising Local Spatial Knowledge. A Bibliography." https://www.researchgate.net/publication/281100923_Urban_PGIS_PGIS_

PPGIS_Participatory_Mapping_in_the_Urban_Context_utilising_Local_Spatial_Knowledge_A_Bibliography

McCambridge, Ruth. 2017. "3 Nonprofits and a Resident Win Environmental Justice Suit for New Pipes in Flint." *Nonprofit Quarterly* (March). https://nonprofitquarterly.org/2017/03/29/3-nonprofits-resident-win-environmental-justice-suit-new-pipes-flint

McDonald, David. 2010. *Saving America's Cities: A Tried and Proven Plan to Revive Stagnant and Decaying Cities.* Bloomington, IN: AuthorHouse.

McLarty, Dustin, Davis, Nora, Gellers, Joshua, Nasrollahi, Nasrin, and Altenbernd, Erik. 2014. "Sisters in Sustainability: Municipal Partnerships for Social, Environmental, and Economic Growth." *Sustainability Science* 9 (3): 277–292. https://doi.org/10.1007/s11625-014-0248-6

Memarovic, Nemanja, Fels, Sidney, Anacleto, Junia, Calderon, Roberto, Gobbo, Federico, and Carroll, John M. 2014. "Rethinking Third Places: Contemporary Design With Technology." *The Journal of Community Informatics* 10 (3).

Meng, Lee Lik, and Tan, Thean Siew. 2002. "GIS for Plan-Making in Penang Island: The Road to Online Planning." *Online Planning Journal* 30: 27. http://www.onlineplanning.org

Metzger, Andy, and Young, Colin A. "South Coast rail service could begin in 2022." *The Boston Globe*, 19 February 2018. https://www.bostonglobe.com/metro/2018/02/19/south-coast-rail-service-could-begin/q7abXi5NItkkFqbNCVaTQN/story.html

Metzger, John T. 2000. "Planned Abandonment: The Neighborhood Life-Cycle Theory and National Urban Policy." *Housing Policy Debate* 11 (1): 7–40.

Midgley, Gerald, and Ochoa-Arias, Alejandro. 2004. *Community Operational Research: OR and Systems Thinking for Community Development.* New York: Kluwer Academic/Plenum Publishers.

Midgley, Gerald, and Ochoa-Arias, Alejandro. 2012. *Community Operational Research: OR and Systems Thinking for Community Development.* New York: Springer Science & Business Media.

Midgley, Gerald, Johnson, Michael P., and Chichirau, George. 2018. "What Is Community Operational Research?" *European Journal of Operational Research* 268 (3): 771–783. https://doi.org/10.1016/j.ejor.2017.08.014

Midgley, Gerald. 2000. *Systemic Intervention: Philosophy, Methodology, and Practice.* New York: Kluwer Academic/Plenum.

Miettinen, Kaisa M. 1998. *Nonlinear Multiobjective Optimization.* Boston: Kluwer Academic Publishers.

Mijs, Jonathan J. B. 2020. "5 Lessons from the Coronavirus about Inequality in America." *The Conversation*, April 27, 2020. https://theconversation.com/5-lessons-from-the-coronavirus-about-inequality-in-america-136024

Mingers, John. 2009. "Taming Hard Problems with Soft O.R." *Analytics.* http://analytics-magazine.org/operations-research-taming-hard-problems-with-soft-or

Mingers, John. 2011. "Soft OR Comes Of Age–But Not Everywhere!" *Omega* 39 (6): 729–741. https://doi.org/10.016/j.omega.2011.01.005

Minner, Jennifer S. 2015. "Recoding Embedded Assumptions: Adaptation of an Open Source Tool to Support Sustainability, Transparency and Participatory Governance," in S. Geertman, J. Ferreira, R. Goodspeed, and J. C. H. Stillwell (eds.), *Planning Support Systems and Smart Cities*. New York: Springer, 409–425.

Mirabella, Lorraine. "Slow Renovation of Baltimore's Harborplace May be Nearing an End." *The Baltimore Sun*, 5 April 2018. http://www.baltimoresun.com/business/real-estate/bs-bz-harborplace-renovations-20180403-story.html

Mitchell, Timothy. 2002. *Rule of Experts: Egypt, Techno-Politics, Modernity*. Berkeley: University of California Press.

Mohl, Bruce. "Double-Whammy for Gateway Cities." *Commonwealth Magazine*, 12 May 2016. https://commonwealthmagazine.org/economy/double-whammy-for-gateway-cities

Moore, Michael. "In Flint, Tough Times Last." *The Nation*, 6 June 1987.

Morckel, Victoria C. 2013. "Empty Neighborhoods: Using Constructs to Predict the Probability of Housing Abandonment." *Housing Policy Debate* 23 (3): 469–496. https://doi.org/10.1080/10511482.2013.788051

Morckel, Victoria. 2014. "The Four Components and Six Essential Pairs: A Framework for Neighbourhood Revitalization." *Planning Theory & Practice* 15 (2): 276–281.

Morckel, Victoria. 2015. "Community Gardens or Vacant Lots? Rethinking the Attractiveness and Seasonality of Green Land Uses in Distressed Neighborhoods." *Urban Forestry & Urban Greening* 14 (3): 714–721. https://doi.org/10.1016/j.ufug.2015.07.001

Morckel, Victoria C. 2017. Using Suitability Analysis to Prioritize Demolitions in a Legacy City. *Urban Geography* 38 (1): 90–111. https://doi.org/10.1080/02723638.2016.1147756

Morckel, Victoria C. 2017a. "Patronage and Access to a Legacy City Farmers' Market: A Case Study of the Relocation of the Flint, Michigan, Market." *Local Environment* 22 (10): 1268–1289.

Morckel, Victoria C. 2017b. "Using Suitability Analysis to Select and Prioritize Naturalization Efforts in Legacy Cities: An Example from Flint, Michigan." *Urban Forestry & Urban Greening* 27 (October): 343–351. https://doi.org/10.1016/j.ufug.2017.09.006

Morckel, Victoria C. 2018. "The Direct Economic Impact of the Flint, Michigan, Farmers' Market Relocation." *Community Development* 49 (2): 161–174.

Morckel, Victoria C., and Rybarczyk, Greg. 2015. "Improving Downtown in a Midsized Legacy City: Examining Responses to Potential Downtown Improvements in Flint, Michigan." *Community Development* 46 (4): 341–360.

Morckel, Victoria C., and Terzano, Kathryn. 2018. "Legacy City Residents' Lack of Trust in Their Governments: An Examination of Flint, Michigan Residents' Trust at the Height of the Water Crisis." *Journal of Urban Affairs* 41 (5): 585–601.

Moskowitz, Peter. 2017. *How to Kill A City: Gentrification, Inequality, and the Fight for the Neighborhood*. New York: Nation Books.

Neema, Meher Nigar, Maniruzzaman, Khandoker Md., and Ohgai, Akira. 2013. "Urban Greening Using an Intelligent Multi-Objective Location Modelling with Real Barriers: Towards a Sustainable City Planning." *Current Urban Studies* 01 (4): 75–86. https://doi.org/10.4236/cus.2013.14008

Németh, Jeremy, Hollander, Justin B., Whiteman, Eliza D., and Johnson, Michael P. 2018. Planning with Justice in Mind in a Shrinking Baltimore. *Journal of Urban Affairs: Special Issue: Promoting Social Justice and Equity in Shrinking Cities* 42 (3): 351–370.

Newkirk, Vann R. 2018. "A Year after Hurricane Maria, Puerto Rico Finally Knows How Many People Died." *The Atlantic*, 28 August 2018. https://www.theatlantic.com/politics/archive/2018/08/puerto-rico-death-toll-hurricane-maria/568822

Next City. 2014. "Building Resilience in Baltimore through Immigration." https://vimeo.com/99063923

New York Times. 2020. "Four Months after First Case, U.S. Death Toll Passes 100,000." https://www.nytimes.com/2020/05/27/us/coronavirus-live-news-updates.html

New York Times. 2020a. "Coronavirus Map: Tracking the Global Outbreak." https://www.nytimes.com/interactive/2020/world/coronavirus-maps.html. Retrieved December 31, 2020.

New York Times. 2020b. "Coronavirus in the U.S.: Latest Map and Case Count." https://www.nytimes.com/interactive/2020/us/coronavirus-us-cases.html. Retrieved December 31, 2020.

Noth, Pierre-René. "Past Times: Life and Strife in the Mills." *Rome News-Tribune*, August 2008.

O'Brien, Daniel T. 2018. *The Urban Commons: Leveraging Digital Data and Technology to Better Understand and Manage the Maintenance of City Neighborhoods*. Cambridge, MA: Harvard University Press.

O'Hare, Michael, Bacow, Lawrence S., and Sanderson, Debra. 1983. *Facility Siting and Public Opposition*. New York: Van Nostrand Reinhold.

Offenhuber, Dietmar, and Ratti, Carlo. 2014. *Decoding the City: Urbanism in the Age of Big Data*. Basel, Switzerland: Birkhauser Verlag AG.

Oswalt, Philipp. 2006. *Shrinking Cities, Vol. 1. International Research*. Ostfildern-Ruit, Germany: Hatje Cantz.

Pamuk, Ayse. 2006. *Mapping Global Cities: GIS Methods in Urban Analysis*. Redlands, CA: Esri Press.

Pánek, Jiří. 2016. "From Mental Maps to GeoParticipation." *The Cartographic Journal* 53 (4): 300–307. https://doi.org/10.1080/00087041.2016.1243862

Pant, Mandakini. 2008. "Participatory Research." In *Participatory Adult Learning and Information Networking*. Germany: UNESCO Institute for Lifelong Learning.

Penna, Robert Mark. 2011. *The Nonprofit Outcomes Toolbox: A Complete Guide to Program Effectiveness, Performance Measurement, and Results*. Vol. 1. New York: John Wiley & Sons.

Perez, Teresita, and Rushing, Reece. 2007. "The CitiStat Model: How Data-Driven Government Can Increase Efficiency and Effectiveness." Washington, DC: *Center for American Progress*.

Perry Abello, Oscar. "How Baltimore's Promising Vacant Properties Program Is Working." *Next City*, 2 November 2016. https://nextcity.org/daily/entry/baltimore-vacant-properties-program-working

Pettit, Kathryn L. S, and Kingsley, G. Thomas. 2011. "Framework: The New Potential for Data in Managing Neighborhood Change." In *Putting Data to Work: Data-Driven Approaches to Strengthening Neighborhoods*, in Matt Lambert and Jane Humphreys (eds.). Washington, DC: Board of Governors of the Federal Reserve System. http://www.federalreserve.gov/communitydev/files/data-driven-publication-20111212.pdf

Phillips, Arthur Sherman. 1946. *The Phillips History of Fall River*. Fall River, MA: Dover Press.

Picchi, Aimee. "12 Major American Cities That Are Shrinking." *Moneywatch, CBS News*, 22 June 2017. https://www.cbsnews.com/media/12-major-american-cities-that-are-shrinking

Pietila, Antero. 2010. *Not In My Neighborhood: How Bigotry Shaped a Great American City*. Chicago: Ivan R. Dee.

Piracha, Awais. 2015. "eDevelopment–Assessment as 'Smart ePlanning' for New South Wales (NSW) Australia." In J. Ferreira and R. Goodspeed (eds.), *Proceedings of the 14th International Conference on Computers in Urban Planning and Urban Management: Planning Support Systems and Smart Cities*. Cambridge, MA: Massachusetts Institute of Technology.

Pollock, Stephen M., Rothkopf, Michael H., and Barnett, Arnold. 1994. *Handbooks in Operations Research and Management Science, Volume 6: Operations Research and the Public Sector*. Amsterdam: North-Holland.

Popescu, Ioana, Duffy, Erin, Mendelsohn, Joshua, and Escarce, José J. 2018. "Racial Residential Segregation, Socioeconomic Disparities, and the White-Black Survival Gap." *PLoS ONE* 13 (2).

Poplin, Alenka. 2012. "Web-Based PPGIS for Wilhelmsburg, Germany: An Integration of Interactive GIS-Based Maps with an Online Questionnaire." *URISA Journal* 24 (2): 75.

Popper, Deborah E., and Popper, Frank J. 2002. "Small Can Be Beautiful: Coming to Terms with Decline." *Planning* 68 (7): 20–23.

Power, Garrett. 1983. "Apartheid Baltimore Style." *Maryland Law Review* 42: 289–329.

Pruett, Natalie. 2015. *Beyond Blight: City of Flint Comprehensive Blight Elimination Framework*. Flint, MI: City of Flint. https://www.dropbox.com/s/f7i0vw00g-

2p9a9d/Beyond%20Blight%20Framework%20Final%20Adopted%202015. pdf?dl=0

The Public Policy Center at UMass Dartmouth. 2016. "Towards an Evidence-Based Housing Policy in Fall River, Massachusetts." Prepared by M. P. McCarthy, J. D. Wright, M. D. Goodman, and D. R. Borges.

Radil, Steven M., and Jiao, Junfeng. 2016. "Public Participatory GIS and the Geography of Inclusion." *The Professional Geographer* 68 (2): 202–210. https:// doi.org/10.1080/00330124.2015.1054750

Raghothama, Jayanth, and Meijer, Sebastiaan. 2015. "Gaming, Urban Planning and Transportation Design Process." In *Lecture Notes in Geoinformation and Cartography*, 213: 297–312. https://doi.org/10.1007/978-3-319-18368-8_16

Ransome, Keisha T. 2007. *Housing Abandonment and Vacancy in Baltimore City*. Baltimore: Morgan State University.

Raymer, Marjory. "Property Values on Rise in Every Genesee County Community." *FlintSide*, 13 March 2017. https://www.flintside.com/features/Genesee-County-property-values-up-in-all-communities.aspx

Real Estate Research Corporation. 1975. *The Dynamics of Neighborhood Change*. Washington, DC: U.S. Department of Housing and Urban Development, Office of Policy Development and Research.

The Reinvestment Fund. 2014. "Market Value Analysis." https://www.reinvestment.com/policy-solutions/market-value-analysis

Reinwald, Florian, Berger, Martin, Stoik, Christop, Platzer, Mario, and Damyanovic, Doris. 2014. "Augmented Reality at the Service of Participatory Urban Planning and Community Informatics–A Case study from Vienna." *The Journal of Community Informatics* 10 (3).

ReVelle, Charles. 1987. "Urban Public Facility Location." *Handbook of Regional and Urban Economics* 11: 1053–1096.

Robert Wood Johnson Foundation. 2008."We Are Where We Live: How Neighborhood Disorder and Crime Impact Physical Activity, Weight and Racial Disparities." Prepared by Mary Nakashian. Princeton, NJ. https://www.rwjf.org/en/library/research/2008/10/we-are-where-we-live.html

Robinson, Jonnell A., Block, Daniel, and Rees, Amanda. 2017. "Community Geography: Addressing Barriers in Public Participation GIS." *Cartographic Journal* 54 (1): 5–13. https://doi.org/10.1080/00087041.2016.1244322

Rocheleau, Matt. "How Rich (or Not) is Your Community?" *The Boston Globe*, 18 December 2015. https://www.bostonglobe.com/metro/2015/12/18/town-town-look-income-massachusetts/cFBfhWvbzEDp5tWUSfIBVJ/story.html

Role of the Lending Industry in the Subprime Mortgage Crisis: Hearing before the Subcommittee on Commercial and Administrative Law, House Judiciary Committee, 111th Cong. 2009.

Rosenblatt, Peter. 2011. *The Renaissance Comes to the Projects: Public Housing, Urban Redevelopment, and Racial Inequality in Baltimore*. Baltimore, MD: Johns Hopkins University Press.

Rosenhead, Jonathan, and Mingers, John. 2001. *Rational Analysis for a Problematic World Revisited: Problem Structuring Methods for Complexity, Uncertainty and Conflict*. Chichester, UK: Wiley Chichester.

Rothstein, Richard. 2017. *The Color of Law: A Forgotten History of How Our Government Segregated America*. New York: Liveright Publishing.

Rust, Edgar. 1975. "No Growth: Impacts on Metropolitan Areas." Lanham, MA: Lexington Books.

Ryan, Brent D. 2012. *Design after Decline: How America Rebuilds Shrinking Cities*. Philadelphia: University of Pennsylvania Press.

Rydin, Yvonne. 2007. Re-Examining the Role of Knowledge within Planning Theory. *Planning Theory* 6 (1): 52–68. https://doi.org/10.1177/1473095207075161

Salzman, Avi, and Mansnerus, Laura. "For Homeowners, Frustration and Anger at Court Ruling." *The New York Times*, 24 June 2005. https://www.nytimes.com/2005/06/24/us/for-homeowners-frustration-and-anger-at-court-ruling.html

Sassen, Saskia. 1991. *The Global City: New York, London, Tokyo*. Princeton, NJ: Princeton University Press.

Saaty, Thomas L. 1980. *The Analytic Hierarchy Process*. New York: McGraw-Hill.

Saunders, Tom, and Baeck, Peter. 2015. *Rethinking Smart Cities from the Ground Up*. London: Nesta.

Sayre, Katherine. "New Orleans Home Prices Up 46 Percent Since Hurricane Katrina; Suburbs More Modest." *The Times-Picayune*, 11 August 2015. https://www.nola.com/news/business/article_ee3ea6d4-4859-59d9-a074-a03c122e192f.html

Schachterle, Stephen E., Bishai, David, Shields, Wendy, Stepnitz, Rebecca, and Gielen, Andrea C. 2012. "Proximity to Vacant Buildings is Associated with Increased Fire Risk in Baltimore, Maryland, Homes." *Injury Prevention* 18 (2): 98–102.

Scharfenberg, David. 2018. "Computers Can Solve Your Problem. You May Not like the Answer." *The Boston Globe*. September 21, 2018. https://apps.bostonglobe.com/ideas/graphics/2018/09/equity-machine

Schilling, Joseph, and Logan, Jonathan. 2008. "Greening the Rust Belt: A Green Infrastructure Model for Right Sizing America's Shrinking Cities." *Journal of the American Planning Association* 74 (4): 451–466.

Schindler, Seth. 2014. "Understanding Urban Processes in Flint, Michigan: Approaching Subaltern Urbanism Inductively." *International Journal of Urban and Regional Research* 38 (3): 791–804.

Schlosberg, David, and Rinfret, Sara. 2008. "Ecological Modernisation, American Style." *Environmental Politics: Special Issue: Environmentalism in the United States: Changing Conceptions of Activism* 17: 254–275.

Schmidt, Deanna H. 2011. "Urban Triage: Saving the Savable Neighbourhoods in Milwaukee." *Planning Perspectives* 26 (4): 569–589. https://doi.org/10.10 80/02665433.2011.601609

Schuck, Amie M. 2015. "Prevalence and Predictors of Surveillance Cameras in Law Enforcement: The Importance of Stakeholders and Community Factors." *Criminal Justice Policy Review* 28: 41–60.

Schwartz, Terry. "PD&R Quarterly Briefing: Challenge and Opportunity of Vacancy," U.S. Department of Housing and Urban Development, 10 April 2014. https://www.youtube.com/watch?v=FiETZZf-UR8&feature=youtu.be

SeaSketch. 2018. Home Page. Seattle. *Tableau Software* 28. https://www.seasketch.org/home.html

Sefair, Jorge A., Molano, Adriana, Medaglia, Andrés L., and Sarmiento, Olga L. 2012. "Locating Neighborhood Parks with a Lexicographic Multiobjective Optimization Method." In *International Series in Operations Research and Management Science*, 167: 143–171. https://doi.org/10.1007/978-1-4614-0806-2_6

Semuels, Alana. "Good School, Rich School; Bad School, Poor School." *The Atlantic*, 25 August 2016. https://www.theatlantic.com/business/archive/2016/08/property-taxes-and-unequal-schools/497333

Sharrow, Ryan. 2018. "Baltimore Puts $10M Toward Vacants to Value Program." *Baltimore Business Journal*, 18 September 2018. http://www.bizjournals.com/baltimore/blog/real-estate/2013/09/baltimore-vacants-to-value-program.html

Shepard, Mark. 2011. *Sentient City: Ubiquitous Computing, Architecture, and the Future of Urban Space*. Cambridge, MA: MIT Press.

Shields, Rob. 2013. "Lefebvre and the Right to the Open City?" *Space and Culture* 16 (3): 345–348.

Sieber, Renee. 2006. "Public Participation Geographic Information Systems: A Literature Review and Framework." *Annals of the Association of American Geographers* 96 (3): 491–507. https://doi.org/10.1111/j.1467-8306.2006.007 02.x

Siefer, Ted. "Fall River's Lightning Rod." *Commonwealth Magazine*, 10 April 2018. https://commonwealthmagazine.org/politics/fall-rivers-lightning-rod

Silver, Christopher. 1984. *Twentieth-Century Richmond: Planning, Politics, and Race*. Knoxville: University of Tennessee Press.

Silverman, Robert Mark, Patterson, Kelly L., Yin, Li, Ranahan, Molly, and Wu, Laiyun. 2016. *Affordable Housing in US Shrinking Cities: From Neighborhoods of Despair to Neighborhoods of Opportunity?* Chicago: University of Chicago Press.

Singleton, Alex David, Spielman, Seth E., and Folch, David C. 2018. *Urban Analytics*. Los Angeles: Sage.

Smiley, Kevin T. 2020. "The Urban Commons: How Data and Technology Can Rebuild Our Communities." *Contemporary Sociology: A Journal of Reviews* 49. https://doi.org/10.1177/0094306119889962bb

Smith, Sandy. "Blight-Fighting Tactic Found to Double Nearby Real Estate Values." *Next City*. 5 October 2016. https://nextcity.org/daily/entry/blight-fighting-tactic-found-to-double-nearby-real-estate-values

Staffans, Aija, and Horelli, Liisa. 2014. "Expanded Urban Planning as a Vehicle for Understanding and Shaping Smart, Liveable Cities." *The Journal of Community Informatics: Special Issue: Community Informatics and Urban Planning* 10 (3). http://www.ci-journal.net/index.php/ciej/article/view/1171

Stanley, Jenn. "Another Ex-Mayor Weighs In on Baltimore." *Next City*, 5 June 2015. https://nextcity.org/daily/entry/former-baltimore-mayors-response-freddie-gray

Steinitz, Carl. 2012. *A Framework for Geodesign: Changing Geography by Design*. Redlands, CA: Esri Press.

Steinitz, Carl. 2016. "On Change and Geodesign." *Landscape and Urban Planning* 156: 23–25.

Steinitz, Carl, and Pinheiro, Rafael L. 2018. Geodesign and the Future of Landscape and Urban Planning. *Disegnarecon* 11 (20). https://doi.org/10.20365/disegnarecon.21.2018.a

Steinmann, Renate, Krek, Alenka, and Blaschke, Thomas. 2004. "Analysis of Online Public Participatory GIS Applications with Respect to the Differences between the US and Europe." In *Proceedings of Urban Data Management Symposium*, 4: 27–29.

Sterbenz, Christina, and Fuchs, Erin. "How Flint, Michigan Became the Most Dangerous City in America." *Business Insider*, 16 June 2013. https://www.businessinsider.com/why-is-flint-michigan-dangerous-2013-6

Stoecker, Randy. 2007. "The Research Practices and Needs of Non-Profit Organizations in an Urban Center." *Journal of Sociology and Social Welfare* 34 (4): 97–119.

Stohr, Kate. "Shrinking City Syndrome." *The New York Times*, 5 February 2004. https://www.nytimes.com/2004/02/05/garden/shrinking-city-syndrome.html

Stokey, Edith, and Zeckhauser, Richard. 1978. *A Primer for Policy Analysis*. New York & London: W. W. Norton.

Stone, Clarence, Stoker, Robert, and Worgs, Donn. 2008. "Neighborhood Inequality and Revitalization: An Exploration of Five Themes through the Baltimore Case." Conference Papers–American Political Science Association, 1–47.

Stone, Deborah. 2011. *Policy Paradox: The Art of Political Decision Making*, 3rd ed. New York: W. W. Norton.

Stone, Melissa M., and Cutcher-Gershenfeld, Susan. 2002. "Challenges of Measuring Performance in Nonprofit Organizations." In *Measuring the Impact of the Nonprofit Sector*, New York: Kluwer, 33–57. https://doi.org/10.1007/978-1-4615-0533-4_3

Sugrue, Thomas J. 2015. *The Origins of the Urban Crisis: Race and Inequality in Postwar Detroit*. Revised edition. Princeton, NJ: Princeton University Press.

Swope, Christopher. "Smart Decline." *Governing Magazine*, November 2006. https://www.governing.com/mag/November-2006.html

Tableau Software. 2013. "What's the Big Deal about Big Data?" http://www.tableausoftware.com/learn/whitepapers/big-deal-about-big-data

Teaford, Jon C. 2000. "Urban Renewal and Its Aftermath." *Housing Policy Debate* 11 (2): 443–465.

Teixeira, Samantha. 2016. "Beyond Broken Windows: Youth Perspectives on Housing Abandonment and Its Impact on Individual and Community Well-Being." *Child Indicators Research* 9 (3): 581–607. https://doi.org/10.1007/s12187-015-9327-1

TheClassroom.com. 2019. "What Are the Seven Regions in the United States?" *TheClassroom*. https://www.theclassroom.com/seven-regions-united-states-7694052.html

Thomas, Kelsey E. "Baltimore Gets $700 Million Blight-Fighting Plan." *Next City*, 6 January 2016. https://nextcity.org/daily/entry/baltimore-blight-fighting-plan-demolish-rowhouses

Timmermans, Harry (Ed.). 1998. Decision Support Systems in Urban Planning. London: E & FN SPON.

Tisma, Alexandra, De Weerdt, Mathjis M., Van Riemsdijk, Birna, Warnier, Martijn, and Van Der Velde, René. 2015. "Smart Phones for a Smart City: Requirements for Context Aware Mobile Application for Landscape and Urban Planning." In *CUPUM 2015—14th International Conference on Computers in Urban Planning and Urban Management*. MIT. Cambridge, Massachusetts.

Todd, Michael. "Reflections of an Activist Scholar: Henry Louis Taylor, Jr." *Social Science Space*, 8 May 2018. https://www.socialsciencespace.com/2018/05/reflections-of-an-activist-scholar-henry-louis-taylor-jr

Torre, María Elena. 2009. "Participatory Action Research and Critical Race Theory: Fueling Spaces for Nos-otras to Research." *Urban Review* 41: 106–120.

Tortorello, Michael. "Finding the Potential in Vacant Lots." *New York Times*, 3 August 2011. https://www.nytimes.com/2011/08/04/garden/finding-the-potential-in-vacant-lots-in-the-garden.html

Townsend, Anthony M. 2013. *Smart Cities: Big Data, Civic Hackers, and the Quest for a New Utopia*. New York: W. W. Norton.

Troustine, Jessica. 2018. *Segregation by Design: Local Politics and Inequality in American Cities*. New York: Cambridge University Press.

U.S. Census Bureau. 2010. *American Community Survey 2010 5-Year Estimates*. www.socialexplorer.com

U.S. Census Bureau. 2013. "Census Regions and Divisions of the United States." *Geography Division*. http://www2.census.gov/geo/pdfs/maps-data/maps/reference/us_regdiv.pdf

U.S. Census Bureau. 2015. American Community Survey. American Community Survey 1-Year Estimates, Table DP04 [housing vacancy]. Generated by George Chichirau using American FactFinder. http://factfinder2.census.gov

U.S. Census Bureau. 2016. *American Community Survey 2016 5-Year Estimates.* www.socialexplorer.com
U.S. Census Bureau. 2016a. *American FactFinder: Population and Housing Characteristics.* Generated by Justin Hollander. https://factfinder.census.gov/faces/nav/jsf/pages/index.xhtml
U.S. Census Bureau. 2018. "Income and Poverty in the United States: 2017."
U.S. Census Bureau. *Census 1970.* www.socialexplorer.com
U.S. Census Bureau. *Census 1980.* www.socialexplorer.com
U.S. Census Bureau. *Census 1990.* www.socialexplorer.com
U.S. Census Bureau. *Census 2000.* www.socialexplorer.com
U.S. Census Bureau. *Census 2010.* www.socialexplorer.com
U.S. Census Bureau. 2000. Census, table H004 [housing vacancy]. Generated by George Chichirau using American FactFinder. http://factfinder2.census.gov
U.S. Department of Housing and Urban Development. 2008. "American Housing Survey: Data Users' Frequently Asked Questions." Prepared by David A. Vandenbroucke. https://www.huduser.gov/portal/datasets/ahs/AHS_%20FAQ_9-9-08.pdf
U.S. Department of Housing and Urban Development. 2014. "Temporary Urbanism: Alternative Approaches to Vacant Land." https://www.huduser.gov/portal/periodicals/em/winter14/highlight4.html
U.S. Federal Home Loan Bank Board. 1940. *Waverly: A Study in Neighborhood Conservation.* Washington, DC: Federal Home Loan Bank Board.
United States Conference of Mayors. 2006. *Combating Problems of Vacant and Abandoned Properties: Best Practices in 27 Cities.* https://community-wealth.org/content/combating-problems-vacant-and-abandoned-properties-best-practices-27-cities
Vale, Lawrence J., and Campanella, Thomas J. 2005. *The Resilient City: How Modern Cities Recover from Disaster.* New York: Oxford University Press.
Verplanke, Jeroen, McCall, Michael K., Uberhuaga, Claudia, Rambaldi, Giacomo, and Haklay, Muki. 2016. "A Shared Perspective for PGIS and VGI." *Cartographic Journal* 53 (4): 308–317. https://doi.org/10.1080/00087041.2016.1227552
Vicino, Thomas. 2008. *Transforming Race and Class in Suburbia: Decline in Metropolitan Baltimore.* New York: Palgrave Macmillan.
Wallace, Nicole. 2014. "Nonprofits Are Taking a Wide-Eyed Look at What Data Could Do." *The Chronicle of Philanthropy.* https://netsquared.org/blog/data-philanthropy-data-visualization-tips-and-data-revolution
Wallace, R. 1990. "Homelessness, Contagious Destruction of Housing, and Municipal Service Cuts in New York City: 2. Dynamics of a Housing Famine." *Environment & Planning A* 22 (1): 5–15. https://doi.org/10.1068/a220005

Wang, Yingli, Touboulic, Anne, and O'Neill, Martin. 2018. "An Exploration of Solutions for Improving Access to Affordable Fresh Food with Disadvantaged Welsh Communities." *European Journal of Operational Research* 268 (3): 1021–1039. https://doi.org/10.1016/j.ejor.2017.11.065

Weaver, Russell, Bagchi-Sen, Sharmistha, Knight, Jason, and Frazier, Amy E. 2017. *Shrinking Cities: Understanding Urban Decline in the United States*. Oxon, UK: Routledge.

Wiechmann, Thorsten. 2008. "Errors Expected—Aligning Urban Strategy with Demographic Uncertainty in Shrinking Cities." *International Planning Studies* 13 (4): 431–446.

Wieckowski, Ania G. 2010. Back to the City. *Harvard Business Review* 88 (5): 25–35.

Wiig, Alan. 2015. "The Empty Rhetoric of the Smart City: From Digital Inclusion to Economic Promotion in Philadelphia." *Urban Geography: Special Feature: Thinking the 'Smart City': Power, Politics, and Networked Urbanism* 37 (4): 535–553.

Wijman, Tom. "Mobile Revenues Account for More Than 50% of the Global Games Market as It Reaches $137.9 Billion in 2018." *Newzoo*, 30 April 2018. https://newzoo.com/insights/articles/global-games-market-reaches-137-9-billion-in-2018-mobile-games-take-half

Williams, Gary, and Holt, Steve. "No Going Back to Normal: Rebuilding Baltimore City after the Uprising." *Nonprofit Quarterly*, 31 July 2017. https://nonprofitquarterly.org/2017/07/31/no-going-back-normal-rebuilding-baltimore-city-u

Williams, Timothy. "Blighted Cities Prefer Razing to Rebuilding." *New York Times*, 12 November 2013. https://www.nytimes.com/2013/11/12/us/blighted-cities-prefer-razing-to-rebuilding.html

Williamson, Wayne, and Ruming, Kristian. 2015. "Who's Talking, Who's Listening: Exploring Social Media Use by Community Groups Using Social Network Analysis." In *CUPUM 2015—14th International Conference on Computers in Urban Planning and Urban Management*.

Wilson, Alexander, Tewdwr-Jones, Mark, and Comber, Rob. 2019. "Urban Planning, Public Participation and Digital Technology: App Development as a Method of Generating Citizen Involvement in Local Planning Processes." *Environment and Planning B: Urban Analytics and City Science* 46 (2): 286–302. https://doi.org/10.1177/2399808317712515

Wilson, William Julius, and Taub, Richard P. 2007. *There Goes the Neighborhood: Racial, Ethnic, and Class Tensions in Four Chicago Neighborhoods and Their Meaning for America*. New York: Vintage.

Winthrop, Bob, and Herr, Rebecca. 2009. "Determining the CO$T of Vacancies in Baltimore." *Government Finance Review* 25 (3): 38–42.

Wolff, Manuel. 2010. "Urban Shrinkage in Europe: Benefits and Limits of an Indicator-Based Analysis." *Working Paper*. http://www.shrinkingcities.eu/uploads/media/Wolff_2010_WP_Shrining_Cities_in_Europe.pdf

Wolfram. Alpha 2018. http://www.wolframalpha.com

Wright, Jeffrey, Revelle, Charles, and Cohon, Jared. 1983. "A Multiobjective Integer Programming Model for the Land Acquisition Problem." *Regional Science and Urban Economics* 13 (1): 31–53. https://doi.org/10.1016/0166-0462(83)90004-2

Wyatt, Ray. 1999. *Computer Aided Policymaking: Lessons from Strategic Planning*. New York: Routledge.

Yin, Robert K. 2018. *Case Study Research and Applications: Design and Methods*, 6th ed. Los Angeles: Sage.

Young, Gordon. "The Incredible Shrinking American City." *Slate*, 16 July 2010. http://www.slate.com/articles/news_and_politics/dispatches/2010/07/the_incredible_shrinking_american_city.html

Zhao, Jianfeng, and Coleman, David J. 2007. "An Empirical Assessment of a Web-Based PPGIS Prototype." In *URISA Student Papers*, 1–12. Citeseer. https://doi.org/10.1.1.134.2531

Zhong, Qing, Karner, Alex, Kuby, Michael, and Golub, Aaron. 2017. "A Multiobjective Optimization Model for Locating Affordable Housing Investments while Maximizing Accessibility to Jobs by Public Transportation. *Environment and Planning B: Urban Analytics and City Science* 46 (3): 490–510.

Zillow. 2019. "Flint Home Prices & Values." https://www.zillow.com/flint-mi/home-values

About the Authors

Michael P. Johnson is professor and chair in the Department of Public Policy and Public Affairs at University of Massachusetts Boston. Dr. Johnson's research interests lie in data analytics and management science for housing, community development, nonprofit service delivery, and climate change response. He is the author, with colleagues, of *Decision Science for Housing and Community Development: Localized and Evidence-Based Responses to Distressed Housing and Blighted Communities* (2016), lead editor of *INFORMS Editor's Cut: Diversity and Inclusion: Analytics for Social Impact, Volume 13* (2019), and editor of *Community-Based Operations Research: Decision Modeling for Local Impact and Diverse Populations* (2012).

Justin B. Hollander is a professor in the Department of Urban and Environmental Policy and Planning at Tufts University. His research and teaching is in the areas of shrinking cities, big data, brownfields, and the intersection between cognitive science and the design of cities. He is the author of numerous books on urban planning and design, including *Polluted, and Dangerous: America's Worst Abandoned Properties and What Can Be Done About Them* (2009), *Principles of Brownfield Regeneration: Cleanup, Design, and Reuse of Derelict Land* with Niall Kirkwood and Julia Gold (2010), *Sunburnt Cities: The Great Recession, Depopulation and Urban Planning in the American Sunbelt* (2011), *Cognitive Architecture Designing for How We Respond to the Built Environment* (with Ann Sussman, 2015), *A Research Agenda for Shrinking Cities* (2018), and *Urban Experience and Design: Contemporary Perspectives on Improving the Public Realm* (with Ann Sussman, 2020). Hollander has collaborated with Michael Johnson on topics at the intersection of urban planning, public policy, and decision sciences for nearly a decade.

Eliza Whiteman Kinsey is an associate research scientist in the Department of Epidemiology at Columbia University's Mailman School of Public Health. Dr. Kinsey's research examines the relationships among the built environment, food insecurity, and urban health disparities. She uses a mixed-methods approach to explore spatiotemporal dynamics of food and health across the urban planning, public health, and social welfare disciplines. Dr. Kinsey earned her PhD in City and Regional Planning, as well as a Master of Public Health, from the University of Pennsylvania. She also received an MA in Urban Planning and an MS in Nutrition Policy from Tufts University. Her master's thesis, on decision modeling in response to decline and distress in Baltimore, formed an important contribution to chapter 5. She also conducted many interviews used in chapter 3.

George Chichirau is a doctoral candidate in the Public Policy PhD program at University of Massachusetts Boston. His research interests revolve around how to best integrate environmental sustainability, social justice, and economic efficiency, with a focus on public transit policy and urban housing development. He served as editorial assistant with Michael Johnson for a special issue of the *European Journal of Operational Research* on community operational research, which appeared in 2018. Chichirau assisted in a redesign of the book project and has contributed original text to chapters 1 and 2.

Charla Burnett is a doctoral candidate in the Global Governance and Human Security PhD program at University of Massachusetts Boston. Her research explores public participation in planning and how technology can be used to strengthen good governance. Using a human security approach, she helps develop public planning tools, such as geographic information systems and virtual and augmented reality, and creates public participatory processes that builds consensus around socioeconomic justice. She is a community-based Planning Fellow at the Marine Science Institute where she is currently assisting environmental scientists and engineers in creating SeaSketch 2.0, a web-based application for planning marine protection sites. Burnett's work has been an inspiration for chapter 6, and some material in that chapter draws from her current dissertation research.

Index

Symbols
"Terf" virtual world, 43, 122
1968 Federal Housing Act, 93
311 System, 42
@Stake, 47, 123

A
Alternative-focused thinking, 158
Alternatives, 43, 56, 117, 128–132, 134, 158–159, 162, 192–194, 196–197, 209
Amazon, 5, 114
Analytics. *See* Data analytics; Decision science; Operations research
 Analytic Hierarchy Process, 192
 Community data analytics, 7, 50–51, 124, 184, 204
 Community-based analytics, 6. *See also* Community data analytics
 Community-based data analytics, 187
 Data analytics, 3, 7, 27, 29–30, 40, 46, 50–51, 61, 117, 124–127, 135, 145, 183–184, 187–188, 204, 208
 Decision analytics, 6, 16, 18, 30, 52, 126, 129–130, 132–133, 172, 175, 178, 184, 208, 210. *See also* Decision science
 Descriptive analytics, 50, 126, 133
 Predictive analytics, 50, 122, 126, 134. *See also* Prescriptive decision modeling
 Prescriptive analytics, 50, 126, 134, 165, 215
 See also Qualitative analysis
 Urban analytics, 6
ArcGIS, 52
Attributes, 15, 49, 78, 131–132, 158, 188, 192–193, 196–197, 202, 204, 209
Augmented reality, 23, 43, 192

B
Baltimore, MD, 1, 4, 8–9, 12–14, 16–17, 19, 21, 22, 29–31, 63, 65, 66, 67–69, 84–103, 109, 116–119, 124–125, 127, 135–136, 139–140, 145–148, 150–152, 154, 160, 162–163, 165–168, 170–176, 178, 182–183, 190, 193, 208, 212, 215–217
 2009 Baltimore Sustainability Plan, 96
 Adopt-a-Lot Program, 96
 Baltimore City Department of Planning, 97, 147–148
 Baltimore City Planning Commission, 86, 96

Baltimore, MD *(continued)*
  Baltimore Food Policy Initiative, 96–97
  Baltimore Sustainability Plan, 96–97
  Dollar House Program, 93
  Growing Green, 96, 147, 176
  Housing Authority of Baltimore City, 147
  Inner Harbor, 90, 94–95, 102
  Neighborhood Garden Committee, 96. *See also* Adopt-a-Lot Program
  Office of Sustainability, 96, 146–147, 174, 179
  Oliver neighborhood, 101, 152, 154
  PlanBaltimore!, 92, 98
  Power in Dirt Program, 97
  Project 5000, 93
  Project C.O.R.E., 94
  Rehab Express, 93
  Targeted Enforcement Toward Visible Outcomes (TEVO), 94
  Vacants to Value (V2V), 96–100, 102, 146, 180
Better Reykjavik, 44, 123, 192, 204
Bioretention areas, 137
Black Lives Matter, 13. *See also* Movement for Black Lives
Blight, 4, 6–8, 9, 10, 13, 16, 18, 29–30, 46, 54, 61, 67, 70, 79, 81–84, 92, 95, 98, 101–102, 113–118, 121, 122, 133–134, 136, 146, 149–150, 152, 153, 159–160, 162, 164–167, 169, 170, 172, 176, 179, 181, 193
  Blight bundling, 79
  Blight elimination, 81–82, 84, 92, 101, 115–116, 153, 159–160, 162, 164–167, 169, 170, 172, 176, 179. *See also* Growing Greener Initiative
Bloomberg's Cities of Service Program, 113

Boston
  Boston Area Research Initiative, 46, 52, 125
  Boston Data Portal, 46, 188, 194. *See also* Data
  Boston Indicators Project, 127
  Boston Redevelopment Authority, 10
  Boston's Mayor's Office of New Urban Mechanics, 52
Building Blocks, 111–113, 126, 159

C
Carticipe, 7, 43, 123, 197, 204–205, 213. *See also* Public participatory GIS (PPGIS)
ChangeExplorer, 43, 123
Child Opportunity Index, 192
Citizen engagement, 39, 44, 184
Citizen trust, 57
CityNexus, 46
Clusters, 98, 100–101, 147–149, 150–158, 162–167, 170, 173–174, 176–180
  Active uses, 156
  Candidate clusters, 156, 180
  Demolition clusters, 101, 147–149, 155
  Passive uses, 30, 136, 156
  Repurposing. *See* Vacant land re-use
  Vacant clusters, 147, 150, 153, 156
Code enforcement, 81, 83, 92–93, 98, 111, 113, 146, 159
Cognitive mapping, 132. *See also* Problem structuring methods; Soft operations research (Soft OR)
Collaborative planners. *See* Collaborative planning spaces
Collaborative planning spaces, 124. *See also* Democratic participation

Communicative/collaborative
    paradigm, 37, 144
Community
  Community and city planning, 33
  Community distress, 2, 12, 29
  Community engagement, 7, 24,
    29–30, 42–43, 48, 55, 62, 85, 124,
    130, 133, 181, 183–184, 186, 190,
    199, 203, 206, 209, 212–214,
    217
  Community gardens, 96, 134, 136,
    156
  Community geography, 49–50,
    184–185, 187, 195, 199, 206
  Community interventions, 33
  Community operational research
    (COR), 28, 124, 131, 136, 177,
    193, 196, 210, 214. *See also*
    Community-based operations
    research (CBOR)
  Community participation, 55, 124,
    181, 189, 193
Community Development Block
  Grant Program (CDBG), 90,
  138–139
Community Development
  Corporations (CDC), 11, 130
Community PlanIt, 47, 123
Community-based, 6, 28, 49–51,
  53–55, 62, 118, 122–125, 131,
  136, 144, 173, 176–177, 186–188,
  193–194, 196, 199, 202–206, 216
  Community-based GIS, 199
  Community-based operations
    research (CBOR), 28, 124–125,
    131, 136, 177, 193, 196. *See also*
    Community operational research
    (COR)
  Community-based participatory
    research, 49, 54
  Community-based research, 49,
    203–204

Community-engaged, 28–30, 40,
    49–50, 124, 130, 131, 173, 181,
    184, 189, 203–204, 206, 214
  Community-engaged OR, 50
  Community-engaged planning, 40,
    124, 206, 214
CommunityViz, 49, 123, 191–192,
  197, 204–205
Compromise solution, 140, 142–143,
  170–171, 172, 178. *See also*
  Multiobjective decision making
  (MODM); Multiobjective
  decision modeling
Computers in Urban Planning and
  Urban Management Conferences
  (CUPUM), 39
Concierge, 191, 195. *See also*
  Facilitator; Public participatory
  GIS (PPGIS)
Constraint, 49, 101, 117, 130, 137,
  138, 160, 163, 165–167, 172, 174,
  176–179, 181, 193–194, 197. *See
  also* Math optimization
Convening construct, 198. *See
  also* Enhanced Adaptation
  Structuration Theory (EAST2)
Coproduction of knowledge, 38,
  62
Corbusian modernist, 34–36, 142
Corner solution, 139–140, 168, 170.
  See also Multiobjective decision
  making (MODM); Multiobjective
  decision modeling
Correira, Jasiel, 114
Cost-benefit analysis, 132, 156, 166
COVID-19, 5, 31, 212
Crime hotspots, 149, 162
Criminal victimization, 54, 59
Critical cartography, 216. *See also*
  Critical GIS
Critical GIS, 216. *See also* Critical
  cartography

D

Dashboard, 42, 122, 124
Data
Big data, 6, 24, 26, 28–30, 41, 53, 58–63, 115, 121–122, 124, 127, 183–184, 187, 190, 203, 205, 208, 216
Civic data, 6
Data analysis, 33, 128, 163, 191, 200
Data exploration, 191, 196, 206. *See also* Spatial data exploration
Data mining, 45, 122, 124
Data visualization, 43–44, 122, 124
Data-driven approach, 28
Data-driven civic engagement, 124. *See also* Game design; Game play
Data-driven decision making, 3
Spatial data exploration, 191, 206
User-generated data, 122, 124
Decision. *See also* Model
Community-engaged decision modeling, 173
Decision alternatives, 128–132, 134, 158
Decision model(ing), 7–8, 26, 28–30, 40, 45, 52, 65, 115, 117–118, 125–126, 128–131, 135–138, 142, 144–147, 149–151, 153, 155, 157–159, 162–168, 170, 172–178, 180–185, 188–194, 195, 196–197, 200, 203–204, 206–210, 213–214, 216–217
Decision problem, 129–130, 135–136, 139, 157, 160–162, 165–166, 168, 172, 176, 180–181, 194, 196, 207
Decision science, 3, 6–8, 27–28, 33, 40, 65, 121–122, 124–126, 184, 189, 207, 214–215
See also Analytics; Operations research

Decision space, 138, 141, 142, 143, 170–171, 197, 201
Decision variable, 137–138, 167, 170, 173, 175–176, 178, 181, 188, 193, 197. *See also* Math optimization
Multiattribute decision making (MADM), 131
Multiobjective decision making (MODM), 131, 135, 160
Smart shrinkage decision problem, 135–136, 139, 157, 160, 161–162, 165, 168, 176, 181
Spatial decision making, 186
Spatial Decision Support Systems (SDSS), 26, 40, 52
Vacant parcel decision model. *See* Vacant land planning model
Decision support system (DSS), 26, 40, 52, 124, 129, 132, 174, 176, 188–190, 201, 209–210
Deliberative planning, 39, 56
Democratic participation, 29, 44, 55, 123, 204. *See also* Collaborative planning spaces
Demolition planning, 45
Desegregation, 37
Design interventions, 25, 45
Design-oriented approach, 36
Deterministic, 167
Disinvestment, 12, 14, 86, 92–93, 102, 125, 145
Distress, 1–2, 7, 12, 16–18, 27, 29, 46, 54, 65, 67, 69, 84, 100, 102, 115, 118, 121, 125, 135, 145, 150, 152, 206, 208, 210–211, 213–214, 216–217
Diversity in participation, 201

E

East Baltimore Development Inc. (EBDI), 95

Economies of scale, 137, 157
Effectiveness, 8, 47, 82, 115, 126–127, 130, 160, 181, 187–188, 201–202. *See also* Efficiency; Equity
Efficiency, 8, 47, 56, 115, 126–127, 130, 160, 162, 181, 201–202, 216. *See also* Effectiveness; Equity
Eminent domain, 10. *See also* Urban renewal
Empowerment, 3, 6, 23, 49, 51, 185, 200–202, 206–207, 213–214
Enhanced Adaptation Structuration Theory (EAST2), 188, 197–198
Environmental justice, 12
Environmental justice communities, 12
Environmental remediation, 136
Envision Tomorrow, 26, 57
Equity, 8, 13, 24, 27, 30, 34, 39, 57, 63, 70, 72, 82–83, 112, 115, 126–127, 130, 132–133, 139–140, 142, 144, 159, 162, 173, 181, 201, 208, 211. *See also* Effectiveness; Efficiency
  Equity indicators, 27, 57
  Equity-oriented, 34

F

Facilitator, 38, 49, 191, 195, 199, 202, 204–205
See also Concierge
Fairmount Innovation Lab, 205
Fall River Consolidated Plan, 139
Fall River, MA, 4–5, 17, 19, 21, 22, 29–30, 63, 65, 66, 67–69, 102–116, 118, 121, 125, 134–135, 138–139, 141–142, 145, 183, 190, 208, 212, 215–217. *See also* Gateway Cities
Flint, MI, 1, 5, 17, 19, 21, 22, 29, 31, 63, 65, 66, 67–84, 91, 102–103, 109, 115–119, 124–125, 140, 141, 163, 190, 208, 212–214, 217

Blight Elimination Framework, 81. *See also* Blight elimination
Community Foundation of Greater Flint, 84
Economic Recovery Task Force, 84
Flint Farmers' Market, 84
Genesee County Land Bank, 84
Grocery Stores Initiative, 84
Imagine Flint Master Plan, 79, 119
Land Bank, 78–79, 84, 118
Participatory budgeting, 81
Food systems, 96
Foreclosure crisis. *See* Subprime mortgage crisis
Foreclosures, 14, 88, 93, 111, 133, 189
Fundamental objectives, 132, 158, 162–163
Fundamental values, 131, 158, 160. *See also* Fundamental objectives
Fundamental values hierarchy, 158, 160, 168–170, 172, 176, 179
Future development, 35, 118, 164, 166–167, 168–170, 172, 176, 179. *See also* Growing Greener Initiative

G

Game design, 123–125, 190. *See also* Data-driven civic engagement; Game play
Game play, 123–125, 190, 193. *See also* Game design
Gaming simulations, 26, 46, 55, 123
Gateway Cities, 17, 103–104
General Motors, 71–72, 74, 77–78
Genetic algorithms, 132
Gentrification, 4, 86, 134
Geodesign, 40, 51–52, 59, 135, 164, 184, 187, 189, 203. *See also* Change model; Evaluation model; Impact model; Representation model

Geodesignhub, 52
Geographic Information Systems (GIS), 6, 26, 40, 48–52, 57, 96, 123, 125, 132–134, 147, 174, 179, 184–186, 189, 191, 194, 198–205, 208–209, 213, 216–217
Globalization, 5, 9
Good governance, 7, 114, 186, 201
Gray, Freddie, 85, 102, 212
Great Recession, 2, 69, 74. *See also* Subprime mortgage crisis
Greedy algorithm, 156, 167
Green infrastructure, 27, 57, 81
Greening, 92, 96–97, 101, 155, 159
Growing Greener Initiative, 164

H

HarassMap, 187
Henson, Daniel P., 94
Hogan, Larry, 94
HOME Program, 138
Homebuyer supports, 92–93
Homegrown Baltimore (HGB), 96–97
Housing covenants, 88
Housing mobility, 28, 132
Human-computer interactions (HCI), 202

I

Idea space, 121–122, 124–126, 144
Incrementalist, 34–35, 142
Inner blocks, 153
Inputs, 44, 59, 117, 126, 175–176. *See also* Outcomes; Outputs
Internet of Things, 23, 25
Interventionism, 34

J

Just City, 36, 38–39, 144

K

Kildee, Dan, 78

L

Landscape architecture, 40, 51
Lefebvre's Right to the City, 13
LinkNYC, 61, 211
London Datastore, 127

M

Machine learning, 41, 45, 122, 124, 134
Madame Mayor, I Have an Idea, 44, 192, 213
Map Your World, 191. *See also* Public participatory GIS (PPGIS)
Maptionnaire, 191–192, 197, 204. *See also* Public participatory GIS (PPGIS)
Market Value Analysis, 133, 136
Marxan, 189, 193. *See also* SeaSketch
Math optimization, 123–125
Mathematical programming, 172, 177, 193
Meaningful engagement of communities, 210
Meaningful inefficiency, 47
Means objectives, 158–159, 162–163
Means-ends network, 158–160, 161, 162–163
Measures of quality of life, 41
Mental mapping, 200
Metropolitan Philadelphia Indicators Project, 127
Mixed-methods, 130–131, 135, 181. *See also* Qualitative analysis; Quantitative analysis
Model
  Change model, 52
  CitiStat, 127
  Citizen-engaged decision modeling, 144, 193. *See also* Community operational research (COR)
  Collaborative model, 159
  Evaluation model, 52

Evidence-based decision model, 181, 214
Facilitated modeling, 132. See also Problem structuring methods
Housing market typology model (HMT), 98–99, 122, 124, 147, 149–150, 165, 175, 177
Human-based decision model, 162
Impact model, 52, 135, 164
Mathematical model(ing), 26, 37, 45, 172, 179
Mixed-methods decision modeling, 135
Model components, 194
Model creation, 174
Model outputs, 140, 142, 194, 200
Model parameters, 194
Multicriteria decision model (MCDM), 192–194, 196–197
Multiobjective decision modeling, 137. See also Multiobjective decision making (MODM)
Neighborhood planning model, 99
Optimization model, 179–180, 196
Planning model, 6, 37, 99, 129, 140–141, 143, 163–168, 169, 171, 180–182
Planning support system (PSS) modeling, 6, 26–27, 30, 40, 183, 216
Policy modeling, 132
Prescriptive decision modeling, 126, 128–129, 163. See also Data analytics; Prescriptive analytics
Process model, 52
Public-sector decision modeling, 28
Qualitative decision model, 131, 158
Quantitative decision model, 131, 145, 184, 193, 195
Rationalist model, 35, 37
Representation model, 52
Smart city model, 23, 24
Structured decision modeling, 136
Vacant land planning model, 163–167, 168, 169, 171, 180, 182
Value-based model building, 178
Model-based problem solving, 173, 214
Model-driven responses, 26
Movement for Black Lives, 13. See also Black Lives Matter
Multiobjective mathematical optimization models. See Multiobjective optimization
Multiobjective optimization, 132, 134, 138–139, 197, 209. See also Multiobjective decision making (MODM)

N
National Neighborhood Indicators Project, 128
Negotiated planning, 34
Neighborhood
 Functionally coherent neighborhoods, 36
 Neighborhood change, 9–11, 210
 Neighborhood change theory, 9, 11
 Neighborhood GIS center, 199, 205
 Neighborhood life-cycle theory, 9–10
 Neighborhood Nexus, 127
 Neighborhood revitalization, 38, 99
 Neighborhood satisfaction, 137, 140–142, 208
 Neighborhood stability, 159, 162
 Neighborhood stabilization, 82, 100, 133, 136, 155
 Neighborhood-level analysis, 142
Neoclassical economics, 35
Neotraditionalist, 34, 38, 144
New Bedford, MA, 4–5, 17, 20
New urbanist, 35–36, 144

262 | Index

Nonlinear multiobjective optimization, 138
Nonresidential development, 208
Nonresidential investments, 137–138, 140–142
Nonresidential land use, 136. *See also* Bioretention areas; Community gardens; Environmental remediation; Land Bank; Nonresidential investments; Nonresidential-focused investments; Parks
Nonresidential-focused investments, 137–138, 142

O

O'Malley, Martin, 93
Objective. *See* Objective function
Objective function, 137–139, 167–168, 170–171, 176, 193–194. *See also* Math optimization
Objective space, 138, 140, 169, 197. *See also* Value path; Visualization
Objectives design, 196
Objective and instrumental rationality, 37
Operations research, 27–29, 50, 122, 124–126, 129–131, 136, 167, 177, 181, 184, 189, 193, 196, 204, 206, 217. *See also* Analytics; Decision science
Operations research and management science. *See* Analytics; Decision science
Organizational effectiveness, 201–202
Outcomes, 11, 14–16, 30, 36, 41, 48, 50, 52–54, 57, 59, 69, 94, 116–117, 126, 128–131, 142, 149, 154–155, 159–160, 163–164, 172–174, 176, 179, 181, 188, 196, 198, 200, 202, 210, 216. *See also* Inputs; Outputs

Outcome construct, 198. *See also* Enhanced Adaptation Structuration Theory (EAST2)
Outputs, 126, 129, 138, 140, 142, 186, 192, 194, 200, 204. *See also* Inputs

P

PAIRS metric, 45, 123
Pareto optimal, 132
Parks, 15, 70, 111, 114, 117–118, 122, 132, 137–138, 147, 156, 165, 173
Participatory, 6–7, 23, 27–28, 48–51, 54–55, 58, 81, 116, 122–123, 125, 174, 184–185, 187–188, 190–191, 195, 198, 201, 203, 205, 208–209, 213, 217
Participatory action design research, 50
Participatory decision making, 188
Participatory GIS (PGIS), 48, 50, 125, 174, 184–185, 198, 203, 205, 208, 213, 217. *See also* Public participatory GIS (PPGIS)
Participatory planning, 7, 116, 190–191, 195
Payne, Patricia, 94
Performance management, 126
Philadelphia's Neighborhood Transformation Initiative, 99
Physical disorder, 14–15, 149. *See also* Physical neighborhood disorder
Physical neighborhood disorder, 14
PolicyMap, 128, 191
Political disengagement, 29, 54, 203–204
Political neutrality, 37
Predictive algorithms, 41
Priority setting, 192. *See also* Problem structuring methods
Problem identification, 144, 181, 196

Problem structuring methods, 124, 131, 132, 192, 196, 204, 206, 216
Problem-driven analysis, 28, 210
Problem-driven approach, 28
Process construct, 198. *See also* Enhanced Adaptation Structuration Theory (EAST2)
Prospective analysis, 142
Pruett, Natalie, 81
Public participation, 36, 38, 48–49, 62, 80–81, 184, 186, 189, 208
Public participatory GIS (PPGIS), 48–50, 174, 184–208, 213, 217. *See also* Planning support system (PSS) modeling

Q
Qualitative analysis, 151, 191–192. *See also* Mixed-methods; Prescriptive analytics; Quantitative analysis
Quantitative analysis, 128, 191. *See also* Qualitative analysis

R
Rationalist planning, 34, 37
Rawlings-Blake, Stephanie, 94
Real estate covenants, 86
Real estate developers, 78, 111–112, 114
Receivership Transition Advisory Board, 84
Redlining, 88, 107
Regeneration, 4
Regulatory change, 111, 173
Relocation, 10, 72, 94–95, 100, 142, 146, 149, 154–155, 160, 166, 180
Residential development, 132, 208
Residential segregation, 12, 41, 54, 85
Responsive cities, 25
Rockford, IL, 5
Rouse, James, 95

S
SeaSketch, 7, 49, 123, 189, 193, 205
Sensitivity analysis, 129, 172, 174, 191, 194, 197
Separation of use zoning, 35
Simulation, 26–28, 46–47, 55, 57, 123–124, 193, 203–204, 206
Slum clearance, 90. *See also* Urban renewal
Smart
 Smart city, 6–7, 23–24, 28–30, 47, 53, 56, 58–63, 115, 121, 183–184, 190, 203, 205, 208, 212, 216
 Smart decline, 13, 136, 183
 Smart growth, 136, 173
 Smart shrinkage, 69, 118, 125, 134–135
 Smart shrinkage problem, 135, 144, 155–157, 158, 163, 165, 172
Smarter Cities Challenge, 58, 61
Social
 Social capital, 15–16, 54, 58, 213
 Social equity. *See* Equity
 Social isolation, 14–15, 29, 54, 204
 Social media, 6, 42, 44, 47–48, 54, 122, 124, 213
 Social Network Analysis, 48
 Social sensing, 25, 45
Soft operations research (Soft OR), 132, 196–197
Soft systems methodology, 132, 196. *See also* Problem structuring methods; Soft operations research (Soft OR)
Spatial inequalities, 34
Stakeholder consensus-building, 201–202
Stormwater management, 70, 117–118, 134, 164, 166–167, 170, 172, 179
Strategic choice approach, 132. *See also* Problem structuring methods; Soft operations research (Soft OR)

Strategic demolition, 101, 159
Subprime mortgage crisis, 14, 86. *See also* Great Recession
Suitability analysis, 45, 134, 156, 163–164, 195
Systems engineering, 26, 46

T
Technology acceptance and adoption, 201
Technology Acceptance Model (TAM), 202
Textile industry, 105
Third spaces, 59–60, 203, 205
Three-dimensional modeling, 43
Top-down policy, 99
Total planning, 36
Traditional rationalist, 34, 37, 142

U
Unequal technology access, 54, 204
University-community partnership, 199
Urban Research-Based Action Network, 53, 125
Urban Spacebook, 54–55
Urban
  Urban agriculture, 70, 81, 87, 92, 96–97, 117–118, 156, 164–168, 169, 170, 172, 176–177, 179
  Urban commons, 44
  Urban greening, 92, 96, 159
  Urban renewal, 10, 13, 34, 90, 95. *See also* Eminent domain
UrbanData2Decide, 44, 123, 213
Ushahidi, 191. *See also* Public participatory GIS (PPGIS)

V
Vacancy, 2, 13–15, 18–21, 22, 45, 66, 68, 75–76, 81, 83, 89–94, 96, 98–101, 108–110, 112–114, 116–117, 133–134, 136–137, 142, 145, 147, 152, 155, 159, 175–177, 217

Housing vacancy, 2, 18, 76, 91, 99, 109–110, 133, 137
Vacant land redevelopment, 146
Vacant lots, 48, 74, 79, 81–82, 84, 86, 96–97, 149, 156, 211
Vacant parcel re-use, 156
Vacant property, 13, 75, 81, 84–86, 93–94, 98, 114, 116, 134, 146, 156, 163, 181. *See also* Housing vacancy
Vacant land re-use, 145–146
Value
  Value path, 139, 168. *See also* Objective space; Visualization
  Value-focused thinking, 131, 157–158, 162, 165, 192, 209. *See also* Problem structuring methods; Qualitative decision model
  Value-laden process, 37
  Values elicitation, 134, 192, 214. *See also* Problem structuring methods
  Values structuring, 196
Vertical gardens, 44
Visual recognition techniques, 41
Visualization, 25–26, 43–44, 54, 56, 62, 122–124, 126, 192, 201–202, 207, 213, 216
Volunteered geographic information (VGI), 184–185

W
Ways2gether, 43, 192
Web 2.0, 185
Weight-sets, 168, 170, 177
Weighting method, 167–168, 177
White flight, 69, 72, 103

Z
Zoning, 35, 37, 79, 107, 111–112, 115

www.ingramcontent.com/pod-product-compliance
Lightning Source LLC
Chambersburg PA
CBHW020643230426
43665CB00008B/295